Rational Recovery
from

h:

The Small Book

Third Edition

by Jack Trimpey, LCSW
Executive Director, Rational Recovery Systems

**The Comprehensive Guide
to Rational Sobriety**

Introduction by Albert Ellis, Ph.D.
President, Institute for Rational-Emotive Therapy, New York

Acknowledgements

There are now hundreds of lay and professional people who have taken sides on the critical issues discussed in this book. They are actively building a rational recovery system in America and around the world. This is a special acknowledgement to those persons, who are making major contributions to their communities. They will be remembered by the many who will find sobriety as a result of their pioneering work as RRS Advisors and Coordinators. Special recognition is also due Mildred McCallister of the Humanist Association of The Greater Sacramento Area, for the critical role she played in 1988, helping RRS enter the mainstream of addiction care. Finally, this is an acknowledgement of the valuable input from those who have supported RRS with their contributions of material, feedback, and finances. Because of you, RRS is truly "of the people..."

Rational Recovery: The Small Book, 3rd Ed.
ISBN: 0-934373-47-7

You are bleeding and the emergency room doctor assures you that you will undergo surgery requiring a transfusion. Relieved, you relax a little and remark that you have type RR blood. As he leaves the room, you overhear him order, "Two pints of type AA to the surgical suite." You jerk upright, blood surging from your wound, and correct the doctor, "I said type RR, doctor." He returns to your bedside and explains, "Type AA will be fine, and you'll be back on your feet in a short time. You will, however, require daily transfusions of type AA for the rest of your life."

"Wouldn't it really be better, doctor, if I were infused with my own blood type?" you ask. "No, not at all," he answers. "Yours is a rare type and besides, that's all we have in stock. You'll be just fine." So, off you go to the surgical suite, wanting to trust, needing to trust -- to avoid the fear you already have. Your personal understanding has always been that blood types usually don't mix, and that your type doesn't mix with type AA. "Has something changed?" you wonder. "Can I really assimilate this substance into my body to sustain my health and life? Will I suffer side effects I haven't bargained for?"

Not being in any position to bargain, you decide to act in your own best interests. Clutching your tourniquet, you spring from the gurny, run out to the street and hail a taxi. A police car stops and the officer sees you bleeding, running from the ER. He restrains you and starts leading you back to the ER. "No, please!" you say, and then you explain about the monolithic blood bank. "In that case, you're coming with me," he says.

Siren on, you speed to the county hospital where you are detained for reasons of incompetence. Even so, you are relieved to have a fresh start on the problem, and you feel that maybe you'll survive to tell the story. But you have become weak -- too weak to defend your point of view. The doctor comes into the ER and diagnoses you and notifies the surgical suite. "Two pints of type AA blood for the new patient..." You feel the loss of hope. You have never felt so low. You surrender your will, and you pass out.

When you wake up, you do not feel well. You can tell there is something very wrong. You seek other opinions, but in this fictional world with the monolithic blood bank the answer is always the same -- "Type AA is good for everybody; it doesn't matter who you are or what your opinion is, we know from long experience that it's the only thing that works." You wish very much that your own type of blood was provided; but underneath it all, it begins to seem that your opinions were probably wrong in the first place. Facing death, and the expert opinions of so many, you come to accept that you had better submit to regular transfusions of type AA blood.

After all, who are you to say what's right for you?

Table of Contents

Introduction

Of the hundreds of helpful books that exist for alcoholics and substance abusers, I find *Rational Recovery from Alcoholism: The Small Book* one of the very best. Like many other writings in this field, it tells alcoholics how to give up, and permanently stay off, imbibing in what for them is liquid poison. Fine! But *The Small Book* goes much further and is unusually solid therapeutically.

As I emphasize with my clients, in the course of my talks and workshops and in my own book, *Rational-Emotive Therapy with Alcoholics and Substance Abusers,* (New York: Pergamon Press), alcoholics usually have three main levels of disturbance. First, they often are basically anxious, depressed, enraged, or self-hating. Why? Because they are easily, naturally that way and have created and accepted a rigid, absolutistic, commanding — or what I have called *mus*turbatory — philosophy of life. They wrongly think they *must* do well, *have* to be approved of and loved, have *got* to be treated fairly and nicely by others, and *absolutely should* be consistently and easily gratified.

Second, rather than confront their problems, and rather than dispute the grandiose philosophies that accompany these problems, alcoholics demand that they immediately feel no pain; because of their low frustration tolerance, they drink instead of think their way out of their difficulties. In resorting to booze, they almost always increase their emotional and behavioral difficulties and become addicted to solving them (at least for the moment) in alcohol.

Third, they sooner or later bring on such bad results with their drinking that they often acknowledge how idiotically they are thinking, feeling, and behaving, and then foolishly damn themselves for their addiction. Their self-hatred then usually drives them to *more* self-sousing.

Rational-emotive therapy (RET) shows alcoholics how to stop drinking and how to deal with all three of these levels of disturbance: First, to undamningly accept themselves as alcoholics but never put themselves (only their poor behaviors) down, no matter how badly they act. Second, to become long-range instead of short range hedonists, and live with the emotional problems they have when they stop drinking. Third, to get back to their original feelings of panic, depression, rage, and self-loathing and show themselves, as the title of my recent book states, *How to Stubbornly Refuse to Make Yourself Miserable About Anything — Yes Anything!* (Lyle Stuart).

Most books on alcoholism touch only on the problems of abstaining — how to get off and stay off the bottle. Good. But *The Small Book,* following the principles of RET, nicely helps alcoholics get to their self-hatred about their alcoholism, to uproot their low frustration tolerance (LFT), that largely drives them to drink, and to tackle the original emotional problems that encouraged them to drink too much in the first place.

The Small Book, therefore, is one of the few comprehensive books on alcoholism ever written for lay readers. Trimpey, moreover, has a rare talent for clear, provocative, and interesting writing. He is in the same ballpark as his readers. Anyone who is alcoholic or interested in helping someone who is alcoholic will find an enormous amount of useful, relevant, and highly understandable material in this pioneering publication.

Since writing the Introduction to the first and second editions of *The Small Book*, Rational Recovery Systems has grown immensely and now has about 70 groups that are active and will soon have, I hope, a great many more. Fine! RRS leads to social change. It means that alcoholics are actively trying to help themselves, help each other, and help their families and others who associate with them and that Rational Recovery groups and their advisors are working collaboratively and cooperatively with each other. With democratic groups like these meeting and discussing regularly, national (and international) freedom and democracy will certainly grow.

Do alcoholics *need* to join RRS to give up drinking and stay sober? Of course not. People throughout the centuries have thrown away the bottle and given up other addictions without any group help. But many have done and will do so much more easily and thoroughly through regular RRS group meetings.

RRS, moreover, is the most effective way to establish a two-party system for helping alcoholics. AA definitely has its place in this system and I have referred literally hundreds of people to it during the last half century, many of whom have been helped to stay off booze. But democracy requires at least two influential parties, not one; and RRS provides a fine meeting ground for great numbers of people who want nothing to do with *any* kind of Higher Power and who want (with the use of RET) to rely only on themselves and other humans to achieve and maintain sobriety.

In our work with many alcoholics at the Institute for Rational-Emotive Therapy in New York City, we consistently find that those who read books on RET improve faster and better than those who do not. I am confident that reading *Rational Recovery from Alcoholism: The Small Book* will greatly help a large number of readers.

Albert Ellis, Ph.D.

Institute for Rational-Emotive Therapy, 45 E. 65th Street, New York NY 10021

8

Preface

For decades, the field of chemical dependency has been dominated by "The Big Book" of Alcoholics Anonymous and its endless spinoffs that also beseech alcoholics to seek God.

Because of the organizational success of Alcoholics Anonymous and its 12-step spiritual healing program, it has become a universal component in addiction care. Unfortunately, millions of alcoholics are not good candidates for that kind of help, and will best be helped to regain control of their lives through a program that starts where they are, making no requirement of moral betterment or belief in a Higher Power, a Supreme Being, or other articles of faith.

Whatever your personal views on theology and religion, you should find the non-theistic Rational Recovery approach to be credible, viable, and a welcome addition to the chemical dependency scene. The author assumes that the reader places a high value on the survival of alcohol and drug dependent people, and would not allow personal preferences to come in the way of a rational alternative for those who are not receptive to spiritual teachings.

Point for point — except for one central point — RR is the *counterpoint* to 12-step spiritual healing and differs sharply from widely accepted views on chemical dependency. RR is in complete agreement that the most reasonable solution to drug and alcohol dependence is usually lifetime abstinence from drugs and alcohol. RR will provide a fresh start for substance abusers who have tried many times to "go on the wagon," only to relapse again and again.

RR is news for the Nineties. Rational Recovery Systems is redefining the nature of recovery from chemical dependence. When you have read *The Small Book* you will have a new and revolutionary viewpoint on the subject of alcoholism. I hope you will also see to it that this book gets into the hands of other people who desperately need to read it. *The Small Book* shows how to achieve your own sobriety, and it shows how to get a group going in your community. Let's see how quickly we can let the whole nation know that it's time for a Rational Recovery (RR) program everywhere an AA group is found!

—J.T.

Disclaimer

This is the third edition of *The Small Book*. A very few who read the second edition were upset by what they read. Richard Hite, a reporter from the *Boston Globe*, called *The Small Book* "...an angry manifesto." One woman who heard me speak for only four minutes (I timed it) said she felt her basic beliefs were being attacked. She demanded equal time to defend her transpersonal beliefs before the audience. Another woman from a clinic where I gave a presentation of RR likened me to Moamar Khadafy. That connection wasn't clear to me, but she was angry. I think her feelings were hurt, too. If you want to hear some public reactions of AA members to RR, listen in on the audiocassette published by Lotus Press, "The Boston Talkshow Event." This set of two ninety minute tapes is a social document that will be heard over and over, by AA refuseniks, by professional people, and by people in positions of social responsibility. Any listener will likely conclude that, if the callers to the talkshow were not evangelizing a religion, then they were representing something very much like one.

Others who read the second edition of *The Small Book* were elated. "I read it with a mixture of fascination and glee," one woman said. Many others said that reading TSB changed their lives and that they are now sober. Still others said that they had gotten sober long ago using the same approach as described in Rational Recovery. But the biggest testimonial for *The Small Book* is the network of Rational Recovery groups that now exist in most American population centers.

All this seems to show what I have been saying for years and has been known for centuries — that there are two general kinds of people: believers and thinkers. Yes, we all do both, but we tend toward one personal style or the other. And we also tend to approach our lives and problems as ones who either have *faith* in unchanging principles or as ones who think things through and use *reason* as the light that shows the way. When push comes to shove, either way will do, but we can't really have it both ways on some central issues of recovery from chemical dependence.

Some may find it hard to believe, after reading this book, that this author has a fundamental respect for Alcoholics Anonymous. I do. When I reached out for help with my own alcohol dependence, they were there — a fellowship of concerned human beings who help themselves by helping others. I have been to many of their meetings and I learned some important information about alcohol dependence. I have personal friends who still attend AA. They do good work, and I know it. I also know that there's a lot that is rational in AA.

But the thousands who leave AA each year, disgruntled and ripe for relapse, are unable to make use of a very good program because the 12-step approach is faith-based. As a means to personal survival, people in AA have faith in something other than, or greater than, themselves, and they implore newcomers to share in that common faith. This is well-intentioned, for it has been an effective way for *some* to halt the self-destruction that results from alcohol or drug dependence. AA veterans, therefore, will use many persuasive means (sometimes coercive means that undermine one's sense of personal worth and competence) in order to induce newcomers to surrender reason to faith. In AA, one's attempts to reason are commonly regarded as "part of the disease of alcoholism" in the sincere hope that, by surrendering to some higher authority or group mentality, one will change for the better.

AA is not *a wrong program,* but for those who examine it and find it unhelpful, irrelevant, or disagreeable, it *is* the wrong program. This is a book for those people — a vindication and at the same time a challenge to them to overcome the ideas of dependency and powerlessness that have been so destructive.

Finally, this is not a book written in an angry spirit (excuse the expression), or one intended to make members of AA look stupid or unethical. To the contrary, Rational Recovery Systems views AA as a victim of its own success — thrust into roles in our society that it is neither designed for, nor able to fulfill. It has been protected from ideological assault by the shield it has borrowed from traditional religions. In its simplest, *communal* form, AA is, as its members say, "wonderful." But when AA comes to us in its *institutional* form, enforced by the military, the courts, social welfare agencies, and when it comprises the single agenda in practically every treatment program in America — well, it's enough to drive one to drink.

In the corridors of public institutions, AA's shield is gone, and *The Small Book* unhesitatingly prints what heretofore was only thought by the many who left it. If America is going to have its institutional AA, then it will soon become necessary for her to have institutional RR as well. It is ironic that when the rational mode of recovery is finally in place — with each and every recovering person afforded a choice between AA and RR — AA will be restored as a program that operates on attraction rather than coercion and remains true to its highest ideal of spreading the word of God (as you understand Him) everywhere.

Step 1: We made a fearless evaluation
of our most personal beliefs
and chose the recovery program
that made the most sense.

Chapter 1

To the "Alcoholic": Take Sides!

In the first edition of *The Small Book* (TSB), I began with "First, let me introduce myself..." and then I gave a three-page account of my own recovery from "alcoholism." Self-critic that I am, I omitted that "drunkalog" from the second edition of TSB for two reasons. First, the discussion of my family served no purpose other than to lend literary color to a book on how to achieve and maintain rational sobriety. Second, and more importantly, "drunkalogs" (the telling and retelling of past alcoholic struggles and misdeeds) are not a part of the rational mode of recovery from chemical dependency.

The second edition (TSB.2) perpetuated the error that a diagnosis is a disease. Some passages that seemed to support the disease/powerlessness concept of alcohol dependence are rewritten or omitted here. While many people may have inherited a talent for getting drunk, we need not conclude that someone's unruly appetite for distilled spirits is a disease. Many medically defined conditions aren't diseases, although, like a broken leg, they may pose serious problems. Also, TSB.2 portrayed the differences between alcohol and drug dependent persons as being greater than they really are. Some social differences may sometimes show up between people who use different intoxicants, but these are insignificant unless much ado is made of it. Recovery is the same game.

The above points serve to illustrate how thoroughly indoctrinated we all are with regard to the affliction now called alcohol dependence and its cure. Before developing the general plan for Rational Recovery Systems, and then for some time thereafter, I accepted many of the irrational assumptions contained in the philosophy of alcoholism. The idea that confession is intrinsically therapeutic and a vital part of recovery from alcohol dependence is one of those assumptions. One other dubious assumption worth mentioning here is that in order to be of help to other alcoholics, one must also have a personal history of alcoholism. In writing the drunkalog in the first edition, I was not only confessing to my readers to somehow do me some good, but I was also trying to enhance my credibility to problem drinkers by saying, in effect, "I am like you. I am an alcoholic, too. I can understand your pain. Therefore you should believe what I have to say." The problem here, of course, is that I am not like you in many important ways, my drinking experiences were probably different from yours, and on top of it all, I am not the originator of Rational Recovery in the first place.

I will tell you this, though. I drank wildly for a number of years. My personal problems mounted. When I finally had enough (not booze, but troubles), I quit drinking. I did so by forcing myself to think rationally. I am not recovering; I am recovered. I am reasonably happy most of the time, and I seldom think about my so-called "alcoholism." Even so, the concepts I shall present in this unique presentation have validity that goes far beyond that which I can bolster by telling you about my own past sorrows and disturbances.

The originator of rational recovery is Albert Ellis, Ph.D., a psychologist with incisive intellect who has made major contributions to the field of humanistic psychology. He is diabetic and occasionally has trouble with dislocated shoulders, but to my knowledge Dr. Ellis has never had trouble with alcohol or any other drug. Even so, he devised a system of self-help, rational-emotive therapy (RET), that is naturally and ideally suited for recovery from alcohol dependence. RET is also a comprehensive system of psychotherapy that is taught in most American universities. Rational Recovery (RR) is the name that I have given to RET when it is used by people wanting to free themselves from alcohol dependence and other substance abuse. Neither RET nor RR "work." They are simply a process of learning to think rationally (effectively) about life and its problems. RR is information about how to stop drinking or using other drugs and stay stopped. Information does not work, fly, dance, or take any other action. It merely exists. If you have a drug or alcohol problem, you may decide to take action based on the information contained here. I hope you do; it will make a big difference in your life.

As you read along you may notice the sensation of mental insight. This is not meant to sound sarcastic, but only to point out that rational thinking is distinctly different from the usual way of thinking. We live in a culture in which irrational ideas have the ring of truth, so when the rational alternative is understood there is usually a quick, pleasant feeling of "Aha!" Some people describe the moment of rational insight, "...as if a flashbulb went off." Many happy flashes to you.

Is "alcoholism" a disease?

A much better question is, "Who cares?" There is much bitter debate over this question, and one would think that the answer would have some great importance to those who habitually drink too much. Alas, it doesn't really matter, because the solution is the same either way. If "alcoholism" is a disease and you have a drinking problem, then continuing to drink is folly. You will almost certainly have to stop it. But, if "alcoholism" isn't a disease, and you are having persistent problems related to drinking, you had also better learn to abstain. Abstinence is simply the final stage in one's effort to moderate, when it becomes easier to quit *for good* than to moderate. Abstinence is also a commonplace thing that human beings have been achieving for millennia without the assistance of Alcoholics Anonymous or any other recovery program. In RR, we know that either way, disease or not, we are not powerless.

But many people *do* care if "alcoholism" is a disease. The disease question is sensitive to many people because their jobs depend on alcoholism being a disease. Others make "I am an alcoholic" their personal identities and the admission passwords to their recovery clubs, and others can forgive themselves for their drunken behavior only if they believe they were diseased at the time. Many accept the disease idea as an article of faith and in normal conversation feel compelled to join the word "alcoholism" with "the disease of..." Some others use the disease idea as a gun to their heads, imagining catastrophic results if they have just a teensy-weensy bit of alcohol, ever, ever, ever. Still others seek leniency in courts of law by focusing on the powerlessness that is said to accompany the disease of alcoholism. So, it is understandable that so much controversy surrounds the disease question, and that so many people care. But in RR, it doesn't really matter.

Historically, alcoholism was a broad term referring to the excessive drinking of alcohol. With the advent of AA in the 1930's, "alcoholism" became a term describing a specific physical disease, although evidence supporting that idea did not come to light until the 1980's. From the start, it was merely assumed by AA that people with extreme dependence on alcohol were physically different, either inherently or as a result of exposure to the substance alcohol. AA not only created a disease entity called "alcoholism" but also defined it and devised a treatment for the disease of its invention. None of this occurred in a laboratory, clinical, or academic setting. It happened in church basements.

Prior to AA and its claim that there is a disease called alcoholism, problem drinkers were seen as morally defective and weak of character. They were of interest mainly to clergy, to doctors who

15

treated the physical results of alcoholic excess, to almshouses, and those who worked in courts and jails. AA gained strength on the idea that if problem drinkers are sick with a disease called alcoholism then who can really *blame* (moralistically condemn) them? This relieved some of the social stigma and personal guilt that problem drinkers encounter, and also had the beneficial effect of attracting many guilt-ridden addicts to AA meetings. "We are powerless over our addictions and our lives are unmanageable," are two beliefs that are cornerstones of 12-step program of AA. They both provide some relief from guilt, but both, as we shall see, are as irrational as can be.

The data are now catching up with AA, and it seems they may be partly right in their claim that problem drinkers are physically different. There are some interesting differences between alcoholics and non-alcoholics in their blood chemistry and in measures of their tolerance patterns. Some sons of alcoholics are seen to tolerate given amounts of alcohol without motor impairment better than sons of non-alcoholics. It also appears there are different kinds of alcoholics who display different patterns of onset and whose patterns of substance abuse differ markedly. Degrees of dependency are also recognized.

All of which points to the conclusion of the American Psychiatric Association. The medical diagnosis "alcoholism" has been dropped from the Diagnostic and Statistical Manual (DSM-3R) in favor of two other conditions, "alcohol dependence" and "alcohol abuse." These two terms now describe the vast majority of persons who experience serious problems associated with the use of alcohol.

The word game

"Alcoholism" and "alcoholic" are *folk expressions* that describe problem drinking and those who drink too much for their own good. Neither word is a medical term; when doctors sign insurance claims for treating someone who drinks too much, they write "alcohol dependence." If the doctor wrote the word "alcoholism" in the space for the diagnosis, he or she would not be properly paid. But the terms "alcoholism" and "alcoholic" are still with us and they will be around for a long time to come.

In this third edition, which we may call TSB.3, I will use the term "alcoholic" referring to people who believe they are powerless over their addictions and act accordingly, and to those who call themselves "alcoholics." Those persons are alcoholics who are practicing the *philosophy* of alcoholism, just as Catholics are ones who practice the philosophy of Catholicism. Throughout TSB.3, the reader may substitute "drug dependence" for "alcohol dependence"; recovery is the same game for boozers and junkies. Usually, I will use the correct term, "alcohol dependence" to describe the problem of persistent,

16

heavy drinking. If you will think about this, you will probably see that alcohol dependence is a much clearer expression. It actually *describes* the problem, i.e., "I am *dependent* on alcohol," and it also even suggests what you may *do* about it, i.e., "I had better become *independent* from alcohol." "Alcoholism" merely labels a person sick. It cannot be shown that people who drink too much are diseased, even though some may have inherited an exaggerated appetite for booze. Eventually, "alcoholism" and "alcoholic" may fall into disuse, but in the meantime we need not struggle to purge them from our vocabularies as long as we realize that we mean dependence on alcohol.

Some other "-isms" come to mind that are not diseases but only patterns of discomfort. Rheumatism is really arthritis. Another is priapism, not a disease but a symptom of one. Most other "-isms" are doctrines or *philosophies*, such as capitalism, communism, Methodism, Catholicism, and catechism. "Alcoholism," like other "-isms" is not a disease, but rather a *philosophy* that has affixed itself to a particular human problem or pattern of discomfort — that of habitual, self-destructive drinking of alcohol. The same philosophy has attached itself to other medical and psychiatric diagnoses, under the various names of "_____ Anonymous," especially when the symptoms of those conditions are morally tinged, social vices.

By recognizing that alcoholism is a philosophy, you may immediately sense a personal change. For example, read once again the title of this book, *Rational Recovery from Alcoholism: The Small Book* Do you see? We are no longer trying to change something that is biologically determined and beyond our control, but rather a mode of thinking — a *personal philosophy* that allows one to slowly self-destruct while under the influence. When you change your thinking about drinking, as I hope you will do, then you are recovered. As with any philosophy, alcoholism is comprised of many beliefs and assumptions. Below is an incomplete list of several assumptions of the philosophy called alcoholism, along with its rational counterpart:

Assumptions of the Philosophy of Alcoholism

1. *One must have a history of addiction or alcoholism ("be one of us") in order to be effective in helping an addict or alcoholic,*
instead of the more rational viewpoint that alcoholics are not so different or so complex that one can be understood only by someone with a similar personal background. There is no necessary intrinsic difference between previously addicted and potentially addicted human beings (other than the efficiency of re-addiction of the former).

"...be one of us" seems an insignificant point but is probably the most tragic error of the addiction care establishment. It segregates

alcoholics unto themselves, incomprehensible and therefore stigmatized, with only an esoteric, transpersonal spiritualism to draw upon as they confront their personal problems. This inbreeding excludes professionals who are committed and well-prepared to empower alcoholics to stop drinking. Among "recovering alcoholics" there is a learned distrust of professionals unless they themselves are adherents to the philosophy of alcoholism. Recovery from chemical dependency thus becomes a *mystery* to those who "haven't been through it." In this context, society at large becomes an out-group that defers matters pertaining to chemical dependency to members of the "recovering in-group." In this way, the 12 steps of AA become the 12 rungs of a career ladder that figuratively if not literally starts in the gutter and often ends up with a position as program director or other position of responsibility in health care institutions. Hiring is preferential, favoring members of the esoteric in-group; consequently, virtually all addiction care in America and elsewhere has come to be based on the AA philosophy of alcoholism.

2. *Special training is required in order to understand, help, or counsel a chemically dependent person.*

instead of the more rational viewpoint that chemical dependency is a common mental health problem that fits well within the existing psychosocial theories of interpersonal helping that are taught in undergraduate and graduate programs in most universities. It has been known for decades that cognitive approaches, specifically the rational-emotive therapy of Albert Ellis, Ph.D., is highly relevant and useful to recovering addicts. The state credentialing programs that provide addiction care certification are redundant in some curriculum areas to other educational programs in counseling and mental health, but in other curriculum areas they are more like seminaries, where faith-based theories and concepts are the norm and thus protected from objective evaluation.

Most people who recover form chemical dependence do so independently, outside of *any* recovery program, as Stanton Peele reports in his, *The Diseasing of America.* That being the case, it would seem more appropriate to "detrain" our legions of chemical dependency specialists who are achieving notably poor results, and introduce them to methods found in mental health curricula or methods that could be learned from interviewing people who have gotten better on their own.

The state-certified substance abuse counselor training programs are usually laden with 12-stepism. These certificate programs also foster low frustration tolerance among their students by providing an unprecedented shortcut to the roles of "counselor" and "therapist." Admission standards are usually compromised so that it appears that

18

counseling alcoholics and other substance abusers requires *less* training and academic preparation than for other client populations. While it is desirable for any counselor or therapist to have *comprehensive* training, as in graduate professional training programs, it is doubtful that any *special* training that circumvents the usual academic rigors will produce counselors that function comparably with practitioners whose skills are the result of comprehensive professional training.

Subsequent to RRS discussions with the State of Maryland Division Alcohol and Drug Abuse Administration in 1990, officials there agreed to, "...revise our regulations to eliminate references to 12-step groups, AA, NA, etc., and to replace those references with the broader category of *self-help groups.*" Cosmetic changes like this are a good beginning, and we will see if other states will go farther than this. The importance in this matter lies in the fact that the state certificates in substance abuse counseling may become licenses, so that one will be required to be *licensed* in order to be of help to a chemically dependent person. Under such an arrangement, training and certification programs would have control over the selection of students, as well as control over the content of the curriculum of the programs, thus furthering the singularity of 12-stepism in health care. With the introduction of the diagnosis, "codependence," which describes 97% of the general population according to one of its chief proponents, John Bradshaw, we see an extension of 12th step evangelism that brings us full circle to pre-Renaissance concepts of mankind suffering primarily from separation from God. With "codependence," the 12 steps are boundless. In real life, one can find ample evidence showing that no *special* training is necessary in order to counsel or otherwise help people suffering from uncomplicated alcohol or drug dependence.

3. It is so difficult to recover from alcoholism that supernatural aid is required.

instead of the more rational viewpoint that quitting drinking and abstaining from alcohol are not such difficult tasks when compared to the alternative of continuing to drink. Recovery from alcoholism is no big thing, and can occur with or without outside help. Spiritual healing with prayer and Higher Powers is an excellent approach for religiously-inclined, recovering alcoholics, but certainly not for everyone. Simply not drinking allows for a return to physical and mental health among spiritual believers and disbelievers alike, but both groups can benefit greatly from some philosophical reconditioning to minimize the chances of relapse.

To convince people that only a Higher Power can restore them to sanity undermines the sense of personal competence that is central to recovery from chemical dependence.

Many people report that when they have refrained form using intoxicants for many months or even years, a subtle change occurs in the quality of their conscious experience. It is as if a mental fog has lifted, many months after one's initial withdrawal from the intoxicant. One person in RR reported it as, "Like the lifting of a morning haze, there was a new *crispness* to my thinking somewhere during my sixth month of sobriety." Comedian Sid Caesar remarked after attaining a good sobriety, "Where have I been?" When this clearing up happens in the rational mode of recovery, we regard it as a return to mental health based on physical health, or good, clean living. In traditional programs it is called a "spiritual awakening," or a gift from God. These two interpretations are really quite different.

4. *AA is the only thing that works and those who reject AA cannot be helped. AA programs have no responsibility to provide for those who object to AA, such as by referring refuseniks to a rational alternative, or by encouraging drop-outs that they may be able to do well on their own.*

instead of the more rational idea that alcoholics can learn to abstain from harmful substances through many means, the chief of which is adherence to certain lines of rational thought. To withhold this information from alcoholics, as is usually the practice in AA-oriented programs, is to discourage motivated people and to invite low recovery rates. When this occurs in public agencies or hospitals, malpractice prosecution or other legal remedies may be appropriate.

5. *Because alcoholics and other substance abusers are fundamentally dependent personalities, substitute dependencies, such as on the AA group and God, are necessary for a meaningful and durable sobriety.*

instead of the more rational viewpoint that chemically dependent people aren't much different from others, except in their physical relationship with alcohol or drugs. Although psychological, emotional, and social problems may certainly be caused by excessive drinking, there are no such things as "alcoholic" or "addictive" personalities. Recovering persons would best pursue independence not only from alcohol or drugs, but also from other dependencies as well.

6. *Substance abusers who express disagreement with the 12-step Program, especially "the God part," are either (a) not quite ready to really get serious about their problems, (b) copping out, (c) making excuses so that they can justify further drinking, or (d) misguided, spiritually deficient persons who, if they are able to stay sober for more than a short period, cannot expect to achieve real happiness.*

instead of the more rational viewpoint that those who "see through" or object to spiritual teachings and requirements of faith should be *commended* for exercising critical judgement. Healthy

20

skepticism is the fundamental strength upon which a durable, meaningful, *rational* sobriety can be based.

7. Alcoholism is a chronic condition characterized by a daily, lifelong vulnerability to sudden, catastrophic relapse, so that a durable sobriety requires constant vigilance, self-consciousness, and introspection as well as endless participation in AA meetings and activities.

instead of the more rational viewpoint that an elegant counterpoint to the spiritual life exists in the Rational Recovery (RET) paradigm; it teaches how to take personal responsibility for what is taken into the body and how to avoid relapses, year after year, without supernatural aid, without daily ritual and prayer, without endless nightly meetings with others who also were once addicted, and without undue self-consciousness about one's past indulgences. Recovery from alcohol or drug dependence is usually an intense struggle at first, but for many it becomes second nature to not drink or use. Therefore, endless dependence on the initial means of recovery is inappropriate. Each person is the best judge of when recovery is complete, although he or she may consider the viewpoint of experienced persons. Sobriety is a matter of self-interest, and the locus of emotional and behavioral control is found within.

8. Recovering alcoholics are obliged to become better people.

instead of the more rational viewpoint that fearless moral inventories, while commendable in some respects, are simply not relevant to recovery from addiction. A fearless inventory of the irrational self-talk that perpetuates one's intoxication cycle would seem more appropriate and a better use of one's time. Simple sobriety seems to be preferable ethically and morally to habitual drunkenness, but one's ethical behavior and moral attitudes are a matter separate from recovery. In RR, we do not become sober in order to become good; we do so because we want some good out of life.

9. Addiction, especially alcoholism, is a symptom of an underlying, practically universal disorder called "the addictive process." The addictive process is a reflection of one's spiritual deficiencies and one's character defects. Those character defects and spiritual deficiencies also underlie many common "sins," i.e., gambling, overeating, overspending, "excessive" sexual lusting, shoplifting, masturbating, child-beating, or even experiencing strong moods or emotions.

instead of the more rational viewpoint that addiction simply means chemical dependency and the focus of recovery is narrowly defined as the return to physical and mental health that usually accompanies abstinence. Intriguing research data suggests that alcohol is selectively addictive or "attractive" to those who are genetically predisposed, rather than to those who are morally or spiritually deficient, or without belief in things supernatural. Dependency on drugs or alcohol is usually accidental, and *some* people seem to be born accident-prone in this respect. There is no "addictive process" other than the appetite-driven self-talk that justifies and demands continued substance abuse. The current use of the term "addiction" seems more related to original sin than to a genuine health issue.

10. *Those closely associated with addicts are almost always sick with an underlying, practically universal disorder called "codependency" and in need of care. The care needed is spiritual healing, AA style, or some closely related approach.*

instead of the more rational viewpoint that it's tough living with a drunk, and dealing with an alcoholic mate or family member requires some tough decisions. The prefix "co-" adds nothing to the meaning of the word "dependent," and in fact *obscures* its meaning, with an anti-therapeutic effect. One cannot really "be" a "codependent," but one may be *so* dependent on the approval of an addicted person that one is immobilized. It is good to recognize one's emotional dependency on an incompetent person, but one need not come to view oneself as spiritually deficient, sick, or "codependent" because of one's present or past circumstances. Instead, one would best decide to be *less* dependent on others and act on the principle of self-interest.

11. *The desire to think independently and be in control of one's life and destiny is one of the character defects that causes the "addictive process" and "codependency."*

instead of the more rational viewpoint that just the opposite is so. Those characteristics are the chief means by which one may achieve rational, no-higher-power sobriety. "Codependency" and "the addictive process" are variations on the theme of original sin, and a way to make the 12-step program seem necessary for everyone.

Confidence, competence, and control of one's emotions and behavior are hallmarks of maturity and mental health, rather than being "sick" or part of the "disease of alcoholism."

12. *"Self-help" in addiction care means separation from the mental health community, except when certain professionals endorse the quasi-religious, "spiritual" agenda of AA.*

instead of the more rational viewpoint that helping oneself can certainly involve sound mental health principles presented by professionals who are skilled in empowering alcoholics and other substance abusers to achieve a healthy sobriety. One goal of Rational Recovery Systems is to bring chemical dependency back home to mental health, where it belongs.

It is worth making the distinction between "self-help" and "support" groups. The expression "support" infers dependence, while "self-help" would seem to be more aligned with concepts of personal independence and empowerment.

13. Recovery is a miracle provided by God, and there are no limitations to what can be accomplished through the 12-steps of AA.

instead of the more rational viewpoint that for many people there are distinct limitations to self-help, and professional help is sometimes appropriate and worthwhile. With God left out of the recovery formula, we are left with human resources to solve human problems.

14. Confession of personal shortcomings and error is inherently therapeutic.

instead of the more rational viewpoint that confession in itself has little value, and actually perpetuates dependency ideas of guilt and the need for external approval. In RR, self-disclosure is not for the purpose of demonstrating one's humility or past degeneracy, but for the self-centered purpose of learning from others about oneself.

15. AA is not a religion; there is room for all degrees of disbelief in the 12-step program. AA is only a huge spiritual organization that encourages belief in a Supreme Being that provides character repairs, views sobriety as a miracle of divine intervention, and expects to make the world a better place for all.

instead of the more rational idea that the facts speak otherwise. The 12-step program is intensely religious and is designed for religious conversion experiences, as reading them will show. The media publishes alcoholic salvation stories every day. Disbelief is regarded as a character defect, and there is an entire derisive chapter about disbelievers in the inerrant AA bible, "The Big Book." Widespread popularity of 12-step programs coincides with a shrinking public health care dollar and the "privatization" of addiction care and related disorders. The result is the encroachment of 12-stepism into publicly funded programs and the emergence of a new mental health establishment based on pseudo-science.

16. People who don't accept a spiritual agenda and criticize institutional AA are invariably angry, crass individuals whose opinions are warped or tainted,

instead of the more rational viewpoint that those whose viewpoints are faith-based are quite vulnerable to objective inquiry, and they often project their own anger onto those who raise good questions.

17. "Denial" is a cardinal sign, or a primary characteristic, of chemical dependency,

instead of the more rational viewpoint that most substance abusers know that they are chemically dependent and wish that they were not so. While they may conceal the extent of their intake from others, they do not typically deny it to themselves. People who voluntarily attend recovery meetings or inpatient recovery programs cannot be "in denial" because they are present. "Denial" is more of a description of 12-step heresy than a useful clinical term.

18. *The 12 steps of AA are intrinsically therapeutic, even when entities other than God are substituted, and, together, the 12 steps are ineffable, containing higher wisdom that is not apparent to the casual observer.*

instead of the rational idea that the 12 steps make little sense without a core belief in a Supreme Being.

The italicized, irrational assumptions above are woven into the policies and practices of alcohol treatment programs everywhere. The purpose of Rational Recovery Systems is to add the rational concepts to existing recovery programs and into public policy so that a two-track service delivery system will emerge in the field of chemical dependency.

In a later chapter, "A Discussion of the Twelve Steps of Alcoholics Anonymous," we will take a close look at some of the inner workings of AA, with the purpose of seeing why so many people reject its spiritual messages.

The beginnings of Rational Recovery Systems

While I was a clinical social worker on a mobile psychiatric team (1981 - 1990), I responded to crisis calls, many of which involved older alcoholics. I observed that virtually all of them had been to Alcoholics Anonymous, yet, when I attempted to refer them to a treatment program, they frequently refused, objecting to the "religious" nature of local addiction care programs. Certainly, many of those who resisted addiction care were poorly motivated for any kind of care, but I became concerned about those who had *specific objections* to the 12-step program of AA. I understood very well what it was like to be offered a program that didn't make sense, because I had been through that same experience myself. But I realized that my reasons for rejecting AA were not the only reasons people don't do well in that program. Others refuse AA because they do not like to talk about themselves in front of a group, because they won't call themselves "alcoholics," because they prefer to pick their own friends, because they don't want to depend on sponsors or groups, because they would prefer to help themselves independently, because they object to the lifetime commitment that the 12-steps require, because they have conflicting religious views, and still others have no real complaint about AA, but continue to fail despite real, often repeated, efforts to use the 12-step approach of AA. I decided that I would go to bat for those who strike out in AA.

Unless you have a specific objection to AA, it can be of *immense* help to you and your family. But alas, many of us *do* have specific objections to AA, and for us an alternative, a *rational* alternative, is desperately needed.

In my own case, I was able to utilize some professional training I had received years before through the Institute for Rational-Emotive Therapy. I learned some simple techniques for thinking *rationally*, and when push finally came to shove, I was able to become my own rational therapist. *The Small Book* is a primer to help recovering alcoholics and other substance abusers to become their own therapists and achieve the "unmiracle" of NHP (no higher power) sobriety. It is smaller than 'The Big Book" (of Alcoholics Anonymous) because there isn't really all that much to be said. It all boils down to this: When you've really had enough to drink, make a plan to knock it off *for good,* and then do it. Use the information in the following chapters to help make your decision stick, and then get your act together like anyone else. Take your lumps, your discomfort, and your disappointments in stride. Avoid what doesn't make sense; *trust your own judgement.* Don't expect miracles.

Mood disorders

If you feel depressed in spite of your best efforts to get your life in order, and no amount of talking, meditating, socializing, or caring from others seems to help, then you may also be suffering from a depressive mood disorder requiring medical care. Spiritual healing programs seem not to recognize that human beings are physical entities, and that the experiences of mind, mood, and manner are complex physiological states and events. RR, however, insists that many alcohol and drug dependent people also suffer an underlying mood disorder that is physiological, and it seems that sometimes excessive drinking is an attempt to self-medicate Depression.

For the present, we are stuck with one word, "depression," that describes two distinct, but sometimes overlapping conditions: (1) normal "depression," which is caused by "bad thoughts," and (2) "Depression," with the big "D," which is caused by "bad chemicals." Normal depression is just that, the ordinary low moods which correspond to the events in day to day life. We can say that this kind of depression is ideogenic, or stemming from ideas we have about things. It is because *we feel the way we think* that RR is such an effective way for chemically dependent people to gain control of the emotions that perpetuate the drinking cycle. Some depression is a natural part of alcohol dependence, partly because alcohol, used regularly, is a central nervous system depressant, and partly because of the great disappointments and failures that go along with impaired, intoxicated judgement. Just stopping drinking for a while will allow some of this kind of depression to lift, and by adopting principles of rational thought,

25

as presented in *The Small Book,* an alcoholic person can expect to achieve a gratifying sobriety in a matter of weeks or months.

However, if you stop drinking and have persistent trouble for over a month with "the blues," have trouble sleeping, eat poorly, or get the feeling that life isn't worth living, then it would be wise to seek professional help. If you are in an RR group, call your Advisor; this is what he or she is there for. If you are not in an RR group, see a private therapist you trust, look up a psychiatrist in the yellow pages, or call the local community mental health center. It is possible that you suffer Depression, and you may benefit from some "good chemicals" to neutralize your "bad (depressant) chemicals." Antidepressant medication is not addictive and does not make you high, relaxed, or anything else. Instead, it acts on a chemical imbalance deep in the brain, enabling you to return to a mood that *for you* is normal.

In clinical settings, rational-emotive therapy has been found to be as effective as antidepressant medication in the treatment of some major depressive disorders. Even though professionals are involved with RRS, they will not provide intensive psychotherapy for major depressive disorders in the RR groups, but they will help to identify when professional care, including medical care, is appropriate.

Over the years, AA has been wrong, often tragically wrong, about psychoactive medicine. They often have discouraged individuals from seeking professional help, and taking any kind of psychiatric medication is severely frowned upon, even in some publicly-run AA programs. The myth about the "dry drunk," for example, is perpetuated by stories of people suffering the serious disorder, manic-depressive illness, which is characterized by erratic mood swings which resemble alcohol intoxication. To AA, these people seem not to be applying the 12-step creed diligently enough, and have not yet qualified for the *miracle* of sobriety. Mental health is not a miracle — it is the result of the proper conditions, many of which are physical, and the rest of which are philosophical.

One thing is certain — there is no such thing as a "dry drunk." In order to be drunk, one must have drunk something. It is true that during withdrawal, people may be irritable, impulsive, intrusive, or obnoxious, but those are withdrawals and not the mysterious condition spoken of by "recovering alcoholics." It is not a medical term or one used in professional mental health jargon. There is no formal recognition that the phenomenon exists, nor are there any documented examples of people experiencing a "dry drunk."

As I have heard the expression used, a "dry drunk" is used to describe periods of irritability, confusion, hostility, anger, or depression that are experienced by people who have not been drinking recently. Sometimes "dry drunk" is used as if it were a diagnosis, at other times it

26

describes the person, i.e., "He's a dry drunk." Usually, the implication is that someone is not working the 12 step program diligently enough, or has stopped attending meetings but is still sober. It is often used to describe those who challenge the status quo in meetings.

Naturally, what goes on in AA meetings is no one else's business, and RRS is aware of that. However, when the public interest is involved and people are treated incompetently in any group setting, there are plenty of precedents for others to make some noise about specific practices. It's called "accountability."

Here is some information about chemical dependence. Alcohol dependence is just *one, single problem*. It may, and often does, co-exist with and lead to several other psychiatric conditions. Bipolar illness, or manic-depressive illness, is an example of one condition that is often seen along with alcohol dependence. People suffering bipolar illness often have symptoms when they stop drinking, sometimes during the first week or month of sobriety, but a bipolar episode may occur years after one sobers up. They might start getting "hyper," talking excessively, not making very good sense, making bad judgements, and being a general nuisance to others. When they appear at support group meetings, they may be sober but doing poorly, so they are likely to get tagged, "dry drunk." Acute bipolar conditions require psychiatric care with daily medication. Traditional support groups don't like the idea of members being "on something," so psychiatric medication is often discouraged.

Major depression is another condition sometimes called "dry drunk." Worsening depression is not part of withdrawal. To the contrary, when alcohol dependent people stop drinking, there may a period of depression and inertia at first, but within a month or so, there is a general lifting of alcohol-induced depression and a return to physical and corresponding mental health. People who feel rotten for more than a month are not "dry drunks"; instead, they should suspect that there may be an underlying depressive illness and seek medical consultation. Major depression can be lethal, as many people get rid of themselves when all seems hopeless. Untreated depression makes alcoholic relapse a virtual certainty, because alcohol does provide fast, *temporary* relief from the worst kind of misery. Major depressions cannot be substantially helped by talking, being cared for or loved, counseling, or by praying, and even psychotherapy may be quite limited in the treatment of major depression. Time and medication with antidepressants, along with cognitive psychotherapy, are known to be the best treatments, especially when in conjunction with each other. Calling someone who is feeling bad, or who is having trouble sleeping or eating, or who is socially inhibited a "dry drunk" can be extremely destructive.

27

Everyone has problems and bad days (sometimes bad weeks). Normal ups and downs do not have to be diagnosed, and it is especially inappropriate to call someone who used to be dependent on alcohol a "dry drunk" because he or she isn't smiling happily. This only perpetuates the myth that there is something inherently different about people who were once dependent on alcohol or drugs; this can be discouraging and frustrating to someone who is already having a bad day.

It is unlikely that with some kind of supervision by mental health professionals practices like the "dry drunk" tradition would have gained such wide acceptance. But with AA unsupervised everywhere, there is a tendency for folk wisdom to be institutionalized into awkward and sometimes abusive practices. Chemically dependent people have a right to appropriate medical and professional care, and RRS stands to help that become more available. Help is where you find it, and in your quest for sobriety you may benefit from professional help, regardless of whether you suffer a psychiatric disorder.

Why Professional Help?

Any therapist worth his salt can help you defeat chemical dependency if that is what you want, and there are far more good therapists than bad. It doesn't matter whether or not the therapist has a personal history of chemical dependency, unless, of course, you make it an issue. The idea that "one must be one to understand one" is just one more example of unfounded tales that are told at AA meetings. You are not a special breed of human being whose problems are so complex that only other former drunks or junkies can understand you. Although you have severe personal problems associated with excessive drinking, you still act the way you feel and feel the way you think, just like non-alcoholics. As you will see later in *The Small Book*, there is little, if any, difference between a "sober alcoholic" (oxymoron) and someone who has never been addicted to something. If anything, you will have a richer variety of life experiences upon which to build an elegant, rational philosophy of life. If you read this page with understanding, then you are quite capable of applying the same intelligence to a relationship with a counselor or therapist.

If you find AA's brand of spiritual healing unsatisfactory after learning first-hand about the program, it may be hard to avoid throwing out the baby with the bath water. During the meetings you have attended, you will have noticed that the groups have a negative attitude toward anything other than AA, and toward professional helpers in particular. "Therapy doesn't work" is a common remark, and each AA member seems to have his or her own example of incompetent professionals who either bungle stupidly or seem to exploit the problems of alcoholics. Counselors and therapists are thought to be ignorant on chemical dependency, offering worthless advice for money — unless, of course, the therapist in question is a 12-stepper himself.

Professional therapists lay claim to the public trust mainly on the basis of their scientific credentials, unless their training was in theology or divinity. The methods used by professionals are usually empirically valid, which means only that the methods are regarded as effective, useful or worthwhile by a faculty of experienced and knowledgeable persons. Persons trained in accredited schools of medicine, social work, psychology, nursing, and counseling are given a broad base of skills in interpersonal helping, skills that apply in any situation. A therapist's skills then develop according to areas of interest, and in almost every community there are trained therapists who do good work with alcoholics. These therapists are sometimes listed under other specialties, such as marriage and family counselors or individual psychotherapists. By shopping the yellow pages as you would for a good barber or mechanic, you may find a therapist who agrees with your view that professional therapy is the best thing for AA refuseniks. If you are fortunate, the therapist will be familiar with cognitive therapy, especially RET. Be clear from the start that you have a serious drinking problem and need help in stopping and staying stopped. That will avoid the common trap of initial misdiagnosis, which is likely when the therapist is not fully informed of the grave nature of your problem.

Part of the problem in finding a good alcoholism therapist is that professionals themselves are sometimes unsure of how they fit into the alcoholism scene. In many communities, mental health services are offered separately from alcoholism services, as if there were some vital difference between alcoholics and non-alcoholics. There isn't, of course, except that alcoholics drink self-destructively, but the funding for the programs comes from different sources, and there are two bureaucracies instead of one. In the mental health bureaucracy, the methods for interpersonal helping are based largely on scientific principles, on theories developed from systematic observation, and upon objective reality. By talking confidentially to a therapist or being in a therapy group, you will come to think and feel differently about some central issues in life. If you go to a community mental health clinic for professional, scientifically-based help with your alcoholism, you may be quickly referred to the alcoholism services bureaucracy, where religious instruction along the lines of the 12-step program is the central ingredient. You will not be asked about your personal views about God, religion, and spiritual healing, because those questions are taboo among most professionals. It will be *assumed* that you cannot be helped through normal means, but only by people who *specialize* in chemical dependency. Professionals, therefore, are often reluctant to accept substance abusers into their caseloads because they believe their training is insufficient to understand or appreciate the *mysteries* of chemical dependencies. One of the purposes of *The Small Book* is to demystify drug and alcohol dependence and thus help professionals make themselves more relevant and more available to the millions of alcoholics who, like you, are not in the market for spiritual healing and higher powers, but who sincerely want to recover from a dread affliction. As stated earlier, RRS is bringing chemical dependency back home to mental health, where it belongs.

Ted's story

The idea that individuals need someone or something greater or more powerful than themselves upon which to rely is a common irrational idea that creates and perpetuates dependency. "Irrational" in this sense means only that there is no evidence to support the idea; on the contrary, there is considerable evidence showing that human beings do best when they have a sense of personal responsibility for self-improvement, and are willing to take the risks of trying to solve their own problems — with some assistance, perhaps, but essentially on their own. In the story below, you will read of one man's encounter with AA. It is quite different from the popular tales of alcoholics who achieve a sublime inner peace through a profound spiritual awakening, or who come to have a personal relationship with a supernatural god. It is a story that is far more common than you might think; tales like Ted's were seldom heard until recently, but they exist in great numbers. Indeed, there is no way to estimate how many millions of Teds there have been, or how many of them have died of alcohol dependence and other addictions for lack of *rational* recovery programs. He is a survivor, and a rare breed, for most people don't have the personal strengths, the intelligence, the opportunities, and the self-discipline to undertake a rational recovery as he did. Many people who have figured out some of the puzzle — that AA is a religious movement disguised as treatment — are unable to discover the insights of rational living on their own. They desperately need a source of information on how to control their emotions, how to resist cravings, how to learn new social concepts, and how to truly accept themselves as fallible, yet inestimably worthwhile, human beings.

Most of all, the public needs to be made aware that there are different roads to recovery, and that the stories we read and hear in the newspapers, magazines, and TV about drunks who "saw the light" and had a spiritual awakening aren't really the whole truth. Read Ted's story with an open mind, and notice your own feelings about what he has to say.

My name is Ted, and I was once addicted to alcohol. I now never drink alcohol, because if I did I would suffer impaired judgement, lose out on the good things in life, and suffer declining physical health. I sometimes think about having a drink, but then I remember that my body is somehow different from most people's, and that taking a drink would almost certainly lead to additional consumption followed by a return to addiction. Since I stopped drinking seven years ago, I have enjoyed life more than ever before, so it would be stupid of me to interrupt my happiness for the brief pleasure of an alcohol buzz. I'm not even sure that taking a drink would be pleasant. I'm not interested in finding out, either.

When things got bad for me seven years ago, I sought help from Alcoholics Anonymous, and, looking back, I can see that I benefited somewhat from the many meetings I attended. At the time, however, I was seriously put off by my perception of AA as a religious cult. I tended to doubt my own judgment about this, since I was wrong in so many other things, but I see now that I was correct: that AA is a religion, complete with deity-worship, a holy book, a creed, confessional rites and the offering, acts of contrition, atonement, and redemption, and for the faithful, salvation in "serenity" — the peace of an AA elder that passeth all understanding.

Raised in a strong Christian home, I once believed in God and Jesus. I thought that there was a way to be saved or elevated in worth by believing very improbable things. I "felt the presence of God" and believed He could read my mind, and I sensed that He was actually interested in me and cared for me. I even expected that I would become a stronger and better person by praying, by reading the Bible, and by trying harder to believe the strange teachings of my childhood religion. During my adolescence I found that I was somehow able to "see through" some parts of religion, especially the idea that it is wonderful that someone good, i.e., Jesus, had died on account of my badness, and that my badness was cancelled because of that death. If anything, I would feel guilty that Jesus had to die on my account, an observation which eventually led me to believe that one of the purposes of religion is to put people down. By the time I was out of high school, I had pretty well figured out that religion is just a lot of superstition put out by churches to make people give money, that gods are all make-believe, and that the universe is big, mostly empty, and has no purpose or meaning of its own. I didn't go around telling people what I thought, because when I did, they would become frightened and angry. I just kept it to myself and secretly marveled at how many people believed in God, in spite of having no proof at all, and in spite of all the weirdness that goes along with it.

During my twenties I drank a lot because I liked booze more than anyone else I knew, and by thirty or so, things got pretty bad. I lost a couple of jobs, wrecked some cars, and had a string of unusual injuries, like cutting myself while cooking, getting beaten up by a street gang, getting burned, and breaking a leg falling out of a tree — all these while intoxicated. When my marriage

31

started going bad and I was out of work again, I ended up lying in a church parking lot, dumped there by my wife who pushed me out of the car with her foot and drove off. Inside an AA meeting was going on; the people who came outside and took me in were very nice and very understanding. They'd all been in the same boat, they said. There was hope, if I would just keep coming back to meetings.

After a few meetings, I was jubilant. Hope returned that I might lead a normal life. I talked freely at the meetings and quickly got to know the regulars as if they were old buddies. One of them, Ben, was mentioned as a possible sponsor because we hit it off so well. But then, something disturbing started to happen, something I first tried to ignore. Eventually it had to come to the surface.

Everyone talked about God, about the "Higher Power" upon which alcoholics must depend to remain sober. They prayed to God during meetings, and the literature I was given contained prayers and religious meditations. I was polite, and explained that I didn't believe in any god, and the members reassured me that there is room for all degrees of disbelief in AA; the important thing is to just keep coming back. During one meeting, while the 12-step program was being explained to me, I asked why everyone wanted me to start believing in God. An older gentleman who had been coming back for twenty-eight years replied, "Because it's the only way to stay sober, Ted. In all my years, I haven't known of anyone who has stayed sober that didn't have some concept of a Higher Power. We are powerless over our addictions, Ted. We must have a Higher Power to give us strength to live the sober life. Do you understand that?"

It finally sank in that I was, in effect, back in church, being pressured to believe very improbable things in order to escape death. As I was starting to withdraw from the group's attention, another member spoke up, attempting to reassure me. "The Higher Power is different for everyone, Ted. The Big Book says we must turn our lives over to the care of God, as we understand Him. It doesn't say the Christian God, or the Islamic God, or the Jewish God, Ted. Anything you understand to be a Higher Power will do." Another man chimed in, "Yes, I didn't believe in God either when I first came to AA. I guess I was an atheist, but I finally accepted that I had better get with the program or end up dead meat, so I found my Higher Power in a bedpan! When I was craving a drink one night, I looked at the pan by my bed that I used to vomit in when I was sick from drinking too much. I thought to myself, "Pan, you're my higher power for tonight." When the night was over, I thanked my Higher Power, and all of a sudden I was thanking God, and ever since then I have known the unfailing love of God Almighty. I guess I am saved. At least I'm still sober." I wanted to ask why, if his God was so powerful, he still felt he had to attend meetings five nights a week, but I was drowned out by several others who were eagerly assuring me that anything can be your "HP"!

I finally stood up and said, "I'm sorry. I'm just not into gods, or praying, or taking moral inventory, and I don't plan to make amends to people I may have disappointed or hurt as a way of helping myself. I'll take care of myself. I don't think I can come back if this is all there is."

As I headed toward the door, Ben followed and pulled me to a side room while the rest closed the meeting with the Lord's Prayer. He told me about a special group of AA that met just once a week across town. They used to be called "The Intellectuals," but were just now changing their name to "We Agnostics." He gave me the address and returned to the meeting.

To make a long story short, We Agnostics turned out to be the same nonsense warmed over. They used the same 12-step program, except that someone had whited out "God" and substituted the word "Wisdom". We Agnostics was more informal than the main group, and it was clear that they were really a group of outcasts who enjoy only second-class membership in AA. No recognition is given them, except as the dumping ground for AA malcontents, and no special program or literature is provided by the national organization. Little is expected of them, since according to AA theology they must surely die.

That, amazingly, is what the AA group told me when I returned and explained that I had decided to leave AA altogether. "We wish you well, Ted, but we must warn you that you are most unlikely to stay sober if you stop coming; you're very sick and you'll need AA for many years to come. Some people don't get straightened out until they've quit and come back several times. If you don't bend your knees, you will bend your elbow. When you start drinking again, you'll probably come crawling back, that is, if you're fortunate enough to survive that long. We'll be here, and maybe then you'll come to believe in a Higher Power that will restore you to sanity."

It's been seven years since that evening, and I am recovered. I have been told not to say I am a recovered alcoholic, but "recovering". I consider that just more doctrine to put people down and make them feel dependent on AA, dependent on the grace of some god. Personally, I feel that AA was more dependent on me than I was on them. Why else would they use all those tricks to pressure me into the God business? With me there was no magic involved in recovery, no "Higher Power," no moral inventory, no confession, no drunkalogs, no AA meetings. Instead, there was a willingness on my part to trust myself and my own ability to reason. Most important, I was willing to tolerate discomfort, anxiety, some initial craving, and some uncertainty and self-doubt. If I drink, I am sick. When I stay sober, I am soon recovered. I learned to love myself by studying rational therapy, and I saw a rational counselor for a while just to get my thinking straight. I am a free man, free to drink or not. I choose not to because I would be injuring myself, raining on my own parade, and who the hell needs that?

Take Sides!

In this small book, you will see that there are two kinds of sobriety. One is HP (higher power) sobriety, built on continuing dependency and supernaturalism. The other, NHP (no higher power) sobriety, is built on the strengths within each of us and inspires us to independence wherever humanly possible.

I have observed many, many people struggle against their addictions in both RR and AA programs, and I have seen people achieve sobriety both ways. But the ones who succeed seem to have some things in common, no matter which program they are in. They are these: (1) they sincerely *want* to get better, (2) they accept the idea of *abstaining* from mind-altering substances, and (3) they are *committed* to a coherent general philosophy that justifies abstaining from those substances.

Much rests on this third point. AA and RR are opposites in many respects; in fact, RR is the *counterpoint* to AA. As you read on, you may come to agree with me that "in between" is not the best place to be. I propose that instead of 12 steps, we have just one, as follows: "Step 1. We made a fearless examination of our most basic beliefs and selected the recovery program that made the best sense."

Chapter 2

Getting Stopped

This chapter will be the shortest and bluntest in *The Small Book*. It will come swiftly and directly to the point. Unless you stop drinking or using drugs, the rest of *The Small Book* will be of little help. You see, persistent use of intoxicants impairs your ability to think in the abstract, and even though you are intelligent and seem to understand much of what you read, you will fail to gain self-awareness of your own addictive thinking. Remember now, addiction is a philosophy, not your self-drugging behavior. As long as you continue to drink or use, you are practicing the *philosophy* you are wanting to change. Because drinking and using feels good, it is very difficult to even criticize, let alone change, the irrational philosophy that produces such gratification. As you will see in the chapter "Voices," there is a *lot* of mental activity taking place each time you drink or use. In order to *hear* your mental voices that lead you to drink, you must stop drinking and at least *intend* to stay stopped.

You are in control of your drinking or drugging every day. You have been in control all along. You may like to think you can handle it and stop any time you want, but deep down you cling to the idea that addicted or "alcoholic" people can't control their behavior. It gives you a perfect "out": Who can blame someone who is "out of control?"

When the pain and losses caused by your habit exceed the pleasure you get from it you will be ready to quit. If you want to stop drinking, you can quit right now and you know it. If you don't stop right now, then you obviously believe you haven't yet had enough to drink. When you have suffered enough, you will finally quit. There is nothing to stop you from doing so.

Quitting alcohol or drugs is simply a matter of making a decision and then sticking to it by stubbornly refusing to indulge. There may be some initial discomfort, but that is just a physical craving and it will fade within seventy-two hours. After that, physically speaking, you are in the clear. You will never again have a *physical* craving for alcohol, unless, of course, you resume drinking.

For most of us, quitting drinking, or heroin, or crack cocaine is no worse than a mild or moderate case of flu. It's no biggie. About one in four or five of us, though, may experience DT's (delirium tremens), with mental confusion, agitation, great restlessness (not just the usual "shakes"), and even weird visions. Those persons are generally over 40, or have been very drunk for a long time. About one-fourth of the persons who have DT's die, so if you suspect, based on your experiences, that you will become ill this way by going cold turkey, then get to a medical doctor any way you can and explain your desire to withdraw from alcohol.

If you believe that you must "taper off," though it is statistically doubtful that you will be better off in doing so, then *do it,* for one day only, consuming only *one* beer (12 ounces) during the entire day. If you drink more than that, you are merely sustaining your addiction, and you will "forget" that you are trying to save your life by quitting. If your problem is with other drugs that have withdrawal syndromes (like Valium or barbituates) go to a drug clinic for professional supervision.

So, pick a time — like NOW, or tomorrow morning — and KNOCK IT OFF!

I'm sure that none of the above comes as news to you.

I've quit a thousand times...
— Mark Twain

Chapter 3

The Difficulty in
Staying Stopped

If most alcoholic people already know how to stop, why do they continue to drink? Essentially, it's because we indoctrinate ourselves with myths and nonsense. Alcoholic people help themselves and each other to drink by perpetuating the alcoholic philosophy that is passed word-of-mouth and hyped by the media. The philosophy of alcoholism holds that alcoholic people cannot control what they put into their mouths, as if their extremities and facial muscles around the mouth are under some strange, alien force that cannot be understood by the common man. It is pure drivel to think that alcoholics are powerless over their addictions. Repeat: drivel, drivel, drivel. Our so-called powerlessness is learned from other alcoholics, from the media, from professionals who as yet don't know any better, and particularly from Alcoholics Anonymous, the organization that seeks a confession of powerlessness from every substance abuser in the world. The difficulty in getting stopped stems, in large part, from the *extremely popular, irrational, alcoholic belief that addicted people cannot choose to become non-addicted.* The truth is that *many* do it, and do it every day. Recovery from chemical dependence is a commonplace thing that has been going on for thousands of years, long before AA came along. Stripped down, Rational Recovery could be called, "generic recovery," because we are using an approach that most people resort to when undertaking some kind of self-improvement. RR is a kind of "uncommon sense" that is very human.

Hal J., an attorney friend of mine, NHP-sober for six years, summed up the issue of powerlessness this way: "I drank excessively for many years, thinking I was basically out of control and unable to stop. I knew I was an alcoholic because I couldn't prevent myself from drinking too much and suffering all the usual consequences. But I'd heard so much! about alcoholics being out of control that I convinced myself that it was natural to keep drinking, day after day, even though it was wrecking my life. The pain of drunkenness became greater than the pain of being sober, but when I tried to stop I would feel *very* uncomfortable; I figured this is why alcoholics can't stop drinking. Then I'd drink and feel better for a while — it was fast, temporary relief. How did I spell relief? B-O-O-Z-E. It was only after I discovered my own "chicken" attitude toward pain that I was able to stop. Withdrawal was nowhere near as bad as I thought it would be, but I was finally ready to *hurt as much as necessary* to get better."

Q: Do alcoholic people have a "chicken" attitude toward pain?

A: Only the ones who drink.

In alcoholism, *pain is the problem as well as the "cure."* Until an alcoholic person recognizes that alcohol is causing more pain than pleasure, he or she has no reason to stop drinking. It is doubtful that any of us have ever quit drinking because alcohol might *eventually* cause some problems. It is mainly when the emotional pain (fear, disgust, remorse, depression, anxiety, and hangover sickness) is finally *present* and exceeds the pain of not drinking that the stage is set for change. Tragically, if the alcoholic believes in powerlessness, there can be no self-inspired change; rather, one is left with the task of submitting to a "Higher Power" of his own imagination, as defined by an external authority such as AA. The odds are worse than ten to one against anyone achieving substantial change in this way. *The belief in powerlessness over addiction can (and does) kill!*

But if, like Hal J., you understand that we have enormous control over what we put into our mouths, and that the pain of withdrawal is entirely tolerable and utterly harmless, you will act wisely and decisively to "stamp out the problem." You will stop your internal whining, which invariably goes like this:

(1) "Oh, how *hard* it is to give up drinking alcohol!"

(2) "It isn't fair that other people can drink without problems and I can't."

(3) "I can't stand this terrible feeling that I need a drink!"

(4) "My love of drinking is so great that I'm powerless to stop. I'm out of control."

(5) "Drinking is one of my few pleasures, and I shouldn't have to stop!"

(6) "I've got to have alcohol. I need it to feel right."

(7) "I can't imagine life without drinking. It would be so *empty.*"

(8) "I can't help it. I'm powerless. I just can't resist drinking at times."

Your job, if you want to stop drinking, will be to *dispute and destroy* this irrational, alcoholic garbage by cashing in a few of your IQ points, as illustrated in the following examples,

(1) "Hard? Of course it's *hard* to change a habit, but why can't I do something that's *hard* for a change? Is it *easy* being drunk all the time and worrying about all the problems caused by my drinking?"

(2) Fair? Who said life is fair? Is there some universal law of fairness? Of course not. The universe doesn't give a hoot about me! Only *I* can make a better life for me, and that means no more booze! Too bad.

(3) It feels terrible? Come on! It isn't half as bad as having a baby. I can't stand it? The hell I can't! Just you watch!"

(4) "I'm powerless? To whose brain are my arms and legs and facial muscles connected? My neighbor's? Who was it who went to the refrigerator and opened that last beer? Hannibal? Who stocked the refrigerator in the first place? Santa? Could *I* possibly have been the one who chose to wrap my lips around the edge of the beer can and guzzle its contents? Am I really out of control, or is that just what I like to think before drinking some more?

(5) It's one of my few pleasures? Awwwwww, poor little me. Can't have my bottle. Waaaaaa! Waaaaaaaa!

(6) I need it? Got to have it? Oh, sure. Likely story. Uh, huh. Yeah.

(7) I can't imagine life without it? Am I *that* deficient, that I can't even *imagine* a normal, full life without alcohol? Of course not. *Maybe I had better start imagining something other than a life of dependency!*

(8) Can't resist it? If that's so, then I'm dead meat on the hoof. Like hell I'm powerless!

To attack your own alcoholic philosophy, you need not attack yourself. If you are an NHP alcoholic, you are quite fallible, yet as worthwhile as you believe yourself to be. There is no reason not to think lovingly of yourself at all times, right or wrong, drunk or sober. Your drinking career is coming to an end, and you needn't feel guilty about any of it. You are in no way *obliged* to stop drinking, but it is quite probably in your own best interest to do so. When you think well enough of yourself, you will stop ruining your life and all its pleasures with booze. Really.

In this next chapter, the above material is presented once again, but in a way that may induce you to stop your chemical dependence in its tracks. You are about to read some passages that may eventually change the character of American-style addiction care.

Go for it; This one's for you!
— "The Beast"

Chapter 4

Voices

Alcohol and drug dependent people hear voices. But then so does everyone else. In the brain there is a noisemaker. As the old saying goes, "Everybody's got one." In the normal consciousness of us all, there are voices, usually sounding like our own. In our "mind's ear," we can literally hear ourselves talking to ourselves. You can hear one of your own voices right now as you read these words. It may sound something like yours, or it may sound the way you imagine this writer would sound. Our mind's ear can also produce a seemingly infinite variety of sound effects, like birds, surf, explosions, engines, music, and so on. Quite often we provide mental pictures to go along with the sound effects. We humans lead such rich inner lives!

Our voices express our perceptions of reality, our ideas and beliefs about life and ourselves, and our evaluations of experience and circumstance. Together, each person's perceptions, beliefs, ideas, and evaluations comprise what we will call a philosophy of life. Everybody has one of those, too. And, while everyone's philosophy is somewhat different from everyone else's, there are also certain similarities and traits worth noting.

Long ago, the philosophers Aristotle and Plato described their visions of man in the universe, and to this day these two schools of thought divide the discourse on human affairs into two very broad categories, the Aristotelian rational and the Platonic irrational. There are two, and only these two, main trunks in the philosophy of human thought, and all others are derived from or branches of these two mainstreams of thought. To (overly) simplify, Aristotle perceived reality as knowable and humans as essentially rational beings — knowers and doers. To him, A=A, i.e., things are pretty much as they appear to be. To Plato, reality is largely unknowable except as revealed esoterically to a learned class; the average person cannot trust his or her own senses and ability to reason — in other words, what you see is not what you get, or A≠A. People seem inclined to one viewpoint or the other, depending on early learning, education, or perhaps innate disposition or cerebral hemispheric dominance. Skepticism is Aristotelian, faith is Platonic. RR is very Aristotelian, AA is very Platonic.

Although each of us is inclined toward one or the other viewpoint, we are also naturally disposed to both rational and irrational thinking. Our folklore is robust with rational gems such as "There's no use crying over spilt milk," and "Sticks and stones may break my bones, but names will never hurt me." But we are also handed down homilies that are at best unprovable, misleading, and sometimes downright false and emotionally disturbing, such as "No man is an island; everyone needs to be loved," or, as often seen on Valentine's cards, "Before I met you I was nothing; now I am everything." Other examples are (in an adolescent love song) "I Want You, I Need You, I Love You," (as if "need" means "want" or "love"), and, "Your Love is Lifting Me Higher" (which implies that your rejection would force me lower). In defense of godism, "There are no atheists in foxholes," and another along this line is "If there were no God, we would have to invent Him." Living as we do in a largely irrational society, our inner voices take on ideas and beliefs that we accept, because of their prevalence and popularity, without much critical analysis. In his *Reason and Emotion in Psychotherapy*, and *A New Guide for Rational Living*, the works upon which Rational Recovery is based, Albert Ellis enumerates a dozen or so "common irrational ideas which cause and perpetuate emotional disturbance." He shows, and research bears out, that disturbed, unhappy people can help themselves considerably by disputing their own irrational ideas and then replacing them with rational ideas that, *by definition*, are objectively true and serve one's enlightened self-interest.

Before examining the common ideas that perpetuate the addiction relapse cycle, we had better acknowledge some significant differences between addicted and non-addicted persons. Foremost, we who are alcohol or drug dependent suffer impaired cognition and judgment while under the influence, even the long-term influence, of these powerful toxins. While non-drugged persons harbor a balance of rational and irrational ideas, addicted persons are profoundly irrational, or unreasoning, when it comes to the continued use of the addictive substance. Because alcohol and drugs act directly on and deeply within the brain, the organ of thought itself, and because alcohol acts on the brain's pleasure centers in its paradoxical way, alcoholic persons are at a severe disadvantage in protecting themselves from the predictably harmful results of overindulgence. Alcoholic persons are powerfully conditioned to the "quick fix" of another drink because the results are so swift, and usually so immediately gratifying; they live on a roller

42

coaster of pain and pleasure. Almost all pleasure becomes associated with the intoxicant, even though the toxin is also the chief cause of the underlying pain. Consequently, alcohol or drug dependent people devise a personal philosophy that is aimed at providing a guaranteed, uninterrupted supply of the precious substance for life. This *alcoholic philosophy* is a subset of the person's overall philosophy, so that one may function quite sanely and rationally in many significant ways and yet have firm convictions regarding alcohol that seem to deny human intelligence.

In fact, there is an animal, or *beastly*, quality to the addict's dominant inner voice. It is a voice which exists only to obtain more alcohol, and it is always drunk, whether its host, the alcoholic person, is or not; its singular purpose is to stay loaded by having its host drink alcohol or use drugs. Under the influence of the intoxicant, "It," this "Thing," or "Beast," is *amplified*, and, operating on the immediate, biological pleasure principle, "It" drowns out other voices of moderation and safety and takes over your decisions and judgments, almost as if you have been hijacked. During blackouts, the Beast is in complete control and capable of grievous antisocial behavior. Upon awakening, the alcoholic person's rational voices return, asking, "What did I do?" along with the common irrational ideas such as, "Oh, what worm I am for having screwed up once again," and "I've *got* to stop drinking (using) so I can feel like a decent human being," and "I'm *powerless* over this thing; I guess there's no hope for me." Heedless and insatiable, the Beast soon intrudes with, "Better have a drink; it'll take the edge off." Your rational voice, which happens to be you, wavers and subsides in the presence of desire for comfort. And so the cycle continues, with the Beast *always* having the last word and the ideal solution to any problem, another drink. It can speak in many tones and is capable of great cunning in its pursuit of booze. It makes and breaks relationships, choosing only those associates who are compatible with its pharmaceutical agenda and spawning distrust of those who are not inclined toward excess. Its motto is, "Never trust a man who doesn't drink (use)." The Beast seethes and rails at those who would attempt to discourage your continuous excessive drinking or drug use, whether it be a spouse, a boss, a neighbor, a doctor, an officer of the law, or, alas, a therapist, and all of these people are declared potential enemies to be tricked, manipulated, faced down, or avoided. Its own survival comes first, even before yours, and its survival means alcohol or drugs, much as you rightly regard oxygen as a non-negotiable necessity of being. The fact that you are growing weak, suffering organ failure, or are broken from beatings and auto wrecks in no way deters the Beast from seeking ever more alcohol to slake its unending thirst. Your body is only a device to fetch booze or drugs, for as long as your body can

43

function. The Beast listens to your rational voices that sometimes challenges its firm control over you, and then it plays word games to destroy any decisions just made.

You can hear it in hour head, saying, "You can quit any time you want to but not just now. You can handle it if you try a little harder. Just use a little discipline — just stick to beer. You're not a real alcoholic, you're just a booze lover who needs to watch it. It's time for a drink. Now. Get some now. You could really use a drink." So you have a drink, or take a drug. "The-r-r-re! That's gooood. Not bad at all. That really hits the spot. Fantastic. You deserved this one. This one's for you." Some friend, this Beast.

Deprived of its nourishment, alcohol, the Beast does not die but it does go to sleep after a relatively short period of struggling against the rational survival efforts of the host. But it does not sleep deeply. It lies in the dimness of pre-consciousness with one eye half open, waiting for the chance — any chance — to catch you unaware at a choice moment. It is then that the Beast will suggest, in the most endearing terms, "Once again, friend, it is time for us to have a drinky-poo," or, "Screw it. Let's do it." Note that the Beast quite often will use the plural pronouns, "us" and "we," as a way of speaking for your better half — the rational you.

There is no such thing as the Beast, of course. It is merely a mnemonic (memory) device to illustrate the exaggerated, extremely irrational, specialized self-talk with which the addicted person relates to certain intoxicating chemicals. These thought sequences continue for months and years after cessation of drinking, but like any habit, "it" gradually loses strength. It is quite useful for any chemically dependent person to recognize that there is some very poor-quality, self-destructive thinking going on with regard to alcohol or drugs, thinking that can be identified, categorized as ego-alien ("That's not me!"), challenged, and corrected.

The following discussion shows *exactly* how to resist the impulse to drink. As you will see, the BEAST memory device is far superior to any Higher Power (HP) you can imagine; HP's are external and not under your control. They are also difficult or impossible for *us* to really believe in. Even if one believes in an HP, he or she may forget about believing in it, and end up forsaken. If you make yourself your own HP, as some agnostic 12-steppers do, then you will pray to yourself, take your own dubious advice, and then go out and take that message to other alcoholics or drug addicts. For many of us, this is silly. The BEAST device is internal and under your control. If you care for yourself, you will not fail yourself.

The rational alternative to the Higher Power

The special memory device, BEAST, allows you to quickly and effectively gain control over your impulses to drink alcohol, provided that the undesirability of drinking alcohol is clearly established in your mind. Your appetite for alcohol supersedes satiation, transcends social disapproval, and proves "irresistible" when you are trying to abstain. An old saying goes, "At times we have *no defense* against the first drink." This saying is just more alcoholic philosophy and is not so. The Beast device is an *excellent* defense, and one that is easily used once one gets the hang of it.

If you feel uncomfortable with the use of the term Beast to describe some of your own thinking, that is good. Some people have commented that rationality means unconditional self-acceptance, so therefore it is irrational to reject what is very much a part of oneself. Alas, RET, in its *essence,* is an effective, systematic means to thoroughly reject irrationalities that are causing personal problems. The use of the Beast concept, as described in this chapter, is thoroughly rational. Now, look below, and you will find a way to finally get firm control over your endless desire to intoxicate yourself.

The Beast Concept

Boozing opportunity

Enemy recognition

Accuse the beast of malice

Self-control and self-worth reminders

Treasure your sobriety

In the absence of a Higher Power, you may call upon the above concept at any time that the desire to drink alcohol occurs. It has the advantages of simplicity and a high degree of relevance to the immediate circumstances. From here on, any idea of drinking alcohol or using drugs will emanate from an irrational ego-alien source, one that you may conceptualize as an ugly, dread enemy that cares nothing for your safety, health, welfare, or even your survival. The addictive voice in your head is a Beast in every sense except reality, for, of course, the "Beast" is only a product of your fertile imagination.

"Boozing opportunity" is any circumstance or time when you are considering drinking alcohol or taking drugs, whether the substance is present or not. It could be at a wedding, a certain holiday or anniversary, a time of day when you are accustomed to drinking, an unexpected event like being handed a drink when out of town and away from familiar people and routines, when passing an old haunt, when a serious misfortune occurs, or one of those "out of the blue(s)" impulses to have a drink. Sometimes alcoholics and drug addicts who have been sober for years will start contemplating future drinks or taking a drug, and this kind of thinking also originates from their Beasts.

Thoughts about any prospective actions (especially drinking actions) come in pairs. This mental dualism can be seen in just about any action, from the simplest — like going to bed or getting up in the morning (should I or shouldn't I?), to the most complex — like getting married or starting college (should I or shouldn't I?) There seems to be some degree of ambivalence about all of our decisions. The alcoholic is subject to two mental commands, "Drink!" and "Don't drink!" A relapse is when the "Drink!" voice prevails and is obeyed.

"Enemy recognition" is the RR self-awareness which defines *any positive alcohol or drug idea* as the "Enemy." During the early months of recovery, recognition of the "enemy" cognitions are difficult, because you are accustomed to the idea that "All of my thoughts are my own, and therefore are accorded equal merit." In RR, you are learning to perceive positive intoxication ideas as "not-me and very dangerous." It is stressed in group sessions that just the fact of *recognizing* the Beast (up to its old tricks) is sufficient to put it on the defensive. Simple recognition of BEAST-ly ideas has a sudden dampening effect on the impulse to drink. At the point of recognition, you are suddenly *thinking about your thinking,* and therefore exercising a *higher order of consciousness* about the use of intoxicants. Recognition allows you to see that rather than being powerless, you have only been obeying a dominant mental command to drink or use, *and a choice point now exists.* Control is now within your grasp.

RR group sessions, if they are available, reinforce the justified fear of any ideas, imagery, or voices which suggest consuming alcohol or drugs, and your current reasons for wanting to remain sober are frequently reviewed. You can do these things on your own.

"Beast" ideations can be subtle, as the following example shows. Supposing you are invited to a social occasion where there is going to be considerable drinking or use of drugs, and there are also some distinct advantages to attending (business contacts, someone you like will be there, or you just want to have some fun). You would really like to go, but remembering the great importance of staying sober, and

46

recalling that you have often given in to the impulse to drink in the past, you may decide to sit at home instead. On the surface, this would seem like a prudent decision, one that serves your rational self-interest. Not necessarily so.

What's going on here is that you may very well be perpetuating the old irrational idea (one that *every* alcoholic and addict is supposed to believe!) that *"If I go to this party where all my old friends are, the temptation to drink may be so overwhelming that I will inevitably end up drinking and ruin my cherished sobriety. Because I am an addict, or one with a history of alcohol abuse, I am powerless at certain times to refrain from drinking alcohol. Therefore, since I may become powerless at the upcoming party, I had better not even go."* If you can imagine a clever creature planting the seeds for further alcohol or drug use, you will also see that concealed in this seemingly prudent viewpoint is the prophetic root of alcoholic relapse, i.e., the idea that "There are certain conditions under which I am powerless over my decisions to drink or not drink or use drugs." The idea of attending the party may even be accompanied with anxiety, stemming from the idea that, "I want to go to the party so much that I may actually go, and if I do, I'll end up getting loaded, and that will be *catastrophic and awful!"*

We think in pictures as well as sentences, so along with the above self-talk one may also "see" himself succumbing to the impulse to imbibe at the party. These visions of imbibing are actually *rehearsals of alcoholic relapse,* so that the "beast" is, in essence, *preparing* you for the time when a relapse will occur. You can just as easily, and certainly more rationally, imagine the more desirable scenario, a rehearsal of *non-relapse,* in which you imagine yourself firmly refusing any alcohol or drug intake — and in living color!

One must wonder how so many Beast ideas have become incorporated into traditional spiritual healing programs. You are clear, I hope by now, that traditional ideas of powerlessness are deadly, and that reliance on anything or anyone else but you to resist temptation is folly. (If not, then read on.) But, how about the old saw, "One day at a time?" Is this really such a good idea, to renew the struggle each day? Doesn't this keep the idea of drinking or using constantly before you, so that eventually you might find yourself "powerless?" If you went "One week at a time," would you be more likely to relapse? Hardly, if you've got the hang of the Beast. Traditionalists may say, "Never is too long; we can handle one day at a time more easily than a whole lifetime." Interesting. That's just what the Beast of drug and alcohol dependence says. *"Never* say never. Keep your options open. You have thirty years of life left; who's to say you'll *never* drink or use again. Maybe I won't do it right now, *but who knows?"*

47

"Accuse the enemy of malice." Various dissociative (distancing) techniques can be used, and there is room here for considerable creativity. Some people find anger toward the imaginary enemy to be effective and appropriate, and others find sarcasm and humor fitting ways of prevailing over the monolithic mentality which would accept suffering and death as a consequence of imbibing. Members learn to *actively and assertively respond* to the coaxings of the beast, typically by answering, "I hear myself thinking about (I can picture myself) taking a drink. I hear you Beast, (I see your video, Beast,) and I know what you're up to. You want me to ruin my chances at sobriety so you can get all the booze you want, but I'm not going to cooperate. You want me to think I'm powerless over alcohol so I'll give in and start drinking. You are crude and ugly, but it is I who have the upper hand. Suffer, plead, and beg all you want, Beast, but you'll not get a drop." One creative and witty woman told how she would tell herself, "Now it's time for a nice drink of gin," and pour water into a small glass. She would then drink the water and maliciously exclaim, "Ha-ha! Fooled you!" She reported sensing mastery over the longing for alcohol by acting out this prank. In my own experience, I (JT) have sometimes chuckled at the absurd ploys I hear from my internalized self-sentences that suggest eventual use of alcohol. With time, it is hard to take those ideas seriously.

"Self-control and self-worth reminders" refer to specific rational antidotes to poor impulse control and self-worth problems, described later as "Common Irrational Ideas that Sustain the Alcoholic Drinking Cycle." For example, some defeat the Beast by holding their hands in front of their faces and simply remember that they have complete voluntary control over their muscles and can easily refuse to move their extremities until the Beast is finally faced down. RR clients learn that they can make themselves feel good at will just by thinking lovingly of themselves, and that they need not change in any way in order to do so. We do not remain sober in order to think well of ourselves; it is because we like or value ourselves that we do not drink. We think well of ourselves, ironically, for the same reason we used to drink — to feel good. Self-worth reminders simply express unconditional self-acceptance and the idea that to drink would be poisoning a friend, oneself.

"Treasuring your sobriety" simply means taking an overview and reaffirming the intrinsic value of sobriety, focusing on how life's pleasures are possible only in a consistently sober state. It is here, that you may appreciate the beauty of an approach that may be based on "One lifetime at a time."

The Beast of RR is a deadly serious entity of your own creation that personifies the biological drives that are an integrated part of your human nature. Our use of the imaginary entity is to bring to your awareness lines of conscious thought that otherwise cannot be identified, remembered and changed. If you will recall your last alcohol or drug binge, you will notice that your only recollection of thinking during the entire binge, which may have been days long, is after you started to become satiated. Until you started coming down, it probably seemed to you that you were under some spell, as if you weren't really thinking at all, "on a bender", transfixed, "tripping," or on automatic pilot. You may vaguely remember going through the motions of obtaining the booze or drugs, but you will have great difficulty remembering anything you thought to yourself as you veered toward relapse and then consummated your desire to feel intoxicated. You "came to your senses" all too late, just as you began to feel the alcohol or drug wearing off. And then, you probably came on strong, with exasperation and guilt, "Oh, now look what I've done. I've really blown it. Why do I always do this? Why? Oh, why? Oh, what an idiot I am!" Those thoughts — the self-downing, hopeless, self-blaming ones — you can remember in vivid detail. "How could I have done that?" you may ask later. "What was I even *thinking* to end up on another binge like this?"

Four useless theories

Here are four equally useless and preposterous theories that attempt to explain what drives us to habitual substance abuse. The first is psychoanalytic, the Freudian school of thought. It views humans as being under the control of unconscious forces, an unconscious mind separate form the being that we think we are, that contradicts our conscious desires and intentions. Someone late for an appointment is said to unconsciously *want* to be late, perhaps as a way of expressing anger to the other party, or to guarantee failure and insure self-punishment. Addicts, along the same line of psychoanalytic thought, are said to be unconsciously doing all kinds of things, like avoiding responsibilities, getting even with Mother, acting out dependency frustrations, meeting oral dependency needs, attempting to regain a lost childhood, or trying to compensate for some real or imagined impoverishment. These explanations not only take the problem out of the substance abuser's hands, but they are also far too clever. They glamorize the mundane far more than they add to understanding and they fail to offer any useful means for learning to abstain. Too often these fancy psychoanalytic interpretations become powerful deterrents to personal growth, as they strongly support the irrational idea that the past is a potent determiner of one's present difficulties. In RR, these explanations of why one is alcohol or drug dependent are regarded as "excuses."

The second theory that attempts to explain compulsive substance abuse is the "no-mind behaviorism" that has attained some popularity in recent years. The idea here is that a stimulus leads to a response as with Pavlov's dog or Skinner's rats and pigeons. While stripped-down behaviorism has made valuable contributions in some areas, the concepts are often used by alcoholics to support their continued bingeing, i.e., "My drugging is caused by such-and-such," or, "My drinking is a conditioned response to _____." This is *stimulus-response* (S-R) thinking, which ignores the central part that cognition (thinking) plays in determining our emotions and behavior. It also removes any effective handle on the problem. Fortunately, we are considerably more thoughtful than pigeons. A variation on S-R, added later to account for different responses to the same stimulus, is S-O-R, where O stands for "organism." "Something's going on in there," early behaviorists said as they pondered the human skull.

And that leads us to rational-emotive therapy (RET), devised by Albert Ellis, Ph.D., who in the early 1950's transposed S-O-R into the ABC paradigm that is now a standard psychotherapeutic method taught in most American universities. As a humanistic approach based in scientific thought, RET has been widely criticized as a refutation of "traditional (irrational) values," but it has been even more widely *copied* by more image-conscious theorists who, after all, would like their professional colleagues to put in a good day's work at the clinic practicing "cognitive-behavioral therapy" and actually helping people to overcome their persistent problems.

The third useless (and preposterous) theory that "explains" personal vice is the devil theory, still devoutly believed in by large numbers even in these modern times. If you believe that the devil is making you do things and are unwilling to dismiss at least this portion of your religious faith, then it would make some sense to seek out a rescuing deity to frighten off your devil or to at least give you some supernatural aid in dealing with it. RR is a program of personal change for those who find spiritual healing unsatisfactory, and those with devil problems would probably be better off in AA, where spiritual values reign supreme.

Some RR members ask, "Isn't the Beast idea basically the same thing as the devil theory?" The answer here is a very definite NO. There is no connection in RR to any realm other than reality — the material world. The devil, I am sure you realize, is an invisible being that is said to *really exist* apart from human beings and is said to be responsible for everything that goes bad in the world. That is an entirely different concept from the Beast of RR, which is only an *imaginary* entity that *personifies* certain biologically driven thoughts. It is no accident that in theology the devil is sometimes also called "the Beast," because some religious ideas of "evil" identify our biological, animal-like drives, most notably sex, but also aggression. As with the Cookie Monster, the devil concept has some fringe overlap with the Beast of RR, but all three entities have very fundamental differences. To sum up this issue, let us say that it is irrational to believe that Santa Claus is a real person, but quite rational to imagine that jolly character.

The fourth useless theory about the cause of chemical dependence is the disease theory. The idea here is that if one "has the disease of alcoholism," he or she is incompetent to choose to become unaddicted. Literature from the 12-step establishment frequently shows pictures of neurons and synapses, with chemical formulae written in the margins. They talk about cell membranes that thicken, so that the cells don't work as well as before. They speak of cells "screaming out for alcohol," implying that because people have no voluntary control over their cell membranes, they are powerless over their addictions. Balderdash.

People have been overcoming patterns of self-defeat for thousands of years, and it is quite likely that *most* of them have approached their problems along the lines of the Beast concept. They first of all make a plan — a big plan — and then monitor themselves very carefully for a while as they overcome previous habits and form new ones. This is really nothing new. Playwright Eugene O'Neill nearly died of alcohol dependence in the middle of his career. When he finally had enough, he simply quit. Then he went on to produce his most esteemed works of literature. That was before AA existed. Recovery is commonplace, and anyone can do it.

The Beast of RR has an advantage over the Higher Power of 12-step programs because it is of our own creation and therefore under our own control. The Beast device is more dependable than Higher Powers that are often fickle, unreliable, easily forgotten about or that disappear just when we "need" them most. Remember, you cannot really *make up* a Higher Power; he, she, or it is really out there — or he, she, or it isn't. It's a matter of *belief*. We, on the other hand, are *always* present in our consciousness and in our lives, and that's the difference. Moreover, the Beast of RR is not a device for externally imposed "morality," as are religious icons like the devil, Satan, God, Jesus, saints, rescuing and punitive deities, and the like. The Beast of RR is only a device that people may intelligently construct as a way to selfishly pursue their own self-defined patterns of abstinence or moderation, as their own painful experiences suggest.

Selecting a self-improvement project, such as learning to abstain from drugs or alcohol, is a very personal decision, and there is no reason why anyone should, ought or must refrain from such risky indulgences. However, when one is finally unwilling to accept the painful consequences of some habitual behavior and is finally ready to get serious about the problem, he or she may choose to call a specialized RR Beast into existence. It is in the spirit of independence and self-determination that lies the beauty of the Beast.

What about the other so-called "addictions" that are said to be sweeping America, like relationship addiction and sex addiction? Here also, the Beast can be employed, but the problem is that those patterns of excess or self-defeat are not really addictions, nor is food. The term "addiction" has been corrupted in recent years in the literature of New Age and 12-step spiritual healing programs so that it has become a buzz word for any bad habit, any pattern of self-defeat, or any morally tinged social vice. In RR, addiction is simply chemical dependency, specifically alcohol and other addictive, mind-altering drugs. Even substances are not really addictive. If there were any truly addictive substances, then everyone would get addicted to them. Heroin is not addictive — 90% of those who took it regularly while in Vietnam stopped doing it when they returned to the states. But many of us addict ourselves to certain chemicals by telling ourselves, "I *must* have this substance so I can feel good and I will do anything I *must* in order to get it." Addicts are, in the words of Albert Ellis, *must*urbators.

One cannot, incidentally, become *addicted* to the activity of sex, although one may very well become habituated to masturbation, promiscuous sexual encounters, or deviant practices so that there are unacceptable risks or consequences. From a rational viewpoint, no sexual act is intrinsically evil or wicked, but in its *context* it may be unethical, coercive, illegal, injurious, exploitive, or carry with it the risk of pregnancy or infection. Since they are biologically driven, sexual desires can attain a compulsive character not unlike excessive drinking, drugging, and overeating, leading one to undesirable outcomes and consequences.

So, one may ask, is there a "sex Beast" cavorting in everyone's head, demanding endless fornication in the streets? Not at all; to view a natural appetite of the human body in that light is sexual moralism and is quite irrational. But anyone choosing to modify his or her sexual behavior as a matter of self-interest (not self-worth!) might do well to start listening to his or her irrational self-sentences and monitoring the mental imagery that invariably precedes the unwanted sexual behavior.

Regardless of which Beast is under discussion, they all have much in common. Here are some Beast parameters:

1. They are repulsive figments of our fertile imaginations, not of any "respectable external authority," that personify the appetites, desires, impulses and urges that get us into trouble.

2. They are almost as intelligent as we are when it comes to continuing the undesirable behavior.

3. They thrive in an irrational psychological environment.

4. They speak to the mind's ear and show enticing pictures to the mind's eye.

5. They are able to change form, using various vocal tones, attitudes, and strategies in the struggle to consummate desire.

6. They revel in the company of other people's Beasts that have the same priority.

7. They fear death and require "that one thing" to survive.

8. They will go to any length to get "that one thing," even though we, the rational hosts, may have to suffer and die in the process.

9. We therefore fear them, accuse them of great malice, and we devote ourselves to learning to recognize them.

10. They maintain power through concealment and they *seem to be us.*

11. They *cannot tolerate* identification and rational evaluation.

12. They often become silent upon recognition, yield readily to reason, and practically always lose strength when their primitive demands are not met.

13. Once established and then mastered by their recovered, rational hosts they don't really die but only half-sleep, watching for any opportunity to revive themselves with a hit of "you-know-what."

14. But the game is up by then, and we rational hosts can easily identify their old, familiar stirrings, and effortlessly squelch them on the spot.

15. Once created, they are permanent features of our rich inner lives, and can never be forgotten.

The Beast, once you get the hang of it, will always be at your disposal, and you need only learn to recognize its urgings. Once this is learned, you will find that relapse is preceded by a great deal of *premeditation,* and that drinking or drugging is the result of a series of highly conscious *decisions.* When you recall your last binge, you will be able, at last, to remember exactly how you relapsed, and how you decided to drink or use. You will *remember* the voice that kicks in when you are in a boozing opportunity, and you will be able to recall its tone, the words it used, and also the pictures the Beast may have flashed before your mind's eye to really get the motor running. Now, for a change, you will be able to *learn from relapse,* something heretofore impossible because your substance abuse has for decades been shrouded in mystery of the demonic or psychoanalytic type.

The myth of alcoholic (or addictive) denial

Most alcoholics and other substance abusers *certainly do* misrepresent to others the extent of their toxic indulgences. And there is little question that this systematic distortion is a defense that helps perpetuate the addictive relapse cycle. This writer does not deny that addicts deny, at least to others. The term "denial", however, is probably used as often in the accusatory sense as in the descriptive, and this development in addiction care often leads to an unnecessary and unfortunate barrier between helpers and addicts. Anyone who has been in an alcoholism or drug treatment program will likely still twinge at the word "denial," so powerful is its use as a presumably therapeutic device.

The early phases of 12-step therapy center around the "addictive defense system," usually with confronting, gut-wrenching interactions between sober people and addicted people. Addicts make statements to others that misrepresent the amount and frequency of their drinking or using, and once-addicted, sober helpers challenge those statements in an effort to make the deniers tell the truth. The sober helpers once themselves "lied" to others about the frequency and amount of their toxic indulgences, but they finally "came clean by confessing the truth," and then went onward and upward to help others with similar proclivities. The ones who persist in their "alcoholic denial" are predicted to continue their addictions with downward personal trajectories.

The attrition that results from the organized assault on the addicts' statements and values is enormous, so that the percentage who remain in 12-step therapy is small. It seems as though the stress of being regarded a compulsive liar is enough to drive one to drink. Some alcoholics leave meetings with the word "denial" still ringing in their ears, while others who survive "denial hazing" by telling the truth gain the powerful support of instant social acceptance.

The following injunctions are common in traditional recovery groups:

"You're an alcoholic, even if you can't see it. You're just denying it."

"Everyone can see that you're really an alcoholic."

"Denial has really *got* you bad."

"You're *in* denial."

"What you just said *was* your denial."

"You're full of shit and you know it."

While many are agreeable to such treatment, it is fair to say that it takes a great deal of pain-based motivation to inspire one to remain in place while the above sort of "interpretations" are made. And, yes, the pain of addiction does inspire many to endure session after session of "defense bashing."

But many (in fact a majority, if recovery statistics are correct) withdraw from the challenge of "denial," and probably often with newly fortified defenses.

In RR the term "denial" is little used, and then in the descriptive sense. By descriptive, we only mean that if someone says something that is improbable, i.e., "I had only one beer last night", we may say that the sayer is implicitly denying having any more than one beer. That is simply what the sayer is doing, denying that he or she had two, five or eight beers or used the one beer to chase twelve shots. But in RR discussion groups it is just fine for alcoholics to deny the frequency or the amount of alcohol they drink, because we focus on an entirely different matter — the advantages of rational sobriety.

It is interesting that in RR groups we do not find people who are "in denial". In a rational context, people speak with their feet — by walking into an RR meeting room, a member is already admitting that he or she is having a problem with chemical dependence, and from then on there is very little to deny. Of course, this may have a lot to do with the ground rule for RR meetings, which clearly state that members make decisions for themselves and do not attempt to persuade others to abstain from drugs or alcohol.

During RR meetings, the participants are seen as being *ambivalent* about further drinking, or having two distinctly different opinions or beliefs (pro *and* con) about drinking at the same time. That is why many people who attend RR groups continue to drink during their "recoveries." Both of those opposing opinions are "voiced" in the addict's internalized self-sentences (thoughts) during and between meetings. One voice says, "Keep drinking. Booze gives you what you really need. You're powerless and it doesn't really matter." The other, and eminently more rational voice says, "Gosh, this boozing is really screwing things up for me. I really should stop. I really wish I could." Both voices are heard during RR meetings, but obviously, the "Keep drinking!" voice is the one that dominates the value system and commands the behavior of all addicts.

In RR, we call that voice "the Beast" as a matter of convenient reference and as a way of clearly separating ideas into two categories: (1) thoughts that support drinking and (2) thoughts that support rational sobriety. Amid the the urgings of the Beast, however, the rational voice of self-interest and survival comes through just occasionally and even then as only a mild, fleeting suggestion. Ironically, the rational voice sometimes comes on most poignantly and clearly during times of sublime intoxication. This is a "safe" time for some to think such abhorrent (to the Beast) thoughts as abstinence and sobriety, when the sense of toxic well-being is at its height, when abstinence is a simplistic wish, and when sobriety is only an abstract, unattainable ideal. Others may cry in their beers, vowing to sober up "tomorrow or pretty soon," but then when tomorrow's withdrawals set in it is so easy to discard the vows of the evening before as the silly whims of a morose drunk. It is *ambivalence*, then, that is the key to rational detox — not denial.

A drinking alcoholic or drug addict can be said to be "all Beast" when he or she is unable to comprehend that the appetite for alcohol or drugs is dictating practically everything he or she says and does. This only means that for the present the addict is ignorant of his or her ambivalence, and has yet to *self-identify as a rational human being*. To help drinking members "break through," the rational self is idealized and portrayed as:

(1) Imperfect, fallible, yet having *intrinsic worth*.

(2) Wanting, because of (1), to *survive*.

(3) Emotionally *independent* from external events.

(4) Thinking thoughts that stand the test of *reason*, i.e., to be "right" or intelligent as opposed to "wrong" or stupid.

(5) Feeling good, and enjoying the *pleasures* of living.

(6) Able to *tolerate* frustration, pain, and discomfort.

Group discussions are aimed at establishing the above conditions as products of reasoning. Addicts are often cynical, but the cynicism is really apathy and resignation to chemicals when other game plans have failed to produce emotional reward. The six central themes of RR listed above are criteria of mental health that transcend most ideologies and can strike a chord in even severely disturbed, addicted persons. What addict would not like to feel better about him or herself, to get more pleasure out of life than the next fix or release from jail, or to figure out how to avoid some of life's most painful problems?

The therapeutic self-help task for addicts is to strengthen their own voice of survival and self-interest, the voice that all but the most brain-impaired addicts still have. Like fanning an ember, those in RR look *inward* for the source of survival, and find a voice within that says, "I want to live a normal life and be happy, and I can't be happy drunk. I am all that I have, and I must survive and be sober to get any good for myself. I will care for myself and respect myself by not drinking alcohol. Any ideas of drinking are my enemy, and I'll call those thoughts my Beast."

But of course this hypothetical alcoholic may very well have a lapse. After all, that is what addicts with untamed Beasts do very well. When asked about recent drinking, some may "deny" having done so. Others may believe or know that drinking occurred, but to accuse the lapser of *lying* would compound the problem. Our lapser probably doesn't yet know that his addictive voice is quite intelligent in the way it will attempt to gain perpetual access to an unlimited supply of alcohol.

"Not only have I gone against what I intended, which was to stay sober, but now everyone can see that I'm lying," our hapless lapser may muse. "And I don't have to listen to these hypocritical bastards rub it in! Maybe recovery's not for me after all. Now it's really time for a drink." The Beast may as well be saying, "Checkmate!"

Therefore, instead of bludgeoning deniers with easily denied accusations of "denial," rational helpers in RR simply remind the lapser of the presence of the lapser's Beast. They share how their own Beasts have gotten them to misrepresent the frequency and amounts of their drinking, and how terrified their Beasts became when they began to really care about themselves, so terrified that sometimes they felt ill, or felt like getting really drunk, or getting mad at everyone and withdrawing from recovery once and for all. The rational helpers might ask, "I wonder if I'm hearing you or your Beast," or, "I'll bet your Beast tried to get you to stay away from this meeting," or "What is your Beast telling you right now?" or "What was your Beast telling you just before you decided to have a drink?"   Helpers may also respond to an unlikely statement by pointing out, "There is a mental voice that directs alcohol dependent people to say dishonest things as a way of guaranteeing itself a perpetual supply of alcohol; this primitive mentality is in sharp disagreement with the line of rational thinking that helped you get to this meeting. You are of two minds about booze, and we call one of them 'you.' The other we call the Beast, and it seems your Beast may be getting you to conceal how much or how often you drink. That's the way my Beast used to work, until I found out how it was ruling my life. Could that be happening to you now?" In real life, though, we are more likely to hear meeting remarks like, "We all have this voice in our heads that keeps telling us to keep doing it. When you get yours figured out, then you'll be in control over what you do. Mine still bothers me sometimes, but I'm getting on top of it."

The lapser may very well *rationally* understand that he is being addressed about something "other than he," something that is alien and ugly within himself that will accept death as the consequence of another drink or hit of something if need be. The lapser will more likely feel as among allies than inquisitors, friends who also have waged battle against primeval, appetite-driven ideas. The rational lapser, then, will have the opportunity to quietly arm him or herself with more *information* about the nature of the inner Beast, the strategies of the Beast, the weaknesses of the Beast, the means to combat the Beast, and finally, when recovery is nearly complete, how to manage the Beast in its weakened, domesticated state. In RR, the awesome power of the human intellect is unleashed upon the Beast of alcoholic relapse.

Targeting the Beast

Getting started on recovery from chemical dependency is usually an on-again, off-again project because of intrusive thoughts that lead to yet more drinking or using. It is quite common for alcoholics and other substance abusers to spend years "getting around to it," i.e., quitting, while addiction-related problems mount and life becomes more and more difficult. A sense of "powerlessness" sets in when repeated efforts to remain sober are unsuccessful. This "powerlessness" would better be called "apathy," since, in the last analysis, one is only choosing to do what one really wants to do at the moment. At the moment, an alcoholic may decide to drink and then soon after regret that decision. And so the cycle goes.

In Rational Recovery, alcoholics are given a powerful instrument to gain rapid control over the impulse to drink or use drugs — the Beast concept. Its use is central to recovering from chemical dependence, and probably is the method most used by those who are successful in recovery, even those who are in 12-step programs. The Beast concept is so simple and obvious that it is sometimes misunderstood and unhelpful. Sometimes ideas or solutions to problems are so simple and obvious that they are overlooked or even considered "too simple" or "too obvious." Below is a protocol to help zero in on your own Beast, in case you are still having trouble resisting drinking or using drugs.

Because you are chemically dependent, you have two ways of thinking about your substance abuse. On one hand, you would like to stop, but on the other, you want to continue. You bounce back and forth between these two ideas, never really coming to a final decision. You are *ambivalent*. If you doubt that you are ambivalent, then do this: make your mind up right now to *never* drink or use again. Now, continue thinking about never drinking again for a few moments, and you will probably notice a subtle change in how you feel. That uneasy feeling is caused by a second opinion about the idea of abstaining from alcohol. What do you hear? If you listen carefully, you will probably hear yourself talking to yourself about the idea of never drinking again. Some of your self-talk will go something like this. "Never? That's along time. I can't really imagine what it would be like to not have the choice. Well, maybe I could still drink (or take a hit) once in a while. I don't think I can say *never*. I'll quit when I'm ready to quit — and maybe even for good one of these days — but not right now. Never say never. Keep your options open." These are Beast thoughts, ones that, *by definition,* support further drinking or drug use.

Now think about the problems related to your alcohol or drug use and about the times you have felt miserable because of drinking or using. After a few moments of this, you will probably hear another voice, a rational one, telling you that you had better knock it off before it is too late. In Rational Recovery, this is the voice of you.

Both of these voices are really you, of course. You are only one thing, and that is you. But, I repeat, you are ambivalent, and you think two ways about your favorite intoxicant. So far, your Beast voice is running the show, and you keep drinking. In RR, you will be strengthening your rational voice (the voice of the "real you") so that you will overpower and eventually master your "Beast" (or however you choose to conceive of that category of your thinking that supports further drinking).

The Big Plan

"Fine," you say, "but how do I get a handle on this and make it really work?" Good question, and here's how. First of all, make your Big Plan — decide that you will never drink or use mind-altering substances again. Now you can *feel* your Beast, and you may feel uncomfortable. You may find it quite difficult to actually make a plan to never drink again because of the interference from your addictive thinking.

Now think about having a drink. (If you're already having one, this exercise won't work; the Beast is often silent when you have sufficient alcohol in your system.) Imagine getting one from the refrigerator, or going to the liquor store. Think of enjoying the drink, and then drinking some more. If you are doing this, then you are *experiencing* your Beast right now. The ideas you are having about drinking as you read these sentences are your *enemy*, and as you become aware of your thinking about drinking, you are starting to *recognize* what the Beast inside of you is like, and how it feels. It wants to defeat your Big Plan.

This moment is a critical one, as we do this mental exercise. At this moment you are thinking about your own thinking. You presently can see that you *always* think before drinking and that you can think about those thoughts, evaluate them, weigh them, and then decide whether or not to go along with them. "Always?" you ask. Yes, always, and drinking is always a choice. When it *seems* that you drink without thinking, it is only because your rational voice is silent; in other words, you are failing to assert good judgement about what you put into your mouth.

As set forth in TSB.2, the Beast is simply that appetite-driven mental voice that seeks the "satisfaction" of alcohol intoxication. Cunning and powerful, it struggles to overcome the rational wishes of abstaining people by taking advantage of weak moments, such as after a hard day's work, after a disappointment or loss, during an emotional upset, or, as the following report shows, during periods of leisure time. The following statement was written by a man who decided to abstain for good after several months of attending RR meetings. Abstaining brought the Beast voice to consciousness, as follows:

"I recently took a week's vacation, and I spent most of it at home. My Beast voice started bothering me, so I decided to *study* it rather than go along with it. Here is what I learned about my Beast:

1. It often starts first thing in the morning, predicting a dull and uninteresting day ahead.

2. Often when it talks to me nicely, I question it and it turns hostile.

3. It offers me dozens of unwise solutions to problems, including drinking, hoping I will take at least one of them.

4. At times it splits into many voices, causing me pain and confusion.

5. When I make a mistake it pounces and blames me.

6. Nothing is too low for it; it speaks crude words and tries to shame me.

7. It loves to exploit my insecurities.

8. It brings up memories of unpleasant events that are distracting and discouraging.

9. It laughs at me when I'm embarrassed.

10. It wants me to accept my beliefs as facts.

11. It tells me to blame others for my griefs.

12. Having carefully questioned the Beast, I can see that it can never really make sense.

13. The Beast, which is just a portion of my own thinking, has no life of its own; this explains its ruthlessness when I try to stop it from using my life. My injury (especially by drinking alcohol) is its only reason for existing.

14. If I worry about my inability to deal with the Beast, I am only falling into another one of its traps."

(Reprinted from *The Journal of Rational Recovery,* Vol. 2, Iss. 4, March - April, 1990)

To make matters worse for alcohol dependent people, our society is drenched with ideas of personal impotence, so that it is very easy to believe that the desire to drink is *irresistible*. A most successful ad campaign challenges the consumer of potato chips, "Betcha can't have just one." Twelve step programs, of course, require an initial confession of powerlessness as an inducement to the remaining eleven steps, and billboards in California last year were graced with a picture of a can of beer zooming under its own power into the waiting hand of a man in his mid-20's who, gathering from the caption, "Get a grip!", was alcohol dependent. Another highway ad for imported (fortified) beer shows a close-up of the the face (eyes only) of a wolf captioned, "It brings out the beast in you." No kidding. Could a committee with the task of drugging an entire population do better than our present crazy quilt of public education on drug and alcohol dependence?

The good news is that we certainly can live sanely in an insane world, provided we learn to recognize the powerful, seductive irrationalities that abound around us.

Chapter 5

The Essence of
Rational Recovery

Anyone can quit drinking, even the most hard-core alcoholic. The problem, as discussed in the earlier section, "Voices," is to *stay* quit. In this chapter, which is really the heart of *The Small Book,* you will find a means to minimize the chances that you will drink, after you have decided that abstinence is for you, but AA is not. (If you are presently attempting to "work" the 12-step program, you may find that the following information is a valuable supplement to the AA steps you find difficult or disagreeable.)

Because you love to be intoxicated, you would like to be able to continue drinking or using drugs, and you would like to reserve this right for the rest of your life. The verdict, "alcoholic," is one you fear because *everyone knows that alcoholics, by definition, cannot successfully drink.* Ironically, if you were not an alcohol dependent person you would not fear learning that you are "alcoholic." A normal person's response to having to give up alcohol would be indifference or a slight sense of loss. He would be jubilant to learn that by making the small sacrifice of refraining from ingesting one substance the major problems in his life could be solved. Yearning to drink successfully or use drugs "just recreationally" is invariably a symptom of chemical dependence. If there were no discomfort when alcoholics cease drinking, there would be no condition called "alcoholism." Down the line, many recovered alcoholic people also come to feel indifferent toward alcohol, and glad that the key to happy living is so simple. But getting there is not so easy, as you may have discovered.

Am I really *dependent* on alcohol?

As long as you have some doubt that you are suffering from the potentially fatal medical condition, alcohol dependence, you will cling to a cherished dream that, "when things get better, things will be better," and then drinking will be just a normal part of life, as it is for most others. But you are suspicious that something is very wrong. Obviously, as an alcoholic, you must be willing to undergo some discomfort and considerable personal change in order to defeat the illness. That is because alcohol dependence is *more* than an illness; it is also a *behavioral disorder*. Part of learning that you are indeed alcohol dependent is to chalk up a long string of failures as evidence that you have not yet figured out how to manage your *alcohol dependent body*. It must become clear in your mind that efforts to drink moderately are futile, and that for you one drink leads to more, and eventually to regrettable consequences. If the question lingers on and on, perhaps you could give yourself a test, not the questionnaire type ("Do you have hangovers? Do you feel guilty about drinking? Have you had a drunk driving arrest, etc.), but an actual test of your ability to drink moderately.

The 30X2 Wager

This procedure is for the self-diagnosis of alcohol dependence and does not apply to users of other drugs. In this procedure, you will simply agree to consume two beers a day for thirty days. That's it. If you do not abide *perfectly* by the terms, you fail, and must accept the diagnosis "alcohol dependent" and the necessity for its proper treatment, which is abstinence. Fair enough?

The 30X2 wager does not allow variances such as (1) "averaging," i.e., one beer Monday, then three on Tuesday, or (2) "skipping," i.e., not drinking at all on some days. The 30X2 wager requires exactly two beers each day — no more, no less.

There are two cautions here. First, this procedure is not precise on the pass end. Some alcohol dependent people may pass the test, but then resume overindulgence. It is on the fail end that the 30X2 wager is more accurate. Very few who fail are not alcohol dependent. In fact, very few who would even consider taking such a test are not dependent on alcohol. Naturally, if you are already sober in response to a drinking problem, there is no point in testing yourself this way.

Second, a month is a long time for an alcohol dependent person to continue drinking the potent, addictive toxin (for us), ethanol, or alcohol. During this test you could be arrested, injured, or killed. The sooner you can arrive at a decision the better, and the fact that you are reading this book is a fair indicator that you are among the 10 percent whose minds and bodies have a profound adverse reaction to alcohol.

The role of intelligence in RR

The expression "rational-emotive" addresses both thinking and feeling. Substance abuse has everything to do with feeling, because we take chemicals as a way of controlling our feelings. Traditional recovery programs address issues of feeling and emotion in indirect ways, such as looking to the past for understanding and personal change. In RR, we learn to take control of our emotions so that we are not compelled to reach for an anesthetic when we are feeling bad.

There is a saying in traditional recovery circles, "There's never been anyone too dumb to get this program, but there's been a lot of people who were too smart." This reflects an anti-intellectual attitude that will not be found in RR. In RR, considerable mental effort is required to change old patterns of thinking and believing. On the other hand, RR is not a program designed for the mentally gifted or elite. Whatever amount of intelligence you have will be sufficient, provided you use it. In other words, bring your mind — the body will follow.

For a glimpse of the process of RR, let's look in on Bert, a fictional but very familiar character at alcoholism clinics. He has come in depressed, despondent because he has failed to stay sober, and has gotten into a heap of trouble since dropping out of AA. He doesn't like to think of himself as "an alcoholic," he doesn't really buy the Higher Power business, he has a vague concept of a god-figure, and he has continued on and off with AA for several years.

Bert: I don't know if I'm an alcoholic or not, but I know I should stop drinking. That much I know.

Counselor: Why should you stop?

Because if I am an alcoholic, that means I can't drink. My drinking gets out of control.

Then why do you continue to drink?

I don't know. It just happens.

What I'm asking, Bert, is why do you like to drink alcohol?

Oh. I drink to relax, when I'm feeling uptight, and when I'm bored. I also like the taste of it.

So you depend on alcohol to feel good, and to relieve boredom?

Yes. I like the way it makes me feel. I guess that means I'm an alcoholic.

Only if you say so, but I don't know how that label will help you. One thing we can say for certain is that you are *dependent* on alcohol. When you're dependent on anything, you can't function very well without it, and there are many bad side effects like the problems you are having.

So, I'm dependent on alcohol. Now what?

That means you can't drink and get away with it. Not only may alcohol eventually kill you, it will ruin most of your fun in the meantime. It's time to quit for good. Now. That's it. Your problem is solved. Case closed.

But I've quit before, many times, and always started up again. I can't stay stopped. I've got to stop drinking and *stay stopped*.

That's right, and it's an entirely different problem from just quitting drinking. You want to prevent a relapse, and that will require considerable change on your part.

I've been able to stay sober for about a month at a time, but I always go back to it. I guess I should stick to one day at a time, like the Big Book says.

It will be necessary for you to *change the way you think.* If you want to get better, you must be willing to give up certain beliefs that seem very important to you, almost as important as alcohol. They are quite ordinary ideas, but they help perpetuate the cycle of drinking that is causing you so much pain and trouble. "One day at a time," is one of them that isn't doing you any good.

But I can't say I'll *never* drink again!

Why not?

Because, well, it's too hard to predict the future, and besides if I say I won't ever drink and then I do, I'll feel like a failure. One day at a time lets me feel like a success every day if I don't drink, and I don't have to worry about the future.

So you still plan to drink some more?

Of course not! I've got to stop for good!

Then why not *plan* to stop for good — for your entire life?

Hmmm. Maybe you've got a point. I'm saying two different things. First I say never say never — one day at a time, then I say I really want to stop for good.

How do you feel right now?

My stomach hurts. Anxious.

What do you think you're afraid of?

Never drinking again.

That's the addictive voice in your head, Bert. It's afraid you will decide to stop forever and make it stick. It's telling you that you may need to drink at times, especially when you really *need* a drink, and it would be *wrong* to say, "Never again."

I don't hear voices in my head.

Yes you do. You think, in your own voice, and you can hear it. I know what your addictive voice said, because you just told me about "never say never." That voice, Bert, is a Beast that will destroy you in order to get you to continue to drink whenever you please.

Oh, that voice. Me.

Yes and no. You are of two minds about drinking. On one hand you want to stop in order to get more out of life. But on the other hand, you want desperately to continue drinking forever. You are ambivalent, and have two opinions about further drinking. If you really intend to stop drinking, then you can go ahead and make that decision for all time. Then, any thinking or ideas that get in the way of that decision will be easy to recognize as an enemy voice. From now on, alcohol isn't really your enemy; instead your enemy is any thinking that supports further drinking. Your job is to learn to recognize your enemy voice in your head and start talking back to it. That voice has been the culprit all along. For example, let me ask you, how did you decide to drink the last time you relapsed?

I didn't decide to drink again. It just happened. The pressure just kept building up at home. I had problems with my wife, you know, and one day after work I stopped at the bank, which is next to a bar. I came out with the money, and, I don't know what happened — but I just automatically walked into the bar and ordered a Manhattan.

The pressure at home forced you to order your favorite drink?

Yes, something like that. The pressure.

What pressure are you talking about? Did you measure it with a barometer or a pressure gauge?

(Angrily) Are you making fun of me? You know what I mean. The pressure from the business with my wife.

The same pressure you feel right now?

(Contritely) I'm sorry. I've been touchy lately. Yes, I feel it now, and I'm irritable at home, too, with my wife.

Fine. Take a rest now, and listen to me for a while. I've learned several very important things about you during the last minute, and they're perfect examples of how your mistaken beliefs are causing you so much trouble with alcohol. First, you have never really decided that you will never drink again. Second, you believe that your feelings are somehow *forced* on you by your wife, like magic. You think you have little control over your feelings of anger and hostility, as if your emotions are caused by events outside your body. You call your emotions "pressure," *as if some outside physical force acts on your emotions,* a force over which you have no control, and from which you can only withdraw, or drink away with booze. Second, you have the idea that you are powerless to refuse alcohol, *even when you are sober.* Third, you believe that what other people think of you is of the greatest importance, that you somehow need the approval of others *for its own sake* in order to feel well. When you thought I was ridiculing you a moment ago, you felt a strong emotion of hurt, as if I saw you as the jerk *you* fear you are. And then you were mad at me, as if *I* had directly caused your feelings. With your so-called "need" for approval, you are quite vulnerable among people wherever you go, and therefore very likely to shield yourself against "pressure" by drinking your favorite anesthetic.

Now, using these three ideas alone, you have a formula that can keep you drinking the rest of your life. You sense no control over your own feelings, you deny responsibility for your decisions to drink, and you have everyone in your social environment to blame for your feelings of worthlessness and subsequent drunkenness. Do you see?

You got my number. That's me, a real jerk.

That's your opinion for now, not mine. Tell me, where did you get the idea that you are a jerk?

Well, look, dammit! My life's a wreck, my car's a wreck, my attorneys' fees for my DUI's and divorce are sky-high, my kids hate me, my business is going down the tubes, and you ask where I get the idea I'm a jerk?

I'm looking, Bert, and all I see is an alcohol dependent person with big troubles. Are you saying that substance abusers are jerks?

Well, maybe, yes. At least the ones like me. Wouldn't _you_ say alcoholics are a pretty scummy bunch? I mean, look at the mess I've made lately — my wife, the kids, the debts.

So, what would it take to get you feeling like a decent human being, someone you enjoy being, someone you respect?

Look, I've told you before, I've got to stop drinking! That's what I've got to do — STOP DRINKING! I'm powerless! I can't control it! And I can't tolerate myself this way! It's been this way for years, and I can't stand it any more! I absolutely must STOP DRINKING!

How would that make you more worthwhile?

Because THEN I could respect myself!

Why not start now?

You must be crazy.

It may sound crazy, Bert, but you must admit that this self-damnation of yours isn't getting any results. In fact, it leads to so much guilt that you continue drinking to ease the pain. Now, listen carefully. What would you think about taking a short-cut, an elegant short-cut to self respect?

Huh?

Yes. Why not just drop all this self condemnation, and concentrate mainly on the tasks of staying sober and getting your life back together? You've already found out that what you're doing doesn't work; give this a try. You have the idea that alcoholics must stop drinking so they can gain self-respect, but that's getting it backwards. People who don't already like themselves aren't very kind to themselves. I propose that you move ahead right now by forgiving yourself for being what you are, a person who is dependent on alcohol, and start recognizing that you are all you have, and you are therefore fundamentally worthwhile. You want to be happy, to get some good out of life, and *you are the only vehicle you have to experience that.* It follows, then, that if you are the only avenue you have to some future good, then you are *extremely worthwhile to yourself,* Do you see?

You mean that I'm worthwhile just because I'm alive?

Excellent! That's exactly the point! You don't need to do *anything,* Bert, to start loving yourself. That's a birthright. You need only to exert your will, your intelligence, your ability to reason, and your authority to establish in your mind that you are as worthwhile as a person can be, whether or not you drink, whether or not other people agree, whether or not your business fails, no matter what develops.

You've got to be kidding. How would loving myself help me stop drinking? Wait a minute. I just thought of something! If I loved myself, I'd have a good reason to avoid alcohol because I know what the stuff does to me. If I drank, I'd be harming someone I really cared about — ME! Is that what you mean?

You've just taken a giant, rational step toward recovery from alcoholism, Bert. If you start to really like yourself and care for yourself, then it's not as if you "have to" or "got to" or "absolutely must" stop drinking. Then you will really *want* to stop, as a kind of gift to someone you care about. You'll stop cracking the whip on yourself and do what you would probably do for any friend — provide some TLC and keep the poison away. I'll be here to help you along the way.

I think I see how this all goes together. If I care for myself, *I will plan to stop drinking for good,* not just one day at a time. Then If I screw up, I can just forgive myself and start over. By using the Beast idea, I can take control of my decisions to drink or not drink.

Sounds pretty good to me.

Analysis of Bert's interview

If the foregoing sounds a little too simplistic, it's only because it is. Bert has been made up for the purpose of illustration, and it's not likely that such a neat turnaround could be effected in a short interview like this. The elements of Bert's interview, though, are drawn from many individuals who have been helped to a durable sobriety using the concepts of rational-emotive therapy. It is interesting that some of Bert's irrationalities are supported in the context of AA, i.e., conditional or variable self-worth, powerlessness, magical thinking, the ideas of need-approval and need-dependency, and the appropriateness of guilt among adults. These irrationalities have consensus in our society and they are the chief strength of AA, the common core of values around which members meet and upon which they build a new life.

The difficulty for AA refuseniks like Bert and for secular humanists in general is that they have little in common around which to gather except their disbeliefs, and disbeliefs are insufficient as a core of values or group philosophy. If I am anti-Republican, do I form or join an anti-Republican club, dwelling on the wrongheadedness of Republicans? No, I would be better off joining a competing party, where there is another version of truth, one which fits my sensibilities better and leads to goals I can comprehend and agree with. AA refuseniks often know very well what they disagree with, such as higher powers, confessions, fearless moral inventories, etc., but does that disagreement supply them with any useful knowledge? Not at all, and that may be why so many who quit AA relapse as expected. To recover rationally from the mayhem of alcohol dependence requires a consistent philosophy, or set of rules, to guide one's thinking and judgments, so that behavior comes under subjective control. As some people become more imbued with AA theology their desire to drink may lessen. But until RR, those who do not buy into that program have had no viable, alternative philosophy in which to become immersed. AA misfits often have their feet planted firmly in mid-air, taking pride in the "Who knows? It's too deep for me" position, playing peek-a-boo with experimental deities. "Who are you," the Big Book asks, "to say there is no God?" They cringe, "I-I didn't. It's just too deep for me."

If one will not become more faithful, spiritual, or humble to gain sobriety, then he or she had better become more rational. Our hypothetical client, Bert, is ready to become more rational, and is shown in the act of doing so. Rational Recovery, derived from rational-emotive therapy of Albert Ellis, Ph.D., provides the motivated alcoholic with an avenue for personal growth, a relatively simple set of cognitive, or thinking, guidelines that are easily learned and comprise a personal philosophy. Just as AA members value religious ideas and work hard at improving their "spiritual" lives, RR clients place a high value on rationality; they strive to be as rational as they can be, as soon as possible. It is important to take sides, because in many ways spirituality and rationality are contradictory. Now for the next logical question:

What is Rational?

This vital term refers to the quality of one's thinking at any given moment, not in a good-bad context, but in respect to the following parameters:

1. Does my thinking in this situation help me to remain sober, safe, and alive?

2. Is what I'm thinking *objectively true*, or am I being judgmental? Is there evidence to support this opinion or belief? Am I using words according to their real meaning?

3. Does my thinking in this situation lead to feelings that I want to have?

4. Does my thinking help me to reach a goal I have chosen?
5. Does my thinking minimize conflict with my fellow man?

These five criteria are listed in approximate order of significance, and it is against these questions that any line of thought can be evaluated. An idea can fail on one or two criteria and still be fairly rational, because rational thought is self-forgiving, or non-perfectionistic.

As you can see, rational thinking in the form of self-talk is something that all of us practice daily in our lives, at least to some extent. We naturally want our beliefs to be true; we want to survive; we prefer positive moods over negative ones, pleasure over pain; and so on. The difficulty is that as human beings we are naturally and biologically prone to gullibility, to magical and superstitious thinking, to short-term pleasures instead of long-term happiness, and, especially, to accept negative evaluations of our intrinsic worth and then think poorly of ourselves and experience feelings of unworthiness. These tendencies comprise the Achilles heel of alcohol dependent persons, whose inherent fallibilities are *magnified* (for example, the "Beast") under the influence of the mind-bending, physically addictive drug, ethanol.

In Rational Recovery we have a comprehensive system of self-help wherein the "alcoholic" can quickly come to terms with the central issues of addiction and recovery. As in rational-emotive therapy, RR identifies several specific irrational ideas and beliefs that perpetuate the addictive behavior of alcohol dependent people, and then RR provides the means to change one's own emotions and behavior. The italicized irrational ideas listed below comprise a personal *philosophy* that sustains the alcoholic drinking and relapse cycle. For clarity, we may refer to that philosophy as "alcoholism," and we may refer to those who believe in and practice that philosophy as "alcoholics." When one has gained insight into the irrational philosophy of alcoholism and abstained for a period, he or she is obviously no longer an "alcoholic," but simply one whose body will not tolerate alcohol in even small amounts.

As you read in the section below about the philosophy of alcoholism and substance abuse, you will probably notice a peculiar feeling of emotional lightness. This is caused by the introduction of rational thoughts into your current thinking. Take note of this feeling if it occurs, as it is scientific evidence showing that *you feel the way you think,* and that you therefore have far more control over your emotions and behavior than you ever dreamed possible. What you are about to read will not cause any shift in mood or feeling, but the changes you notice are caused directly by *your own thoughts.* You can accentuate the "rational high" by shifting back and forth between the irrational (italicized) and rational phrases in each numbered idea. Enjoy yourself as you read.

71

Central Beliefs of Alcoholism

1. I am powerless over my alcoholic cravings, and therefore not responsible for what I put in my mouth,
     instead of the rational idea that I have considerable voluntary control over my extremities and facial muscles.

2. In order to feel like a worthwhile person, I must stop drinking,
     instead of the rational idea that it is <u>because</u> I am worthwhile to myself that I will decide to stop drinking and build a better life.

3. My painful emotions and alcoholic cravings are intolerable, and therefore must be controlled by drinking alcohol,
     instead of the rational idea that some discomfort is a necessary, inevitable, and entirely harmless part of becoming sober and remaining so.

4. I have little control over my feelings and emotions, which are somehow forced upon me by certain persons or by external events,
     instead of the rational idea that I feel the way I think, and so have enormous control over my emotions, sorrows, and disturbances.

5. It is a dire necessity for adults to be loved, respected, or approved of,
     instead of the rational idea that adults do not have to get what they want including love, respect, and acceptance; rejection is just another person's opinion of my worth, one with which I may gullibly agree or rationally disagree. I choose to love myself simply because it feels better than to dislike myself. In this matter, mine is the final word.

6. Because I have committed certain acts, or behaved offensively, or harmed someone, I should therefore moralistically blame and condemn myself and feel worthless and guilty,
     instead of the rational idea that as a human being I am uniquely fallible, and while I may feel regrets, remorse, or sadness for my alcoholic behavior, I need not conclude that I am a worthless person.

7. Other people should not behave poorly, and when they do they should be blamed, moralistically condemned and punished for their misdeeds,
     instead of the rational idea that everyone makes mistakes and it makes no sense to blame others for their imperfections. For me to think others are not as they should be is a failure to accept reality. If I condemn others, I will apply similar measures to my own worth and end up with personal guilt.

72

8. *In order to feel like a worthwhile person, I must be competent, intelligent, talented, and achieving in all possible respects, and to fail in any significant way, such as having an alcoholic relapse, constitutes proof of what I have always suspected and feared — that I am a defective, inferior, worthless person,*

instead of the rational idea that doing is more important than doing well, trying is the first step toward succeeding, and accepting myself now as a fallible, yet inestimably worthwhile human being is entirely possible. Succeeding does not make me into a success, and failing doesn't make me into a failure.

9. *If "things" aren't the way I very much want them to be, then it's terrible, horrible, awful, and catastrophic,*

instead of the rational idea that "terrible" and "awful" are magical words meaning "worse than most unfortunate." Since nothing can be more than 100 percent bad or completely unfortunate, "things" don't have to be any particular way for me to remain sober and relatively calm. If I cannot change or control conditions, I can accept any misfortune, including, when finally necessary, death.

10. *It is easier to avoid than to face squarely certain self-responsibilities, such as eliminating alcohol from my diet and concentrating on personal growth,*

instead of the rational idea that the "easy way," especially continuing to drink, is invariably much harder and more painful in the long run.

11. *Because I am sober, I absolutely must not drink, no matter what, because one drink would lead to my downfall,*

instead of the rational idea that as time goes by drinking appears increasingly stupid because of the obvious selfish advantages of sobriety, but, if I ever stupidly relapsed by drinking, it wouldn't be awful because I would very likely recover again — selfishly, guiltlessly, and probably very quickly.

12. *Because I am an alcoholic, I need something or someone stronger or greater than myself upon which to rely,*

instead of the rational idea that dependency is my original problem, and it is better to start now to take the risks of thinking and acting independently. I cannot really "be" an "alcoholic," but just a person who has believed some of the central ideas of alcoholism.

13. *Because alcoholism once greatly affected my life, it will continue to affect me frequently and indefinitely,*

instead of the rational idea that because rational sobriety is self-fulfilling, and because there is so much more to life than a constant struggle to remain sober, I can gradually close the book on that sorry chapter in my life and become vitally absorbed in activities and projects outside of myself that are unrelated to my former alcoholism.

14. *Somewhere out there, there is a perfect solution for life's problems, and until I find it, I am doomed to a life of uncertainty and turmoil,*

instead of the rational idea that uncertainty is the spice of life, and seeking a perfect solution is silly and a waste of time. I will do better to view life as an enjoyable experiment, seeking my own pleasures and cultivating my own personal growth.

By reading and rereading the ideas above, you may immediately notice their interconnections. This insight is the rational consciousness that supports sobriety and provides the basis for continuous personal growth. In the next chapter we will examine each rational concept in a little more detail in order to establish sobriety as rooted in reason.

Chapter 6

Relapses

A "relapse" implies that you have gone against an earlier decision to stay sober. With your new understanding of the Beast concept, you now have a powerful tool to prevent relapses. But all the help in the world will not help unless you have made a clear commitment to abstain from intoxicants — for good. In RR, we speak not only of the Beast, but also of "The Big Plan." Very often, when someone has had a relapse, we find that he or she is still ambivalent about further drinking. When asked, "What's your plan for drinking (using) in the future," the answer might be vague, for example, "I guess I'll start sobriety over again." Or the relapser might say, "I've got to be more careful." These statements are not about plans to abstain. They are actually coming from the Beast, which is quite fearful of ideas of quitting intoxicants forever. So, if the relapser is pressed, "Do you plan to stay off intoxicants for good," or "Do you think you will be relapsing in the future," the answer will likely be further waffling like, "I can't really know the future. I hope I stay sober." The door, here, is wide open for the next boozing opportunity, and the Beast is placated.

The Big Plan is simply a decision that a person makes to never, ever, use intoxicants again. It is a final, decisive act of will that is a covenant with oneself. The Big Plan scares the crap out of anyone's Beast because it fears deprivation and eventual death. The idea of "no more of anything," i.e., alcohol or drugs, is like a death threat that you, the rational host, can *physically feel*. In RR groups around the world, people are learning that it takes a bit of nerve, somewhat like jumping off a high dive, to swear off intoxicants forever. People report anxiety, stomach aches, headaches, and even panic — all of which are symptoms of stress caused by the addictive voice in one's head screaming protest, crying out for mercy. But when one does finally make The Big Plan and decides, "I am willing to suffer as much as it takes in order to get better," there is usually a calm that shortly follows. The Beast has been faced down., and it is in retreat.

75

But the struggle is not over. Relapses are a normal part of recovery. You may choose to never have one, but if you do get faked out by your Beast, recovery is made much, much easier if you already have a Big Plan working. It goes like this:

Under The Big Plan, you will quickly come to see yourself as a person who simply doesn't drink under any circumstances. If you should have a slip, you will be acutely aware that you are violating a covenant with yourself that is next to sacred. Alright, let's call it sacred. You can say that your life is sacred if nothing else is. Biologically, this makes sense, because we are programmed for survival. So, when you drink or use, you will be extremely self-conscious of what you are doing, and therefore you will be able to interrupt your relapse at will. As we say, drinking (using) is always a choice, but *even more so* when you have a Big Plan in effect.

Relapses don't just happen. They are made to happen. Even in cases when alcohol is accidentally ingested, such as at a party where the punch has been spiked, a relapse is a full-fledged conscious decision. Every time. A lapse, where a drink has been accidentally or impulsively taken, is not a relapse.

The first and most important rule regarding relapses is "Don't have one." A relapse, or a return to drinking alcohol, is a serious personal setback, because the meter goes back to "zero time" since the last drink. As we learned in the "Voices" chapter, an *imaginary* being, the Beast, lurks in the mental twilight zones of former substance abusers, sullenly awaiting an opportunity to re-energize itself with alcohol or other drugs. The Beast will take advantage of any situation and use cunning and subtle tones to gain access to the precious intoxicant. It is a voice that grows weaker as time since the last drink goes by, and one that each recovering alcoholic learns to *recognize* more readily with each passing sober day.

Consider the case of Leonard S. After five years of pleasant NHP sobriety, he was driving home on a country road. It was Friday evening and his wife was to be out of town for a few days. Passing through a village, he noticed a bar with its door propped open, jukebox music coming from within. Within seconds he had parked his car and was approaching the bar on foot.

How did Leonard happen to be walking toward a bar in the country on a Friday evening when his wife (who had only recently come to trust him again) was out of town? It would seem that he was falling victim to a strange phenomenon, when, for mysterious reasons, he "lost control," and suffered an alcoholic relapse. After all, Leonard was a recovering alcoholic, subject to powerlessness at times, wasn't he? Could he have lost touch with his Higher Power? Would he order up and begin a drinking spree that would result in violence, incarceration, and/or the end of his cherished marriage?

As Leonard drove by the bar, he peered inside, heard the music, and felt the Beast stirring. He later recalled that he distinctly heard a mental voice, resembling his own, whispering, "Take a look inside." He drove past slowly, then heard it again: "Go back. See what's inside. You don't have to order anything. Just go back and look. It won't hurt to look around. It should be interesting. See the drunks. Remember old times." Looking back, Leonard remembers that he knew that the voice was somehow "not really me" but he nevertheless did a U-turn and parked at the bar. The voice, his own thinking voice, continued, "This should be interesting. Go in. You don't have to order. Just go in." As he got out of the car and started walking to the bar, he recalls feeling anxious and asking himself, "Am I really doing this? Going to a bar?" He also remembers the response, "Why not? You don't really have to drink anything. Go in just to mingle with the people."

Well, Leonard is still happily married. He didn't get arrested. He didn't order up. He didn't even get inside the bar, and he didn't suffer a relapse or even a lapse. He stopped in his tracks, and said, in the strong voice of his rational self, "Hello, Beast. So, it's you again, you old son-of-a-bitch. You're a sneaky bastard, but I caught you this time. I know what you are and what you're up to, and I can take care of you any old time. And next time, I'll have an even easier time recognizing you and putting you out of my mind." Leonard recalls that the irrational Beast went totally silent, and he continued home, very pleasantly NHP sober.

In this example, Leonard S. has *personified* his alcoholic self-talk, which still (though only occasionally) argues the case for a drink. He says that lately when he hears it, he is amused rather than upset; on one occasion he was asked what he was smiling about.

Some readers will notice the connection in this to demonology, which would have it that people are sometimes possessed of evil spirits or suffer character defects which cause them to run amok. In that scenario, one must appeal to a "good" spirit, usually God or Jesus or some saint, as an antidote to the "evil influence." In AA theology, one must appeal to the Higher Power, God, to magically protect against "temptation" by the evil forces. From the Leonard S. illustration, it is easy to see how Rational Recovery and NHP sobriety are based on one's desire for happiness and survival rather than upon "spiritual awareness." To personify alcoholic self-talk is akin to thinking of Jack Frost as the personification of winter; it is a convenient and effective way to conceptualize and categorize certain life-threatening cognitions which will naturally and harmlessly occur in recovering and recovered alcohol dependent persons.

The stories below of Lloyd and Todd, however, illustrate a vital principle that is overlooked in much of the literature on alcoholism.

"So now I've had a drink," Lloyd recalls thinking, as he lay in his hospital bed. He attended a cocktail party, an autumn celebration where "cider and donuts" were on the list of refreshments. Sober via HP for three years, going one day at a time, he had no plan to drink alcohol now that life had become more satisfying than ever before — a happy condition he attributed to sobriety. He also had no long-range plan — no Big Plan — in effect, and he devoutly believed that there are certain times when "recovering" persons such as he have no defense against alcoholic relapse. A good slug of bourbon had been added to the cider. For reasons best known to biologists and chemists cider blocks the taste and to some extent the odor of bourbon. Only after Lloyd had consumed over eight ounces of "cider" did he realized that he was becoming intoxicated.

"Oh, my God!" was his first conscious reaction, and he was flooded with *fear*. "This is terrible!" he thought. "I've just had some BOOZE!" he catastrophized to himself. Lloyd was quite unready for what was to follow. The alcohol quickly made its way to his brain, the permanent residence of the Beast, which exploded into life, as it had not done for three long, dry years.

"So now you've had a drink!" Lloyd heard. And Lloyd repeated it: "So now I've had a drink."

"And you know what *that* means, don't you?" the inner voice went on. "That means that you will have some more! *You're over the line!* There's no turning back now, Lloydie baby! Let's see who's looking, and then get back over there to the punch bowl. That's it, and dip another. Very good, now, down the hatch. Ahhhhh! Yes. It's been a long time. It's o.k., Lloydie, you'll be o.k.. You can handle this one. Just act normal and no one will notice that you're so buzzed you could piss your pants. Let's have another, Lloydie, and get the hell out of here, away from all these office assholes, and get to where the real action is! It's party time!"

Four hours later, Lloyd was beaten to a pulp outside an inner city bar, where he had made a pass at a big-time biker's girlfriend. He didn't lose his job, but he was depressed for months about being so vulnerable, and he worried that he would soon be out of control again. He perceived that he was powerless over alcohol after having one drink, and in effect he was.

Well-intentioned Lloyd had never built rational defenses against the intrusion of alcoholic self-talk. He had never rehearsed in his mind what he would do if he accidentally drank alcohol. He assumed that his rescuing deity would shoo away harm and protect him from evil. He was unaware that all drinking actions are self-directed by powerful mental commands. And poor Lloyd never had a Big Plan in effect. He was unprotected, and he never had a chance against the thirsty Beast living in his head.

Todd, however, a high school teacher who had been sober NHP for five years, drank again quite voluntarily. It was summer vacation, and he simply decided to drink a beer. He recalls that he was at a friend's cabin, everyone was drinking, and he went to the refrigerator; a little mental voice, his own, said, "Why not? Have one. It's OK." Within about five seconds, he had popped the can and drunk from it. As the beer went down he heard, "Verrry good. Mmm. More." He took several gulps and soon felt the buzz. He walked outside, finished the can, and tossed it. Todd recalls hearing two separate, somewhat different voices that even seemed to come from the different sides of his head. One said, "Grab that six-pack and row to the middle of the lake. Relax in the sun and really enjoy yourself." Having been sober NHP, Todd was quite familiar with the Beast and its ways. He also recognized that he had done something quite stupid, and had violated a sincere promise he had made to himself five years before. "I hear you, Beast, and you got me to have one beer," Todd thought back, "but now you're out of business. Just because I would *like* to have another and still another doesn't mean I *have* to. For the rest of today, I'll just *stubbornly refuse* to drink. The first thing I'm going to do is talk to Chuck over at the woodshed. He knows what the deal is about booze, and that'll be a help. Then I'll let this one wear off by taking a nap, and after that I may go home if I hear any more booze ideas." The point is that although Todd had a lapse, he did not have a relapse. He proved that an alcohol dependent person need not continue drinking after one drink; in fact, one may stop after even more than one drink, if one chooses to do so, to get off the slippery slope of re-addiction.

This power of self-determination is greatly enhanced when one takes full responsibility for what is taken into the mouth, and when the internalized Beast-sentences that argue for more booze are recognized, challenged, and authoritatively denounced. A rational person will recognize that an impulse to drink is only a feeling that will shortly pass, and that the impulse will pass rapidly when the irrational thinking behind the impulse is identified and challenged.

One may ask, "When does a lapse become a relapse?" An objective measure is difficult to establish because the results of drinking or using drugs are insidious and variable. For Lloyd one drink was a relapse. For someone else, two might trigger a surrender of resolve to abstain. But if a sober alcoholic spends an evening getting drunk or a former drug addict starts a "chipping" pattern of "occasional lapses," it would seem to this writer that there has been a serious relapse, and he or she had better join a recovery group or seek professional care immediately.

When a relapse does continue for a period of days or weeks, we can say that there has been a return of the addiction. Until the threshold of addiction is reached each drink makes withdrawal more difficult, until finally the benefits of sobriety are lost and the problems of recovery are at the former level, i.e., back to square one. Conversely, the sooner the alcoholic ceases drinking after the first drink, the easier recovery will be. Each drink drives the barb deeper, but there is no time when it is not *relatively* easy, in comparison to the alternative of addiction, to stop. Refer to the chapter "Getting Stopped" and review your own reasons for wanting to stop drinking or using drugs

Intentional relapse

A familiar pattern is developing in many RR groups concerning ambivalent individuals who have not made a Big Plan to abstain for good. The following illustration is drawn from two actual meetings in California during 1990. One of the characters was alcohol dependent, the other dependent on heroin. They responded to the rational milieu exactly the same say, as far as this observer could determine. "Ron" is the name that describes both men.

Ron: I've had it. I don't feel like going any further with this recovery stuff. My old lady is pissed off at me for screwing up, I have constant headaches, and I've been transferred to a job location twice as far from home. I'll tell you, if I had $20 right now, I'd go get me a bottle (bag) of good stuff and fly away. I really mean it. If a $20 bill floated into my hands right now, I'd just leave this meeting and get high. I just want a little peace and I'm going crazy.

Member #1: So you're planning to relapse.

Ron: Damn right.

Member #2: Can anyone think of why Ron shouldn't get loaded again?

Member #3: You know you could get busted again, Ron. And this won't really help things at home. I hope those things don't happen, though.

Member #4: I hope you don't get busted. I'd hate to see you on the ropes in court again. I also hope you can work things out with your wife. I really hope your getting loaded doesn't ruin everything.

#1: I hope you get away with what you're planning to do. All you want is some peace, and I honestly hope that you enjoy your high while it lasts.

Ron: What is this? You guys are trying to *talk me into it* or something?

#2: No way. We only make decisions for ourselves. In RR, we aren't our brothers' keepers. If you want to take your chances, that's up to you.

#1: Why did you come to RR, Ron?

Ron: I've been in the 12-step program for years, and I'm getting nowhere. It doesn't agree with me at all.

#4: What didn't you like?

Ron: You know, the powerlessness part, and the Higher Power stuff.

#3: Well, you can see that this group isn't going to be your Higher Power. Do what you think is best. If you get loaded, come back and tell us about it. No kidding.

Ron: Man, this is really different! I mean, this is strange. It's just me, then. Is that right?

#1: You got it. Taking drugs or drinking alcohol is an extremely personal decision for all of us, and no one made the decision to abstain because they were talked into it by someone else. We all know what the consequences are for us, so we just don't do it any more. It's not easy at first, but it isn't hard, either. It just takes a Big Plan and a lot of hard work for a while.

Ron: What about this Big Plan?

#2: Have you ever told yourself you'd never get loaded again?

Ron: Millions of times.Probably every time I do it. Like they say, "One day at a time." Right?

#2: Well, then what happens?

Ron: Then I change my mind, that's what. I think, "Screw it. Do it."

#2: That's what we call the Beast. It talks in your head, and waits for a chance to get you loaded again. What we do here in RR is learn to master that voice that keeps us relapsing. The voice is our enemy — not drugs or alcohol. Now that we know what our real enemy is, we can zero in on it and defeat it. Your Beast tells you, "Never say never! Keep you options open! You'll never know when you really *ne-e-e-e-d* another fix. Do it just one day at a time."

#3: When you do it one day at a time, you're telling your Beast, "Not right now. But try me later."

Ron: Damn. I've always thought that voice was me.

#1: It is, but you can make it "not you." As soon as you have a Big Plan to abstain that is based on how much you value your own self and your happiness, then anything you think that goes against that Big Plan is what we call the Beast. "You" don't want to drink, but "it" is dying to get loaded.

Ron: So that's what you meant by "I own my own hands and feet?"

#1: Right. You own your muscles, and the Beast is just a poor, disembodied voice, all alone in there (points to his head), and has to convince you to use your muscles to get what it wants.

#4: It takes some practice at first, but when you get the hang of it, it gets easier and easier. But you have to have a Big Plan to never do it again to put your Beast in the corner. That's the really hard part.

81

Making that decision. It's really very personal, and no one can make that decision for you.

#2: That's why we hope you don't really mess up when you get high the next time. What's good for us may be bad for you. Maybe you can keep on using and have a happy life. Who knows?

Ron: I don't like it when you guys keep giving me best wishes. I feel like I'm at my own funeral. I think I've changed my mind about relapsing — you know, getting high again. For now, at least.

#1: No Big Plan, yet?

Ron: I'll have to think real hard about that one.

#4: That's what we all did.

Sobriety rehearsal

Being prepared for vulnerable moments is a key strategy for the recovering alcoholic, and RR provides a means for this. It is very important for you to know two things in order to manage relapses: (1) you can always refuse to drink alcohol or use drugs in the first place and (2) you can stop any time you choose to if you have had something. Imagine, for example, that you have just been forced at gunpoint to have a good-sized drink, and then the gunman leaves you locked in a room with a supply of alcohol, but there is also water and food. You have the choice of mentally rehearsing two outcome scenarios: (1) you proceed to get drunk on your own, using the coercion as an excuse to continue drinking or (2) you decide that you will not make matters worse by continuing to drink. With your eyes closed, try to visualize these alternatives as vividly as possible, focusing on the room itself, the sounds of the gunman, the smell of alcohol, the brand of beverage, and your subjective feelings about being forced to drink and then about the choice of continuing to drink or not. Listen most attentively to what the Beast is telling you. Imagine yourself when help comes to unlock your room, and how you feel about the outcome of being drunk and then about how you feel about being sober at the time of rescue.

Imagine you are recovering from alcohol dependence and you are a member of a large family of heavy drinkers. You are six months sober and there is a family reunion. You arrive and everyone is two sheets to the wind and things are getting loud. You love your parents, brothers and sisters, drunk or not, and now your father welcomes you with a hug and a drink. Your family converges to where you are, raising their drinks to give a toast to you, "Hooray, he's (she's) here! Over the lips! This one's for you!" Your father hands you the drink and all await.

How do you feel? What can you do? What can you say? It is *easy* to imagine a drunken outcome. After all, it's a family tradition. But you

82

may also imagine something very different. You could raise the glass and not drink its contents. Just start talking or laughing when everyone is sipping, so as not to call attention just now to your sobriety. Then, everyone would overlook it and everything would be ok. Right?

Wrong. They know you too well. They are all waiting to see if you drink, because they all have the same problem — alcohol dependence. They won't drink until you've downed yours. They're still waiting.

How do you feel now? Well, you might feel anxious, fearful of ridicule, rejection, and mean teasing. If so, then the Beast is urging you not to offend your loved ones by not drinking. "Go ahead," the Beast is urging, "you can sober up later, but do what you have to now. It won't hurt you much to drink, but this is a reunion for your father, and he's old and sick and won't understand if you reject the drink he's handing you. Don't make waves. Take the drink. You feel awful anyhow, and you need a drink. It'll take the edge off. They're all in a good mood and you're all uptight. It's just like always. Nothing's changed, and I haven't changed. I'm an alcoholic just like them. Who am I trying to fool with this sobriety stuff? They're looking at you like there's something wrong with you. Get a grip. Take a drink."

Pretty powerful stuff. Downright Beast-ly. Fortunately, the simple application of native intelligence will show that all of the Beast ideas are absurd. To wit: (1) you do not have to do *anything*, let alone drink poison. (2) "Sobering up later" may be more than you are bargaining for. (3) It will likely hurt you immensely to drink for any reason. That's why you've been abstaining. (4) So what if your father doesn't understand your refusing a drink? What did he ever understand anyhow? And what do you care if he approves of you anyhow? Are you a child, needing daddy's love to feel like you're worth something? (5) For that matter, why do you need *any* of these relatives to accept you? Did you come to this reunion to love or to be loved? (6) Good question. Maybe I'm here just to have some fun and enjoy old times if I can. But if I require their approval, then that's no fun, because I'll have to do what they expect of me. No way. (7) Although we share the same family genes that may make us alcohol dependent, the similarity stops there. I know something they don't, and I'll be damned if I'd do what they do.

So, in your sobriety rehearsal, you may imagine yourself naming the toast, "Here's to my sobriety!" And then you may securely sit back and imagine the look of horror on their faces as they realize that someone has just left the fold. You will know that they are all quite fearful of their own alcohol dependency but really hate to take a close look at what the family has been doing for decades. And that's their problem. Cheers.

83

Another relapse rehearsal has to do with finding out that you have only a short time to live. Would you use that as an excuse to resume drinking? Or, would you rather be sober during your final days so that you could get the most meaning out of the time left? Is drinking as a prelude to death part of your Big Plan? Do you really *have* a Big Plan, to never again drink or use drugs? It is worth pondering imaginary situations like these from time to time so that when you really are confronted with stressful or tempting conditions, you will already have your mind set on a favorable outcome for yourself. You really do have an enormous amount of control over your decisions to drink or not.

Disulfiram

The trade name for disulfiram is Antabuse, truthfully named as a combination of the words, "anti-" and "abuse." In the military, nerve gas is made "safe" by keeping the essential ingredients apart until lethal effect is desired. Antabuse is a self-administered tablet taken each day that contains half of the chemicals needed to poison you. Antabuse therapy is the use of chemical weapons on the Beast. Here is how it works.

When it is taken (250 - 500 mg.) for about two days, the Antabuse level in your blood is high enough to give the full, "desired" effect. If you drink any alcohol, even small amounts, this is what will happen. First your skin will tingle a little, and then you will get itchy. Your skin will break out in large red blotches, and your eyes will water and it will be difficult to focus your eyes. Your heart will speed up, and breathing will become difficult. You will feel like you are suffocating. Then you will feel weak and nauseated, but you may be afraid to lie down for fear of passing out and dying. You may vomit. The effect lasts for several hours, during which time you may actually die, especially if you have other medical problems. Some say that niacin alleviates the reaction, but one is well advised to go to an emergency room during an Antabuse reaction. You may resume drinking alcohol about five days after discontinuing Antabuse, but even then there may be some unpleasant symptoms.

On the up side, Antabuse works beautifully, for all of the reasons above. In effect, you are telling your Beast, "Look, I'm tired of losing all of my arguments with you, so take *this!*" So you, somewhat rationally, take the tablet. At first, you will probably not hear a peep from your addictive voice. Knowing there is disulfiram in your system, you will be able to enter the most tempting boozing opportunities confident that you will not be carried out on a stretcher. After all, you aren't *completely* stupid.

84

Antabuse is an excellent therapy for people who do not have a Big Plan in effect, or who are without an appropriate recovery program. Some people use it intermittently, as "insurance" while on vacations or during periods of personal crisis or stress. But there is a down side.

Antabuse is harmful to your liver, and extended use is questionable from a medical point of view. Extended use is also questionable from your Beast's point of view, and you will soon realize that you have many "reasons" for not taking it. The most common are, "I forgot it at the regular time, so I'll wait for tomorrow's regular dose," or, "I'll just take half the prescribed dose because it is hard on my liver," or, "I'll see how it feels to go without it," or, "There is a high risk situation coming up, so, even though I don't really plan to drink, I'll stop taking it because just in case I did drink I wouldn't want to end up in a hospital," or, "I'll take an Antabuse vacation to give my liver a break," or, "This stuff is just a crutch; it's time to go it alone."

In RR, taking Antabuse is an admission of powerlessness over your addictive voice, but nevertheless a fine way to buy time while getting your act together. This therapy, when voluntary, is an expression of sincere motivation and determination to overcome alcohol dependence. However, Antabuse only puts off the inevitable showdown between your rational self and the irrational thinking that argues endlessly for more booze. Users of Antabuse are *prime candidates* for Rational Recovery, and they are in an excellent position to finally take control over what they place in their mouths using rational principles of self-reliance, rather than through a continuing siege mentality.

Chapter 7

The Unmiracle of
NHP Sobriety

The 1990s will go down in future history books as a time of controversy in the field of addiction care. Issues of politics, money, religion, social policy, science, law, and health care will be analyzed for readers of those future history books, and our present ignorance will be obvious to them. The data now coming in suggest a possible link between alcohol dependence and several other physical traits (EEG patterns, blood chemistry, etc.), and as the mysteries of the DNA helix are unraveled it is possible that we will find certain markers that will identify the alcohol dependence syndrome. Watch the newspapers and see. For some people alcohol dependence appears to be a genetically transmitted metabolic and appetite disorder that disposes one to self-destructive and self-defeating drinking. However, if ten people are seated in a recovery group, there is no way to know if all or any of them have some inherited trait that is responsible for their unusual appetites for alcohol. If those ten people are also inpatients in a hospital alcoholism unit, it would seem that treatment personnel or third party insurers would want to know which ones have a physical basis for being there.

Blood tests for the alcohol dependence trait may become available to the public in coming years. One such test, the ADMAST (alcohol dependence MAO suppression test) may be available to the public in 1991. Even the ADMAST is only one measure and does not rule out other physical reasons for alcohol dependence. And, it will not be surprising if we find some people with positive ADMASTs who have no difficulties drinking alcohol. In traditional 12-step programs, it is assumed that everyone present is diseased, and every effort is made to convince them so. In RR, as mentioned in Chapter 1, we are not concerned about whether alcohol dependence was written in our

87

genes at the time of conception, because that wouldn't make one powerless even if it were so. Whether dependence on alcohol is a primary physiological disorder, it is neither a symptom of personality or character defects, nor caused or perpetuated by one's lack of spirituality or belief in supernatural beings. The good news is that, of all the major, chronic, life-threatening conditions, alcohol (drug) dependence is the one that has the simplest solution — abstinence. But this goal is usually difficult, because the behavior disorder of alcohol dependence is one result of an appetite for alcohol that is not under one's voluntary control.

In Rational Recovery, you are provided everything you need for maintaining sobriety except the desire to do so. You must perceive a *good reason* to abstain from your all-important beverage in order to succeed, but in the large majority of cases, "alcoholics" such as yourself are not motivated enough to endure the pain — the discomfort of physical withdrawal, the psychological craving, the social emptiness, and the perceived boredom of a life without alcohol. People do largely what they want to do, and most alcoholics, preferring the transient pleasure of intoxication, simply do not want to stop drinking. The promise of a "better life" falls on deaf, alcoholic ears, because life on booze, despite some discomfort, tummyaches, annoyances, and hassles from "them," is at times subjectively pleasant, agreeable, and, strange as it seems to observers, "meaningful." Drinking alcohol *does* have its rewards, however shallow and temporary they may be; only pain and fear seem to interrupt the sublime moods of intoxication, so that recovery becomes a possibility.

During the years of alcohol or drug dependence very little emotional growth is possible, because personal growth is usually the outcome of mastering fears, discomforts, and anxieties. The use of drugs or alcohol to cope with negative emotions, including "boredom," prevents you from learning independent ways of feeling good. *You are emotionally dead while you are artificially "feeling good."* With the removal of alcohol you are in a strange new world, one into which you feel forced, one devoid of the fulfillments, however austere, associated with alcohol use. Current approaches to recovery accept the inevitability of continued emotional dependency; you are expected to form new dependencies to replace alcohol. In RR, you are given the means to reject dependence as a matter of principle and to form a personal philosophy that is by definition conducive to a durable, fulfilling sobriety in which you will *independently* pursue your own (i.e., self-defined) goals. Following, is an expanded discussion of the central ideas of alcoholism and their rational antidotes. You will see that RR is thoroughly unmiraculous in its content as well as in its general outcomes.

1. *I am powerless over my alcoholic cravings and therefore not responsible for what I put in my mouth,*

instead of the rational idea that I have considerable voluntary control over my extremities and facial muscles.

The popular definition of alcoholism in the 1980s incorporates the idea of *uncontrolled* drinking. This is unfortunate for those who think they can't stop. I have heard many alcoholics, including myself during the years of my alcoholism, explain that the reason for all their drinking is that, "I can't stop it. If I were able to stop drinking," the argument goes, "then I wouldn't be an alcoholic." By drinking inappropriately and excessively, despite the disastrous results, the alcoholic seems to *prove* that he is powerless. But, ironically, he would be right in saying, "When I finally stop drinking and learn to abstain, I won't be alcoholic." Alcoholism, remember, is just a philosophy that justifies continued alcohol use. Alcoholics are those who believe in that philosophy, especially its central ideas.

Substance abusers find it easy to forget that each time they have a drink there are very specific, *conscious* antecedents to the drinking behavior, actual conscious thoughts that they hear with their "inner ears." If you are still drinking, listen to your own thoughts and you will hear yourself talking to yourself about having a drink. You will hear things like, "Beer. Time for a beer. Refrigerator. I'll get a beer." You may imagine yourself walking to the refrigerator, or even driving to a carryout or bar, where, in your mind's eye you will see yourself obtaining and consuming the alcohol and subsequently feeling very good. Instead of your spouse's or your own company, you may imagine other merry drunks who will commiserate with you about life's misfortunes, about the depravity of married life and/or employment, and who will graciously assist your inner alcoholic voice by saying, "Have another. I'll buy." As you achieve a rational sobriety, these Beastly voices and images will continue for some time, perhaps the rest of your life, but by practicing rational thoughts and images in your head, you will find that the ideas of drinking gradually appear more and more absurd. Once the Beast is discovered, it loses its clout, psychologically speaking. Much as in the game of "hide and seek," when you are found out, the game is over.

Better yet, you can think of your relationship with your Beast of Booze as like a chess game. You will have to use a lot of your intelligence, because the Beast is quite intelligent in pursuing its one-item agenda, and it is used to winning every game with you. It uses many strategies to get you to add the intoxicant to your blood, and that is when you are checkmated. To turn the tables, you will want to learn and to recognize your Beast's *opening moves,* and be prepared for a better move of your own. One of the Beast's favorite opening moves is to get you angry about something. Then it will offer you a drink or a hit of something as a cure for your angry feelings. It won't know what to do if you refuse to blame fate or some person for whatever, and you will find it quite easy to abstain. Another opening move of the Beast is to convince you that you are incompetent to refuse the intoxicant, especially for more than a day at a time. (There are reports that there are some recovery groups that go along with this Beast-ly idea. Perhaps the Beast has infiltrated the organizers of those meetings.) It doesn't take much of your intelligence to understand that drinking is a voluntary, premeditated act, every single time, and that the Beastly idea of powerlessness is common horseshit. With this insight, your countermove against the Beast is to unleash the awesome power of your own intellect against a clearly inferior mentality. You might even say to yourself, "Checkmate, you bastard — set up a new game!"

Internal images and voices about drinking are quite inconsequential and have nothing to do with your final decision to drink or not to drink. They are merely ideas, and that's all. You can think about drugging yourself until you're blue in the face, and you won't get high. Ideas of drinking or using drugs are entirely harmless, and having them does not mean that you are therefore compelled or even more likely to drink or use. It is only when you *decide to move some part of your body for the purpose of obtaining or consuming the intoxicant that you may become intoxicated or drunk.* At any time, even after the grave error of "the first drink," you are free to reverse your course of action by turning away from the beverage, and refusing to drink it. Even if you hold a container in your hand you can still put it down, or refuse to open your mouth, or roll the joint. Or, you may perform other voluntary acts that will guarantee that none of the toxic substance gets into the bloodstream and is carried to the brain where it will act with destructive effect. For example, you may get rid of your drugs, dump the liquor down the sink, leave a party where everyone is intoxicated, etc.

2. *In order to consider myself a worthwhile person, I must stop drinking,*

instead of the rational idea that it is *because* I consider myself a worthwhile person that I will decide to stop drinking and build a better life.

If you believe that your self-worth or self-esteem will be increased through sobriety, you will be in the large majority. You will also have great difficulties in staying sober.

For example, suppose you are sick and tired of the drunkard's or junkie's life, feeling rotten for all the trouble you've caused, and feeling like a failure for all the opportunities missed or ruined. You feel

90

worthless, as if you deserve nothing better than suffering, death, and another drink or hit of drugs. But inside there is this glimmer of hope that maybe, just maybe, you could start life over without drinking and be able to hold a job, or stay married and regain some of your physical health, or have enough money to pay the bills and be a respectable human being. "Wouldn't that be a wonderful thing," you might think, "and all I have to do is just stop drinking! I'll stop being an ugly, worthless drunk, and then I'll be more successful, and people will be able to see that I'm a decent person, and then will I ever feel good!" So, you stop drinking. Weeks and then months go by, and all is well. But then you apply for a job, and you find out later that you didn't get it because of your reputation as a drunk. Later, the neighbor, whose garage you ran into last month causing $900 in uninsured damage, meets you on the street and calls you an "irresponsible drunkard" in front of a dozen people. And the police, who know you well, pull you over and give you a field sobriety test, even though you've been sober a long time. So you call up an old friend for some sympathy and he is more interested in going to a drinking party than in talking to you and tells you so. And you call your ex-wife, but she's still mad and hangs up. You get to feeling very low, and start seeing that even after you've done all the right things, you *still* feel like a worthless, lonely, inadequate worm. The urgings of your alcoholic voice now become dominant. They point out that at least while drinking you had *some* pleasure, *some* fun, and *some* friends, if only at the bar. You tell yourself, "So what the hell? What's the use of keeping up this act as if I'm something special? Why not go tie one on like the alcoholic that I really am? Who am I trying to kid? At least I can feel *something* that's good."

This is the great difficulty of staying sober, and the Beast is a patient creature. AA will provide a loving, encouraging Higher Power and a ready-made circle of friends to get you through the tough times. RR will provide you the means to love and respect yourself (even though others may not); to build a new social life among non-drinkers; and to find the capacity to stubbornly refuse to drink or use drugs as a willful act of self-love even when it would be tempting to have something. Where RR groups are established, you will also have a circle of friends who understand the difficulty of sustaining sobriety in the face of great frustration.

If you are still drinking and considering a better life, the time to start feeling good about who you are is *now*. Better a self-respecting drunk than a guilty one. If you believe that achieving sobriety will magically confer upon you a sense of goodness and give you the feeling that all is well with the world, you will be disappointed with the early stages of sobriety. The idea that you'll have more intrinsic worth sober than drunk is a bigoted, fascist view that holds that members of certain groups are intrinsically less or more deserving than others — a view that probably has caused more human suffering than any single idea. The opposite and rational idea is that individual human worth is self-defined, is unprovable, is distinctly separate from the opinions of others, and is the lowest common denominator of mental health. Without an unswerving sense of personal worth we become dependent on others for approval, upon success for self-esteem, and we subject ourselves to variations of mood that put sobriety at risk.

Q: So, what do I have to do to feel like a worthwhile human being?

A: *Nothing,* except to simply understand that your worth cannot be proved or disproved; you have the final word.

Q: But, if I'm already worthwhile, why should I stop drinking?

A: When you love yourself, that is a powerful reason.

3. *My painful emotions and alcoholic cravings are intolerable, and therefore must be controlled by drinking alcohol,*

instead of the rational idea that some discomfort is a necessary, inevitable, and entirely harmless part of becoming sober and then remaining so.

If you have been sober for a week or more, you are no longer having a *physical* craving for alcohol or drugs. Your urge to drink or use more drugs is called "psychological dependency," or a desire to obtain fast, temporary relief from emotional discomfort. This discomfort is usually perceived as "boredom," and the imagery about using drugs or alcohol is vivid and powerful. You are a creature of habit, and for many years you have dealt with much of life's frustrations by introducing powerful anesthetics and stimulants into your body. When you are sober and feel "bored," you are feeling your habitual dependency, and that dependency can be very strong. "Boredom" is one feeling that characterizes alcohol and drug dependence. In reality, boredom is a demand that life provide constant, spoon-fed pleasure. Boredom is simply an admission of one's incompetence in finding meaning or fascination at a given moment. Boredom usually signals that one is most uncomfortable with one's own company. Boredom also may mean the presence of negative emotions caused by dwelling on irrational ideas.

In spite of the folklore, an emotion is most unlikely to kill you. You can have strong, painful emotions, and suffer no lasting ill effect. Most emotions, by their nature, are transient. They fade away of their own accord, unless you renew them with catastrophic thinking, or with depressive ideas about yourself and about life. If you believe irrational idea #3 you will actually feel *more* distressed or bored at times when you are tempted to use or drink; you will feel *compelled* to drink since there seems to be no other alternative to persistent discomfort. On the other hand, if you understand that your emotions (including boredom) are self-induced feelings that are harmless in themselves, you will be able to interrupt your disturbed emotions by asking yourself, "Stop! Wait a minute. What am I telling myself to cause myself all this grief?" If you listen to your feelings you'll hear your own voice, or that of the Beast (or however you conceive of your internalized addictive voice), and you'll hear yourself thinking at least one and possibly several of the irrational ideas that are listed here or at the end of the chapter "To The Families." By working on your ABCs (and not forgetting D and E) you can rid yourself of painful moods far more effectively and lastingly than by drinking any amount of alcohol.

4. *I have little control over my feelings and emotions, which are somehow forced upon me by my past, by certain persons or by external events,*
    instead of the rational idea that I feel the way I think, and therefore I have enormous control over my emotions, my sorrows, and my disturbances.

Although listed fourth, the idea that emotions are externally caused is the beginning of RR. As long as you believe that your emotions are externally caused, you will have practically no control over your inner feelings. For example, if you believe that your spouse "makes you angry" by nagging you to do chores and then complaining about how you do them, then you are *emotionally dependent* on that person to change before you can feel better. In believing this, you grant the other person enormous power and control over you, and then become angry at him or her for exercising or "abusing" that power. It's almost as if your spouse holds a remote control device, like the ones used with TV sets, but the buttons are for anger, pouting, guilt, drinking alcohol, and various other miseries. In order to remain sober for very long, it is vital that you be able to minimize your negative emotions. You can gain control of those emotions only by understanding how your brain works. Below is a simple scheme by which you can visualize your habitual disturbances, and by which you can immediately begin changing how you feel.

The following demonstration of the ABC's of RET are the chief means for effecting personal change in RR. Read the example below carefully, not only for content, but also to learn the form and structure of this potent self-help device. The Sobriety Spreadsheets provided at RR meetings are blank forms on which you can do your own ABC's, especially when confronted with a boozing opportunity. This is preferable to calling a sponsor because you are recovering *rationally*. When you write down your reasons for wanting to have a drink or a fix, you will have an opportunity to decide for yourself if it is a good idea or a stupid one to go ahead with it. Not only will you then be in a position to choose whether to relapse, but you will also be able to take full credit for your choice.

The ABC's of the Intoxication Cycle

Activating Event: My wife nags at me. (Or, "My boss yells at me," or any other scenario of interpersonal conflict.)

Beliefs: 1. I *can't stand* her constant nagging! 2. She just nags like this to get to me, to make me mad. 3. She *shouldn't* treat me this way. 4. I *shouldn't* have to put up with this! I deserve more peace in my life!

Consequences: I feel angry, hostile. I argue and withdraw. *Then I want a drink to calm my nerves and forget.*

Dispute "B": 1. *Can't stand* nagging? Does this mean I'll fall over? What's so terrible about her nagging at me? It's just sound waves, isn't it? Is her nagging really *constant?* Or is it just more than I would *like* or *prefer?* Is her nagging really *intolerable?*
2. Is she really making me mad? Or am I the one who is making myself mad by telling myself how awful and unfair it is that she nags? Is she nagging just to make me mad, or does she simply want me to be more helpful? Wouldn't it be easier to comply, than to sustain my end of this conflict? If she does want me to get angry, will I cooperate with her?
3. Why *shouldn't* she treat me the way she does? Do I really need her continuous approval to feel all right? Why *shouldn't* she be just the way she is?
4. Why *shouldn't* I have to put up with her behavior? What universal law exempts me from this kind of frustration?

Effects: 1. *Of course* I can tolerate her complaints, if I choose to. She's not exactly pouring hot lead on me. Her nagging is annoying, but actually harmless. Therefore, I am less threatened by her outbursts.
2. She is not responsible for how I feel — I am. If I blame her for my feelings, I am in error, because I feel the way I think. It's my *blaming* her and *condemning* her that causes my anger, not her behavior. Realizing this, *I feel less angry toward her.*
3. She really is just the way she should be, faults and all, because she is the product of everything in her biological and personal background. If I want her to change I'll have to try various means, including a positive approach; my present negative approaches aren't working at all. In the meantime, I don't absolutely need her approval, even though it would be nice to have it. *Therefore, when I don't need but*

94

only desire or prefer her approval, I feel more secure and less irritated when she is nagging or rude toward me.

4. There is no reason anything *should* be any different from what it is, because everything in the universe is caused by conditions to be exactly as it is. Everything, then, is just as it should be; I may not like the way things are, but I can accept reality (any circumstance) without becoming severely disturbed and demanding that reality shape up to my expectations. This way I feel more comfortable and my efforts to get what I want are more effective.

5. The general effect of all of the above is that I have greatly reduced my own emotional disturbance far more effectively than by cracking a brew, and with long-lasting and far-reaching results. Although a stiff drink would probably erase my disturbed emotions temporarily, I would still have to deal with them, and with her, later on. For me to splash flammable alcohol on inner fires of my own making is truly the height of insanity, and I choose not to abuse myself and others in this absurd way.

Hydraulics and generators

If you are willing to take the risk of being different from others in order to overcome your emotional dependence on alcohol or drugs, then this author suggests that you recognize the different ways to conceptualize your emotions. The "hydraulic theory" of human emotions goes something like this, given that there are many variations.

"An emotion, especially anger, is 'something down there that bothers me.' It is a pressure or force in me that makes me feel upset or behave poorly. It is caused in the present not only by frustrating events, but also by past disappointments, especially bad experiences in childhood. I have no direct control over my anger because it is just there; therefore all I can really learn to do is manage it the best I can. Anger occupies space in my guts and can build up into pressure that somehow has to get out. Other people can increase the pressure in my guts by doing things I don't like. If I erupt into yelling or telling people off, I can reduce the amount of anger I have — like "letting off steam." When I feel the anger coming up, I can stuff it back down, and this is repression. But the anger is still down there, building up pressure for later. When my guts are sore from too much anger, I can take away the discomfort by drinking alcohol (or using drugs)."

Sound familiar? Perhaps. It is quite likely that you think of your guts as a container for anger, swelling with pressure piped in from the past and from the outside world until your emotions build up and finally erupt. If so, then compare this with the *generator* theory of human emotions, to follow:

Imagine several colored electric lights wired to an electric generator. The generator represents your brain, where thinking occurs, and the colored lightbulbs represent your various emotions, somewhere in your abdomen. When you have a thought, the lamps light up, in different combinations and with different intensity. The red light is anger, the blue one is depression, the green one is affection, the pink one is humor, the purple one is sexual feeling, and so on. Imagine yourself blaming someone for "being a jerk" and thinking of how intolerable this "jerk's" behavior is. Now imagine that the red light is glowing, representing your anger. The more you blame, the brighter and redder the red light gets. The thoughts in your brain are generating your anger. Now, imagine that you find reason to accept what has happened and forgive the character who displeased you, and see the red light dim and then go out. Now, picture an attractive someone of the opposite sex, and see the purple light start to glow. Now think of something funny, and notice the pink light flicker and glow. Now think something gloomy and hopeless, and see the blue light throb in cold hues. You feel the way you think. Do you see?

This last example is the generator theory of human emotions. Simplistic? Yes, these illustrations are simplistic, but the generator concept is far more accurate in describing how the brain works than the hydraulic theory noted earlier. Not only is it more accurate, but it provides individuals with a means to finally grasp direct control over their emotions. When it is seen that emotions, like the glowing lights, are directly activated by thoughts that are occurring in the present moment, then the next logical insight is that "I may now control my emotions by thinking in a purposeful way." This purposeful way is called rational thinking, and is the essence of the rational-emotive therapy of Dr. Albert Ellis that is the heart — the substance — of the Rational Recovery self-help movement.

5. *It is a dire necessity for adults to be loved, respected, or approved of,*
instead of the rational idea that adults do not have to get what they want, including love, respect, and acceptance; rejection is just another person's opinion of my worth, one with which I may gullibly agree or rationally disagree. I choose to love myself simply because it feels better than to dislike myself. In this matter, mine is the final word.

This idea that adults need to be loved is a pivotal issue in Rational Recovery. Because we are biologically inclined to function as social creatures, and possibly because of the extended years of early dependency humans have on parents, it is very easy for us as adults to be convinced that love or approval is *a necessity for its own sake.* Probably more than any other idea, this one can lead you to a dependent lifestyle that is highly conducive to alcohol and substance abuse. If you honestly believe that you need to be loved, admired, appreciated, or approved of, then you will sense that you are an incomplete being without the favorable or loving opinions of others. Love, after all, is essentially someone else's opinion of you. Being suggestible, we tend to respond to loving opinions with a corresponding self-opinion: we feel lovable or *worthy* as a result of someone's love. Accordingly, when we are unloved, or rejected, we tend to accept that opinion also, and feel *unworthy*. Serious trouble can ensue when one is highly dependent on another person's loving opinions. It is irrational and relationship-defeating to allow your own sense of well-being to be determined by another, even one whom you love. It is also an avoidable problem and worth learning about.

By giving some serious thought to this issue — applying your intelligence — you may learn to become *independent* from the loving or accepting opinions of others. When you accomplish this, which need not require much time, you will have made a great stride toward *emotional independence from alcohol and drugs!* People who unconditionally like or accept themselves usually feel well and are in a state of mental health that is conducive to abstinence. If one is prone to moods of worthlessness, guilt and depression, one is also far more prone to short-range preoccupations such as drinking or using drugs.

The difficulty, of course, lies in the fact that early on, as little kids, we all really *were* dependent on others, and for everything. Biologically speaking, love is the bond that prevents the starvation of infants and little kids. The connection between love and food is clear in this context, and it can easily spill over into adult life in the form of dependence on the acceptance and loving opinions of others. This kind of emotional dependence is common, but nevertheless it is an obstacle to adult happiness. With some effort it can be overcome at practically any age after adolescence. Simply being aware of the problem, as you are becoming here and now, is more than half the battle.

Psychologically speaking, love is the classroom of self-worth, wherein one gathers from the loving opinions of the parent that one is, indeed, a worthwhile being. The difficulty here is that very often parents are less than clear on the issue of whether their children are essentially worthy, essentially worthless, or somewhere in between. Many, therefore, enter adulthood with serious doubts about whether or not they are worthy souls or ones who must now set about to prove, through various culturally-prescribed means, that they are really worth their daily bread. Few young adults figure out that one's intrinsic, self-declared worth is a matter entirely separate from the opinions that others may have of them, and that everyone has the capacity to simply like oneself because it feels better than hating oneself and because no one can stop them from doing it.

Most young children are psychologically dependent on the loving opinions of others largely because of their small, undeveloped brains. Children are like "believing machines" that uncritically accept information provided them by adults, especially their parents. Were this not so, Santa Claus would have little popularity. If I confide to a child of four that I am capable of independent flight, and there are pretty wings concealed beneath my shirt, there is a good chance I will be believed. Children do not play with a full deck; considerable gray matter is missing.

That same child will believe that he or she is morally defective, inferior, worthless, unlovable, or ugly if I also express those honest *opinions*. Those unprovable ideas may then become the foundation of the child's personality; the child has no way of checking them out, and no way to establish a more rational truth — that simply being alive is sufficient to infer his or her own worth. That's too deep for little kids to figure out in the face of adult authority.

As the brain fills out neurologically, the capacity for independent thought and reasoning emerges. The stage is set for the child to suddenly "see through" the problem of personal guilt and worthlessness and exclaim, "Eureka! I'm not worthless! That's just my crazy mother's opinion!" But no-o-o-o, we live in a culture that *perpetuates* the nutty ideas of our ancestors, ideas of externally defined, variable, personal worth, the good-kid-bad-kid syndrome, the fears of disapproval, the idea that adults need love for its own sake, and, in effect, a philosophy of perpetual childhood.

When people discover that as adults they no longer need, but only desire, or prefer, to be loved or approved of by others, an important transition takes place — the transition from emotional dependence on the opinions of others to emotional independence, based on rational, *unconditional* self-acceptance. The results in one's social and personal lives are invariably gratifying, and chemically dependent people are finally prepared to take control of their addictions and their lives.

6. *Because I have committed certain acts, or behaved offensively, or harmed someone, I should therefore moralistically blame and condemn myself and feel worthless and guilty,*
     instead of the rational idea that as a human being I am uniquely fallible, and while I may feel regrets, remorse, or sadness for my alcoholic behavior, I need not conclude that I am a worthless person.

We live in a society that is steeped in this idea, and we can see its signs everywhere. There is a popular ad in which a smiling man sits at the wheel of a fancy car with the caption, "Feel good about yourself." Another urges people to become blood donors with the caption "Feel Good About Yourself — Give Blood!" Many religions are based on the idea that we are all worthless unless some deity forgives us for being rotten. Judges stiffen sentences for those who don't express ideas of personal worthlessness (guilt — not to be confused with remorse, sorrow, regrets) for having committed offenses. Abortion foes believe that healthy pregnant women have feelings of personal wickedness and badness following that procedure; therefore abortion, the "cause" of emotional suffering (actually an Activating event), should be outlawed to protect hapless mothers from emotional turmoil (the irrational Consequence). The idea that not all that many women who have had an abortion choose to condemn themselves completely escapes these protectors of the public morality. Other examples of institutionalized irrationality are endless.

Each chemically dependent person knows the extent of his or her dependence, but desperately wants to avoid the shame of what that dependence means. Ours is a harsh, moralistic society that does not treat substance abusers kindly. The stigma associated with alcohol or drug dependence is severe, even though the philosophy that perpetuates alcoholism and drug dependence is widely accepted and even promoted in programs intended to combat the problem. Even though no one wants to be alcohol dependent, those persons are blamed and condemned as though they planned each social offense while sober. It is little understood that the only planning that may be going on is for the next drink or hit of something. It is not hard to see why alcoholics are so hard on themselves, so self-despising, and so hopeless for anything better that only the companionship of someone similarly afflicted provides comfort. It is also not hard to see why traditional recovery programs have such an emphasis on the disease/powerlessness concept and the importance of making amends (seeking the forgiveness/approval of others).

Alcoholism is like the "A" in *The Scarlet Letter*. It is a word of shame, guilt, ostracism, and what is sometimes called "shithood" in RR. "Now look what I've done!" is a common refrain of the morning after. And the common remedy is another drink.

In RR, one is encouraged to accept *full responsibility* for every action that one has taken, drunk or sober, but to stubbornly refuse to *blame* oneself for having committed it. "What?" one may say. "Suppose your relative was killed by a drunk driver. Wouldn't you want *him* to feel guilty as hell?" From first hand experience, I (JT) can say that I don't care what a drunk driver felon feels as long as he is safely behind bars for a long time. My uncle Dick was killed by a drunk driver. Dick's family went through great pain from that tragic auto accident. Dick's family and I will always grieve over what happened; the driver's guilt feelings will change nothing. I hope that the driver is not taught that he is powerless over what he puts into his mouth, and that he must do fearless moral inventories because he killed my uncle. I sincerely hope that if he gets out of prison he will have overcome his alcoholic philosophy. I hope that if the driver who killed my uncle Dick gets out of prison, he will hold *himself*, and not some Higher Power, accountable for what he puts in his mouth for the rest of his life.

It is common to think that guilt over one's misdeeds does some good. It does not. The guiltiest people are the ones who are making the same mistakes over and over and over again. If guilt had any utility for adults, the world would be a far better place than it is. When one is thinking about what a worm he or she is for his or her imperfections, there is no real problem-solving going on; we can only do one mental task at a time. While we are stewing and blaming ourselves we are not thinking constructively about how we got into this mess, and about how we can avoid similar mistakes in the future.

Guilt, the gift from our parents that keeps on giving, is an emotion of childhood that would easily be outgrown if it were not powerfully reinforced throughout society. Originally, guilt is a useful, although often harmful, device for parents to control the behavior of their children when they leave the room. Later, guilt serves as a kind of "superego" or moral restraint for certain forbidden, antisocial, or illegal activities. But as one reaches adulthood the need for self-rating as a central ingredient of one's "conscience" fades, and ethical behavior may be derived from one's own human experience. Humanistic philosophy takes a far more positive view of human nature than theologically derived perceptions of the human condition.

At the heart of the traditional, Judeo-Christian view of human beings is the Doctrine of Variable Human Worth, which has it that one's intrinsic worth (worth in the universe) is a varying, quantifiable essence that is somehow to be conferred, earned, or proved. We may imagine a scale of zero to ten, representing how much worth one has at a given moment, and the indicator will slide between the numbers according to a set of rules given by certain respectable authorities. These religious rules, derived from old writings and interpreted by clergy, form what is known as "doctrine," or the conditions under which one may be grudgingly permitted to feel marginally worthwhile to himself or herself. Doctrine then becomes a wedge between *love* and *self*, so that the two are never really united but only conditionally exposed to each other. The result is lifelong shame over one's personal self — an underlying feeling of badness or rottenness or inferiority that Albert Ellis wittily calls "shithood."

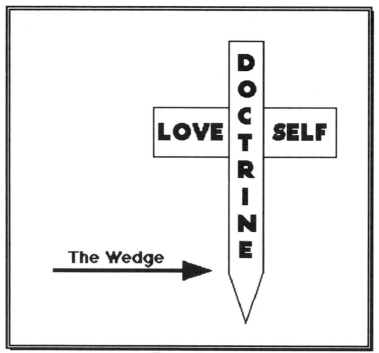

Figure 1

The elegance of Rational Recovery lies in its simple antidote to the doctrine of variable human worth. We learn, through a process of reasoning, that we can neither prove nor disprove our inherent goodness or badness, so we therefore take an elegant shortcut to self-esteem by *making it up!* That's right, we simply break certain rules because we can see that they are bogus rules. Instead of *proving* or *demonstrating* our decency, goodness, worthiness, or self-esteem, we *declare* it. Why do we simply accept ourselves, even though we are quite fallible and others may angrily condemn us? For four reasons: (1) it feels better than to hate or condemn ourselves, (2) no one can stop us from doing it, (3) it makes no sense to rate ourselves according to our performances or according to the opinions of others, and (4) it is not guilt that prevents us from behaving in antisocial or unethical ways, but our own enlightened self-interest. Guilt and shame (which are essentially the same) fade away in the light of reason. With this rational insight, self-forgiveness easily replaces self-condemnation, and the struggle for self-worth is over. Try it. You'll like it.

7. *Other people should not behave poorly, and when they do they should be blamed, moralistically condemned and punished for their misdeeds,*

instead of the rational idea that everyone makes mistakes and it makes no sense to blame others for their imperfections. For me to think that others are not as they should be is a failure to accept reality. If I condemn others, I will apply similar measures to my own worth and end up with personal guilt.

If an offensive person is real, then it would behoove us to accept reality. If one believes that others are not as they should be, then it is the same as saying that reality is not the way it should be. This is an absurdity. People who behave offensively, antisocially, or against our interests do so for specific reasons, some of which we can understand and others we cannot. For example, suppose you see a man kicking a black dog. It yelps piteously. You might think, "Look at that SOB! He kicked that dog for no good reason. He shouldn't have done that! I can't stand people who mistreat animals. What he needs is the same treatment. Someone should teach him a lesson. Maybe I'll teach him a lesson if he keeps it up!" But then, suppose you learned that just yesterday his son was mauled by a black dog. Your response to this news might be, "I see. I guess I can't blame him. But I still don't like his kicking dogs." There is a rational French expression that I'll not cite literally that translates, "To understand all is to forgive all."

Even if the man were only kicking the dog for amusement, wouldn't that only show how deeply disturbed or emotionally impoverished he is and how much he is in need of external restraint or professional care? Can we really add anything constructive or good to this sorry incident by proclaiming that the perpetrator is "bad" or an "SOB?" Aren't we actually increasing his control over others by upsetting ourselves over his deplorable acts? Is the dog helped in any way by our anger and moralistic condemnation of its kicker? "But," one may ask, "doesn't this rational thinking just lend itself to passivity and set the conditions for dog-kickers to take over the world?" Hardly. Angry people function poorly, and they often get hurt or killed while teaching others unsolicited lessons. A quick yell to let the kicker know he is being observed might help to protect the dog, but if we are truly interested in the welfare of dogs, we do have a law enforcement system that is far better qualified to deal with malicious dog-kickers than any of us. And it is good to recognize that even malicious dog-kickers may have positive traits like being able to invent a medicine that may save your life. Our purpose is not to rid the earth of malicious dog-kickers, but only to discourage and restrain that particular practice and perhaps help them come to terms with their abhorrent behavior.

In the preceding paragraph, try substituting other forms of disagreeable behavior that you find angering for dog-kicking, i.e., wife beating, drunk driving, gossiping, war-starting, lie-telling, money-stealing, and notice your feelings ebb and flow. Seek a realistic perception that minimizes your negative emotions, keeps you out of unnecessary conflict with others, while increasing your effectiveness in dealing with the offensive behavior. It's a matter of mental focusing at first, but with practice comes naturally.

8. *In order to feel like a worthwhile person, I must be competent, intelligent, talented, and achieving in all possible respects, and to fail in any significant way, such as in an alcoholic relapse, is to prove what I have always suspected and feared, that I am a defective, inferior, worthless person,*

instead of the rational idea that doing is more important than doing well, trying is more important than succeeding, and accepting myself as a fallible, yet inestimably worthwhile, human being is entirely possible.

It is hard to grow up in our society without learning to associate one's self-esteem with successful performance. The grades given in schools are often taken by the students as a rating of the student rather than the performance; a student's feeling of worth is often strongly affected by ratings of his or her performance. Parents often berate children as part of administering discipline. It is an unusual parent who is capable of conveying consistent self-worth to the children. "Someday you'll amount to something, Johnny," some children are told, and the implication is clear that one's intrinsic worth is somehow to be proven through various acts of compliance, achievement, and conformity. Much of religion is premised on a doctrine of variable human worth, whereby one must gain the approval of deities and church authorities in order to consider one's self a worthy soul. The idea of arbitrary and unconditional self-love is considered wrong, impossible, decadent, evil, sinful, sick, conceited, and offensive in our culture, yet it is the essence of mental health. Rational self-worth is an intellectual insight which, once understood, you can apply to yourself with increasing ease.

The idea that self-worth is self-defined rather than proven or defined through approval is difficult for many to grasp, but when the insight finally does occur, rapid gains are usually made in personal growth. The benefits of rational self-worth, such as (1) reduction or elimination of social anxiety, (2) greater spontaneity in social situations, (3) increased ability to express oneself honestly and openly in public or in intimate relationships, (4) greater willingness to tackle difficult problems or projects where the risk of failure is high, and (5) virtual immunity to negative or low moods in response to rejection or failure, quickly become apparent to those who have made this most important breakthrough.

Some typical reactions to gaining rational insight into the problem of self-worth are, "It was like not seeing the forest for the trees. How simple!" and "I always suspected something like this was true, but I could never get it straight."

9. *If "things" aren't the way I want them very much to be, then it's terrible, horrible, and awful,*

instead of the rational idea that "terrible" and "awful" are magical words meaning "worse than most unfortunate." Since nothing can be more than 100 percent bad, or completely unfortunate, "things" don't have to be any particular way for me to remain sober and relatively calm. If I cannot change or control conditions, I can accept any misfortune, including, when finally necessary, death.

Understanding that nothing truly terrible can possibly happen is a rational insight that can have a *greater calming effect* than belief in a rescuing deity. Understanding reality is manifestly more useful than trusting an ethereal being. When threatening circumstances develop, ask yourself, "What's the worst thing that can happen?" and then know that your worst fears are unfounded; you are built to accept, tolerate, or endure great hardship without dying, going insane, or suffering injury or loss which would preclude any further good in life. For example, you may fret and worry endlessly about the possibility of **A**, going bankrupt. "Look at these bills!" you say, telling yourself at point **B**, *"Isn't it awful* that I don't have enough money to pay them off this month! How will I ever take care of this? If I don't get control of my finances, I'll go bankrupt, *and that would be horrible!"* The **Consequence** is considerable anxiety and an inclination to drink alcohol; the financial problem is in no way helped. Your rational alternative is to **D**(ispute) the **B**(aloney) by asking yourself, "Supposing I can't pay all of this month's bills? Is that my problem, or my creditor's? And if I get dunned, or lose my credit rating, would that really be *terrible*? Or would it just be a pain in the ass for a few years and prevent me from accumulating more debts? And suppose I go bankrupt? Would I die? Would I even have to suffer? If I had to live in a small apartment instead of this nice, big house, would I have to be miserable? Hell no. I can have some great times, no matter where I live, and no matter how much money I have. I would be more restricted, and have more inconveniences, and fewer luxuries, but I doubt that my family or I would starve. Millions of people go bankrupt, and life goes on reasonably well for many of them. Even if I had to go on welfare, I could still get lots of good out of life, even though that would not be ideal. But the chances of bankruptcy are small anyway. If I pay a little to each account each month, maybe I can prevent it. But, if the worst happens anyway, I honestly believe that I can handle it!" In this rich vein of rational thinking, one turns one's life over to *oneself* instead of to some higher power or to the whims of fortune.

By disputing the irrational ideas behind your disturbed emotions as above you will "see through" your problems and experience the Effect of feeling relieved and being able to think about creative solutions to your money problems. You will no longer be able to "awfulize" what is really just an unfortunate, perplexing problem. This step-by-step approach can be applied to virtually any problem, and the general effect is to drastically lower your anxiety level as well as any inclination you may have to drink alcohol. Always remember your ABCs.

For many, it is difficult to grasp that nothing terrible happens in life and only thinking makes it so, and they view the rational viewpoint as a denial of reality and a position of cold detachment. "Terrible things *do* happen," they say, "What about the Vietnam War, or the Armenian earthquake? Suppose your house burns down? What about when a loved one dies, or you're sued for everything you have? Suppose you're sent to prison? Aren't *those* things terrible?" To answer this with a question, for whom, and how much, and for how long? The victims in a natural disaster all react differently. Some are immobilized with *panic* or *despondency,* but others who are relatively unfazed by the urgent situation function as leaders and heroes. In a natural disaster the victims are *startled* and there is much *excitement* and *alarm.* Those who are *mourning* the *loss* of their homes and *loved* ones feel great *sadness* and *helplessness,* and this may be followed later by *depression.* The injured feel *pain* and they *fear* for life and limb. Their lives may never be the same, and they may *grieve* for their losses for many years. Do we really add to our understanding of human tragedy by saying "It's terrible?" We can compassionately recognize the emotions of those who are suffering without calling a natural disaster "terrible" or "awful." (Besides, natural disasters create work for people, who are often paid handsomely for their efforts. It is hardly terrible for them. Children are sometimes seen playing happily in the ruins of earthquakes. Many of them seem little perturbed at the devastation of their community. They somehow have missed that "It's terrible." Would a Martian or lunar earthquake be terrible? Of course not; "terrible" is a human perception, one which always over-generalizes and always exceeds reality.

Certainly, we feel strong emotions over loss, and grieving is basically the "de-awfulization" of what we originally perceived as terrible. When grief is complete, one has concluded that the loss is no longer terrible. The intensity of grief and the duration of grief are measures which can be strongly influenced by reason. In fact, grief, often thought of as a pouring out of sadness until none is left, can better be seen as a process of reality testing wherein one changes one's belief from "I can't live happily without so-and-so" to "I may always miss so-and-so, but I guess I can still enjoy my life." Consequently, the ability to reason aggressively, (think rationally) can decrease both the intensity and duration of personal grief.

10. *It is easier to avoid than to face squarely certain self-responsibilities, such as eliminating alcohol from my diet and concentrating on personal growth,*

instead of the rational idea that the "easy way," especially continuing to drink, is invariably much harder and more painful in the long run.

Drinking alcoholics must struggle with this self-defeating idea because the addiction is perpetuated by the desire for immediate gratification. Enough has been said on that. But RR is more than a get-sober program; it's a program for *staying* sober.

Happiness cannot be achieved through inaction and inertia. As a recovering alcoholic you will find that alcohol played a very central role in your life, and that it is hard to have fun. You will continue for some time to think that drinking alcohol is fun, and that it is important to be loaded in order to enjoy yourself. If you are unable to have fun, you are likely to start drinking.

Consequently, it is critical that you overcome that which stands between you and fun. Most of us find pleasure in other people, in special relationships, and in social and recreational activities. Others find great enjoyment in creative pursuits, in aesthetic pleasures, in special projects such as organizations and politics, or in physical fitness projects.

Let's face it, making new friends is hard. But it is far easier to take the risks of meeting new people, people who are not necessarily alcoholic, by eliminating the perceived risk of rejection. All through *The Small Book* and in idea #5 above you will find something that is unique and delightful about Rational Recovery. You will find that by just loving yourself as the real, living thing you are, for no particular reason than it feels better than *not* loving yourself, you will be much more at ease around others, that you will honestly not care greatly whether they like you or approve of you. By not needing the approval of others you will be able to *be yourself,* to say what you think, and to express yourself without shyness, apprehension, or fear of rejection. The pleasant irony here is that the more you are just yourself, dropping all pretensions and just being what you are, the more people will tend to like you, accept you, and value your company. Conversely, the more you think you *need* friends, approval, companionship and affection, the more you'll put people off and the *fewer* friends you'll have.

In NHP sobriety you have an obligation to yourself to pursue your own self-defined goals; because you're already certain of your individual worth, you won't be tackling projects for the purpose of proving that you're as good as other people. If, for example, you were to return to school, it wouldn't be to erase feelings of inferiority about your lack of academic achievement but rather to open the door of opportunity to goals that you, in your own opinion, want and deserve. Your sexual strivings will be for your own personal gratification rather than to prove your masculinity or femininity or prove to yourself and others that you're lovable rather than sexually defective. Your very life, then, becomes an opportunity for self-fulfillment, a time for getting the good things in life for yourself, enjoying others, and for meaningful activities and pursuits. It is difficult to imagine a more valuable contribution to society than a meaningfully engaged, sober NHP alcoholic — you. Go for it. This life's for you!

11. *Because I am sober, I absolutely must not drink, no matter what, because one drink would lead to my downfall,*

instead of the rational idea that as time goes by drinking appears increasingly stupid because of the obvious selfish advantages of sobriety, but, if I ever stupidly relapsed by drinking, it wouldn't be awful because I would very likely recover again — selfishly, guiltlessly, and probably very quickly.

This irrational idea, that having one drink will lead to a catastrophic downfall, may serve to deter some of us from drinking, but for others it is probably just a self-fulfilling prophecy. The idea, incidentally, is irrational because it fails the test of objective truth. Many alcoholics have impulsively or accidentally taken a drink and then stopped without returning to their addiction. Those people are the ones who understand that alcohol for them is a poison, and that they are exceedingly vulnerable to alcoholic downfall, and they therefore have no illusions about returning to a "normal" pattern of moderate drinking. They understand the "chipping" phenomenon, where the addict continues to tempt fate by occasionally drinking, only to return slowly to complete addiction. Too often alcoholics, after sipping a forbidden drink, hear the resurrected voice of the Beast, saying, "There! Now you've really gone and done it! There's no use stopping now. You are out of control, just like 'The Big Book' says! It's time to tie one on, so you might as well enjoy it."

In RR, you will be encouraged to reject ideas of ever achieving moderation, even though there is no evidence that you cannot succeed. You will be helped to recognize your yearnings to drink moderately as a symptom of your original appetite disorder that you don't wish to indulge, and as a continuation of your original chemical dependency. For you, with a history of alcohol dependence, moderation is very probably as unattainable and unrealistic as becoming an Olympic gold medal winner, not just once, but thrice.

12. *Because I am alcoholic, I need something or someone stronger or greater than myself upon which to rely,*

instead of the rational idea that *dependence* is my original problem, and it is better to start now to take the risks of thinking and acting independently. I cannot really "be" an "alcoholic," but just a person who has believed some of the central ideas of alcoholism.

All through *The Small Book,* you will find references to *dependence* as a chief culprit in alcohol and drug dependence. As you re-read *TSB.3,* you will become more aware of how various dependencies sabotage your own best interests. Below, are several dependency angles you may have overlooked thus far.

Why do you want to stop drinking or using drugs in the first place? Is it to please others, or yourself? Is it because someone thinks you should? Are you trying to impress someone else, or yourself? Do you have a "right" to drug yourself into indifference or oblivion? I hope you understand that you *do* have the "right" to do anything you please in life — as long as you are willing to accept the consequences. That is the "catch."

Do you involve others in your struggle against chemical dependence? Your chances of learning to abstain are far less when you are depending on someone else to keep your balance. The next time you think of saying to your spouse, "You should go to a codependency meeting to get your act together," or "How do you expect me to stop drinking with the cupboard full of your liquor?" imagine yourself and your spouse walking a tightwire, tugging and pulling at each other to keep each other from falling. It might be nice if "true love" could serve the personal interests of both partners in a marital relationship, but that's the stuff of romance novels — fiction, and certainly not real life. If yours is a loving relationship, then it would be more appropriate to express your devotion by not dragging your loved one into an issue as personal as what you put in your mouth.

Another dependency that may needlessly complicate your efforts to not drink or use is dependence on a rescuing deity. In Rational Recovery, *belief* in some Higher Power or Supreme Being is a different matter from *dependence* on such an entity. In RR, we leave whatever gods there may be to their other godly duties, like creating universes, tending to the courses of rivers, and seeing to it that each flower is the proper color. To depend on a God or Higher Power to stop us from intoxicating ourselves not only sets that deity up for failure, but also fosters dependence in an area of our own competence. This is neither character-building nor useful.

For a great many people, God images seem to intrude into everyday problems in ways that are unhelpful. For example, many substance abusers think that they are being "tested" or "punished" by a cosmic being, or that eventual sobriety will result from submitting to such a being. This kind of belief system usually gets started in childhood and remains resistant to change throughout life, but many people *overcome* their religious beliefs as a matter of self-improvement. The famous 12 steps start with a confession of powerlessness over one's addiction, and then the program unfolds as a deepening dependency on some Higher Power. People who don't accept supernatural ideas are encouraged to accept the group as a Higher Power, which, from a rational viewpoint, would seem a most unwise choice. On many crucial points AA says just the opposite as theologically neutral RR, so people of different opinions about rescuing deities now have a clear choice on the road to recovery.

If you find the spiritual teachings of AA difficult or objectionable, then, in all likelihood, the rational alternatives will make more sense. Because it is so important for recovering and recovered alcoholics to have firm roots in a highly relevant, consistent, and coherent philosophy, the following comparison between godism and rationality is included in *The Small Book*. In order to achieve NHP sobriety, you will want to become very rational, and that means being willing to examine issues by following reason to its conclusions.

How "the God part" works:

We humans can imagine damn near anything. Most of us are also surprisingly capable of thinking analytically, critically, and logically. Recovery from addiction calls for considerable effort and purposeful thought, no matter how it is approached. While AA and RR are contradictory in some regards, there is considerable overlap, and it is only fair that in *The Small Book* we examine the core philosophies of both systems of thought.

The key to understanding AA spiritualism is to understand the part that "God" plays in recovery. *The key to understanding NHP sobriety is to grasp the role that the human intellect, or intelligence, plays in recovery.*

Guilt is a central theme in most addictive and compulsive disorders, and alcoholism is no exception. Repeat from above: the guiltiest people are the ones who are making the same mistake over and over again. Unfortunately, guilt has practically no value in effecting personal change, because people generally act the way they feel, and people who feel rotten tend to act in rotten ways. Moreover, when one errs, he would best devote his energies toward planning how to avoid the same mistake in the future or to analyzing how he got into his predicament in the first place. Guilt-prone people, especially addicts, do none of these constructive things; instead they dwell on how stupid, inadequate, and worthless they are. The addictive cycle is one of "error-guilt-error-guilt," and the pattern continues forward indefinitely toward eventual self-destruction. Only through some dramatic or radical change can the error-guilt cycle be interrupted. Because guilt does not reduce error, guilt must go.

To get rid of guilt, however, you must know what it is. For our purposes, guilt is the feeling of worthlessness or badness which results from self-blame and self-condemnation. By making yourself believe in a loving Higher Power, your ideas of shame and worthlessness are cancelled out by an *authority* higher than yours, a "Supreme Opinionated Being" whose opinions are by definition absolutely true. As an alcoholic, therefore, you may be thoroughly despised by your family, your neighbors, and the rest of the community, but yet disregard those opinions in favor of your Higher Power's opinion. After all, he is a perfectly wise deity who, in spite of all of your abuses and misdeeds, forgives you and loves you anyhow. If God loves you, then who are you to disagree? Your worth, then, is *conferred* on you by "God's" approval.

But that's not all you get from your Higher Power. If you're willing to regard yourself as powerless over your actions, fraught with character defects, unable to manage your life, and having insufficient will to resist temptations like drinking or snorting cocaine, your Higher Power will become a special pal to you and actually use his supernatural abilities to reduce your appetite for intoxicants, to protect you from high-risk situations, to improve your moral character, and to infuse you with fine moods. When you think of Him, you will feel calm, because you will be reminded of your inherent worth (to him at least) as a human being, and you will have faith that you will easily pass up boozing or bingeing opportunities. Your future is now "charmed" with supernatural aid in your daily life. Your Higher Power may even offer the bonus of continuing your existence after you are dead, so that you can continue to be with Him and finally reach spiritual perfection and perpetual bliss. Since this is a very good deal, indeed, AA spiritualism works beautifully for those who are able to believe in a rescuing deity. I urge anyone with a serious addiction to give it a serious try — and I'm serious in suggesting it.

No Higher Power sobriety achieves the same result, except for the promise of an afterlife. The God part is missing; *you* will play the part of God. Yes, you read that correctly. *You* will correct your error-guilt cycle with the radical, dramatic insight, *"I am worthwhile and lovable because I say that I am, and I am the final authority here!* There is no evidence in the universe that because I am an alcoholic I am worthless.

Although I've behaved wretchedly toward others, that doesn't make me a wretch, and my miserable behavior does not make me a bastard. I'll never be able to *prove* my goodness (or badness), so I'll love myself just as I am, *for no other reason than it feels better.* It is *because* I love myself and want the better things in life for myself that I will stop abusing and defeating myself by drinking alcohol. I will also stubbornly refuse to blame myself for anything I have ever done. Being human, I reserve the right to be wrong — even seriously wrong — without a twinge of guilt. Sadness and regrets? Of course. But will I blame and condemn myself for being a fallible human being? I will not."

By adhering to this very rational position, even if you are intoxicated as you read this, you will immediately feel better about yourself, and you will notice your feelings of shame and guilt fading away, just as if some Higher Power had magically erased those feelings. But the credit for this vital change is due *you; you* are in control of your feelings, your behavior, your thinking, your life. You have performed the unmiracle of self-redemption, the act of self-forgiveness resting on your own reasoning and authority. By reading further into *TSB.3,* you will find that it isn't so hard to immediately start loving yourself — even though you may be failing in various areas of your life, and even though others are angry and fed up with you. Remember that your inclination toward guilt and worthlessness has been powerfully conditioned since childhood; to unlearn your habitual moralizing and self-depreciation will take conscious effort, an open mind, and lots of practice. Within you right now are all the necessary ingredients for gaining a durable, meaningful, guiltless sobriety.

13. *Because alcoholism once greatly affected my life, it should continue affecting me frequently and indefinitely,*

instead of the rational idea that, because rational sobriety is self-fulfilling, and because there is so much more to life than a constant struggle to remain sober, I can gradually close the book on that sorry chapter in my life, and become vitally absorbed in activities and projects outside of myself and unrelated to my alcoholism.

For those with a year or more of NHP sobriety, an appropriate motto is, "It's no big thing." When a substance is absent from the body for a period of time the appetite for it wanes and eventually disappears. Formerly carnivorous vegetarians report that the appetite for meat is one that must be fed to be sustained, and those who refrain from sugar for various reasons often remark how repulsive the thought of sugar now seems. Something just like this occurs in the alcoholic body, so that the subjective feeling of "temptation to drink" gradually lessens and eventually disappears.

But we do know that the Beast of RR usually doesn't disappear altogether. It may reassert itself even after many years of pleasant sobriety. Even so, we do not feel threatened by the mere thought of drinking, because of the *sense of mastery* that we have achieved over our old nemesis.

RR is unique in that members are expected to fully recover in a reasonable time, and then leave the group. While traditional programs tend to dwell on human weakness, frailty, and incompetencies, RR holds a vision of the human being that is affirmative. We look within to find strengths and competencies that form the foundation for sobriety and continuous personal growth. For these reasons, RR is correctly viewed by many people as a way for long-term members of AA to kick the recovery habit. In this sense, RR is a preparation for quitting recovery altogether even after many years of 12-stepping. During this time, one may address some central dependency issues that very likely may have developed during the years that one attended 12-step meetings.

14. *Somewhere out there, there is a perfect solution for life's problems, and until I find it, I am doomed to a life of uncertainty and turmoil,*

instead of the rational idea that uncertainty is the spice of life, and seeking a perfect solution is silly and a waste of time. I will do better to view life as an enjoyable experiment, seeking my own pleasures and cultivating my own personal growth.

There are many "-ism's" besides alcoholism that promise a perfect solution to life's difficulties, usually based on perfect truth. These plans for perfect harmony and inner peace offer happiness as a miraculous gift to those who believe in and subordinate themselves to some ideal, some ineffable essence, or to some spiritual being. Rational Recovery holds out no such promise, but does provide a means for being reasonably happy — most of the time. In a rational context, ecstasy seems to suggest some mental abnormality or to be briefly associated with rare moments of extreme good fortune, and there seem to be no circumstances when one would be compelled to feel desperately unhappy.

Recovery from the philosophy of alcoholism is a limited although intense struggle. When one finally has a reasonable expectation that he can live a normal life without the use of the "perfect solution," alcohol, and when he feels confident that refusing alcohol is second nature, recovery is complete. Personal growth, however, is never complete and there are infinite ways to add meaning to life.

Chapter 8

A Discussion of The 12-step Spiritual Healing Program of Alcoholics Anonymous

This is the chapter of TSB.2 that caused all the outrage and controversy. It has been interpreted by many as a direct attack on AA, as a needless, fruitless, angry put-down of "a program that has helped millions." High ranking officials of the public alcoholism and drug abuse administrations have said the following pages are "...offensive..." and "...makes people defensive," and "...threatens the credibility of RR."

Let me say this. Chapter 8, which follows, is intended to do two things. First, it is intended to summarize the common objections that literally millions of people have to the 12-step program. These are not my own personal objections, but a summary of the objections of the thousands of frustrated people who have contacted RRS and told us their stories. Second, this chapter is intended to bring to the public eye what is happening in our national addiction care system. It is not my intention here to persuade AA members or devout theists that their views are wrong, or to discredit any successes of the AA treatment approach. Instead we will simply examine each of the steps from the perspective of an inquiring mind, asking the questions that come naturally to *anyone* who is not already convinced of the overall correctness of the 12-step creed.

The idea that an author must be angry in order to criticize or express dissent is an *ad hominem* response that overlooks what the author is saying. It is also typical for proponents of faith-based systems of thought to believe that there must be something wrong with someone who disagrees. There is an AA pamphlet titled, "AA: An Interpretation for the Nonbeliever" (Jon Weinberg, Ph.D., Hazelden Foundation), that is worth getting and reviewing first hand. On the front cover of this 14 page booklet, a "nonbeliever" is depicted in caricature, and one must see it to believe it. This is an ugly person — his mouth is twisted into an ugly scowl, his eyeglasses are slipping down his nose, his double chin protrudes over his collar, and his entire face is furrowed with deep, angry wrinkles. He is pitiful. He is a stereotype that is central to AA tradition, and we may find the image of this troubled soul described throughout "The Big Book." He is "the angry one," a pathetic dumbbell who denies God, then sees the error of his ways, surrenders to his Higher Power, has a spiritual awakening and then lives happily ever after.

One of the barriers to progress in addiction care is what we might call "blasphobia", or the morbid fear of being associated with anything that could be construed by anyone as being blasphemous, anti-God, anti-Christ, anti-religion, satanic, demonic, etc. As it stands, AA represents America's "traditional values" — the good, the true, and the beautiful. What could be more publicly appealing than a secret society of altruists who themselves were redeemed from iniquity through faith in God? But I must ask, "What is the state's interest in protecting the 12-step ideology from meticulous scrutiny?"

As you read this short critique of the 12 steps, you will notice that taken together they comprise a philosophy in which one is powerless, submissive to authority, unequipped to function independently, and in endless need of external support and guidance. This should not be surprising to anyone, and to take offense that this is pointed out would seem to be a *denial* of reality. The 12 steps are derived from an ancient philosophy with which we are all familiar. Like it or not, the twelve numbered ideas below reflect just one of the major philosophical traditions of American society. They have often been held up as an ideal for the entire world. From a rational viewpoint they are a negative, irrational philosophy that we may call "alcoholism."

Step 1. *"We admitted we were powerless over alcohol — that our lives had become unmanageable."*
Step 1 actually teaches addicts that they are not responsible for what they put into their mouths, that they have no capacity to refrain from ingesting alcohol. Could it be that alcoholism is largely a *result* of this idea? That is, isn't the alcoholic already expressing the idea that his desire for alcohol is an *absolute* need, that a craving is *irresistible* or *intolerable*, and that, when the desire to drink occurs, it *must* be gratified *immediately* and *completely*? To the extent that this is so, the message in this first step could be counterproductive to those who are concerned enough to attend a few meetings but not really inclined to adopt the social or theological elements of AA spiritualism.

Learned helplessness from Step 1 often can be a self-fulfilling prophecy in which the addict retains this central spiritual principle of surrender even after quitting AA. For example, after attending a few meetings you may decide that AA isn't for you, that you can get sober on you own. So you stop attending meetings, resolved to quit drinking. However, something lingers in your thinking and it won't go away. When you feel like having a drink, you think back to what was said at the AA meetings, and you remember the sincere people and their stern warnings:

> You are powerless over alcohol and you have no control; only a Higher Power can restore you to sanity. We all tried it on our own and none of us could remain sober until we found our Higher Power. You can't resist the overpowering urge to drink, and if you leave this group you will drink again; then it's all downhill. This group is a lifeboat; leave us and you'll sink. There's no escape except through our loving God, who gives us the strength to stay sober, one day at a time.

This kind of indoctrination does *nothing* to help your resolve to not drink; it is probably *the worst thing* to tell someone who is having problems with impulse control and who does not believe in a rescuing deity. If you are seriously tempted to have a drink and all those experienced people say you're powerless over alcohol, who are you to argue the point? "Down the hatch — Cheers." Your decline is highly predictable.

The chief problem with the idea of powerlessness, even greater than the negative psychological impact it has on certain addicts, is its utter falsity. There are simply too many examples of alcoholic persons, including this writer, who "wise up and sober up" when the consequences of chemical dependency become too costly, too risky, or too painful. Self-initiated sobriety is far more common than generally supposed, and I have encountered many such persons in both my personal and professional life. It is doubtful that any of us could have helped ourselves if we were really convinced of the truth of Step 1. Some people find within themselves the ability to stop drinking independently, while the large majority of us achieve our goal of sobriety and abstinence by getting professional help or attending AA. The charge that when an alcoholic seeks help for his problem he is admitting powerlessness is simply not true; reaching out for help is in itself a powerful act of self-determination.

Step 2: *"We came to believe that a Power greater than ourselves could restore us to sanity."*

It should be noted that "The Big Book" of Alcoholics Anonymous devotes an entire derisive chapter to "agnostics." That book, about three inches thick, is the central document of the AA movement, and its influence on thinking about alcoholism is pervasive and profound. It was written by the founders of AA fifty years ago, three men who attained sobriety following the Christian plan of salvation. Several of their contemporaries, members of "The Oxford Group," attempted earlier to found a sect of recovering alcoholics based on a more orthodox interpretation of Christian theology. They failed, partly because of the explicit religious dogma they sought to incorporate, leaving the "Akron Group," with its ambiguous "Higher Power," to evolve into the dominant theistic organization it is today.

It is important to address "The Big Book's" aspersions upon atheists, agnostics, skeptics, "disbelievers," and those whose religious views do not include a rescuing deity. "AA bashing" (a euphemism for "blasphemy!") is not our purpose in challenging "The Big Book"; our concern is for the desperate persons who are harmed by its dogmatic stance. The 12-step program is a *direct attack* on the nonreligious groups listed above. With our constitutional guarantees, all's fair in the discourse between religionists and humanists, but little attention is paid to the intellectual violence done to sick people who do not endorse God, Jesus, the Bible, Christianity, or religion in general. One purpose of *The Small Book* is to validate those individuals — to insure that each person, regardless of personal philosophy, has a maximum opportunity for recovery.

Major problems develop when a particular branch of medicine is given over to a treatment approach that includes divine intervention, or what is commonly called "faith healing." Simply put, there is not a shred of objective evidence for the existence of a sentient, supernatural being in the universe. If such evidence existed, there would be no need for religions to endlessly indoctrinate people into such an idea. People would have no trouble in comprehending the obvious, proven truth. Deities, gods, and the like are imaginary, and people must *make* themselves *believe* in them because there is no evidence that they exist. For many people making believe this way comes easily, while others find it virtually impossible to believe in improbabilities such as supernatural beings. It is such a being, a benevolent, rescuing deity called "God," upon which AA rests.

"But," the AA elders insist, "there is room for all degrees of disbelief in AA. Anything can be your Higher Power! Your HP can be a wrench, a tree, music, the AA group, even Wisdom, but you

116

absolutely *must* place your faith in something greater than, and outside of, yourself."

This tactic is, in a word, unethical. It is practiced everywhere in the AA spiritual network, and obviously has the sanction of key AA leaders. This is a cult tactic which, in the view of many, detracts from the dignity and credibility of the Twelve-Step program. It's a bait-and-switch head game in which the real intention is to convert a neophyte to hard-core belief in God Almighty. Suppose a doubting newcomer accepts a bedpan as his Higher Power on the advice of well-intended members. Granted, he may get through detox while meditating on the finer dimensions of the bedpan, but what about the next hurdle, Step 3?

Step 3: *"We made a decision to turn our will and our lives over to the care of God, as we understand Him."*

Ah, now — it isn't the bedpan, is it? Would you turn your will and your life over to a bedpan? Now our newcomer is faced with the task of reconciling his newfound sobriety with a new, poorly-understood "God." Bye-bye, bedpan. Maybe it's time for a drink.

The Higher Power of AA is a flexible "training deity" devised to 1. help neophytes complete early detox and withdrawal, 2. avoid disclosing the inflexible theism behind AA, and 3. provide a progressive relaxation of critical judgement so that neophytes can be further indoctrinated in AA theology. Notice that there is still equivocation with "...as we understand Him." Even though "He" rates a capital letter, you are led to believe that you are still at liberty to make "Him" what you believe "Him" to be. Sure you are.

Step 4: *"We made a searching and fearless moral inventory of ourselves."*

Here we find that recovering alcoholics are expected to become better people. Is adult life really a struggle to "be good?" Come on, now. If some folks define adult life that way, then fine for them, but it would seem that there are far better reasons for seeking sobriety than to "be a good person." We find here also the pernicious idea that good people are less likely to suffer a relapse than less "moral" people. Why should an alcoholic be required to search introspectively for "moral defects" in himself? Is this really relevant to alcohol dependence? Do we want alcoholics to become "good people" or just sober people? Are alcoholics bad, in need of moral betterment? (Good people, of course, never get hooked on alcohol.) Are diabetics similarly obliged to make searching and fearless moral inventories? If not, why not? If an alcoholic stops drinking through a chemical dependency program but still robs banks, was the treatment successful? Of course it was!

117

The Christian roots of AA are most conspicuous here, where the neophyte is required to debase himself, to grasp downward at "humility" as an avenue to spiritual redemption through faith. "We are all sinners" supposedly gives way to moral ascendency.

Step 4 presents difficulties for many disturbed persons whose defenses against self-condemnation are poor. There is speculation that persons are most prone to suicide or self-destructive relapses during this phase of AA indoctrination, when the inductee is flooded with conditioned guilt and remorse and is unable to stem the tide of his self-condemnation. Unfortunately, data regarding this problem is scarce because of AA's lack of accountability and disdain for keeping records of persons experiencing such difficulties. Keep in mind that most of AA group activity occurs in church basements and social halls under lay leadership (the strongest ego dominates the meetings), and few persons served by AA ever come to the attention of professional caregivers. "The Big Book" does give a vivid example of an individual who did commit suicide while trying unsuccessfully to "get his Higher Power together," and the writer describes this incident almost cavalierly as *something to be expected when one fails the test of faith.* The wages of sin is death. This all gets very, very Christian, which is fine for Christians. But can we really expect most substance abusers to accept Christian theology? Wouldn't a fearless inventory of irrational ideas that perpetuate the intoxication cycle be more appropriate?

Step 5: *"We admitted to God, to ourselves and to another human being the exact nature of our wrongs."*

The idea here is that by confessing our sins, the listener will forgive (accept) us in spite of our having committed the misdeed. Forgiving is the opposite of blaming (or condemning) someone for committing an antisocial or other unacceptable act. Forgiveness by God is a temporary antidote for guilt because its message is, "God says you are still a good person even though you acted badly, and who are you to question the opinion of God?"

At this point we come to the AA sponsor system. Briefly, it is a "buddy system" of interpersonal dependency, where the neophyte "borrows the ego" of a program veteran, and attempts to identify with one who has "been through it." There are many inspiring stories about how a faltering neophyte called his sponsor in the wee hours and found strength and encouragement to resist the temptation to drink. I have also spoken with alcoholics who believe that their dependency on a sponsor was unwarranted (considering that sponsors have no special training or skills) and alcoholics whose emotional entanglement with a sponsor led to serious problems. One case involved a member whose sponsor resumed drinking and died, leaving him disillusioned and demoralized. Another account is of a sponsor who took on the role of spiritual therapist, financial advisor and vocational counselor with a susceptible member. While there will probably be occasional abuses in any kind of human relationship, it is worth pointing out here that emotional dependency among normal adults is categorically self-defeating, even when one party is deemed the helper. The sponsor system seems to encourage the irrational idea that one needs someone other or greater than oneself upon whom to rely.

Sponsors hear confession from newcomers with the understanding that confession is intrinsically beneficial and healing. This assumption is contradicted by the fact that confession programs are interminable, open-ended affairs in which the confessor never attains personal liberation from guilt *or from the confession ritual*. In AA, God listens to and forgives confessions eternally. In Rational Recovery, individuals confess nothing; instead, they learn to accept themselves as imperfect yet worthy beings who seek only self-forgiveness and who reject guilt as a matter of principle. Self-disclosure, then, is simply a means of identifying problem areas for self-improvement.

Step 6: *"We were entirely ready to have God remove all these defects of character."*

It is probably difficult for religious persons to imagine why this idea is so offensive to some people who are not religious, but I will attempt to explain anyway. What is being asked for in Step 6 is a miracle. Members must believe that miracles are possible and theirs for the asking. Accepting the miracles of sobriety, survival, and serenity from a Higher Power while other group members fail to qualify for miracles is thought to be character building. In Step 5, there is some connection between what the neophyte is being asked to do and a potential benefit. If you confess, you may be forgiven, and that may help somewhat. But now the neophyte is being asked to get ready for a miracle — entirely ready. Well, suppose he's only *partly* ready? Or *almost* ready? Would this rescuing deity hold out on a sincere person who is not *entirely* ready? Is "entirely" inserted to cover for when the rescuing deity, in His infinite wisdom, *doesn't* come through with the desired character repairs? Why did this rescuing deity endow us with "alcoholic" genes in the first place — just to stir up a little trouble? So he could show off later with character repairs? To test our mettle? To lead us to AA?

The "wrongs," or mistakes, or misdeeds, that one confessed to in Step 5 (after the "fearless moral inventory" of Step 4) have now been converted to "defects of character," which are to be removed through divine intervention after some additional qualifying steps. The passive-dependent theme in this step is apparent.

Step 7: *"We humbly asked Him to remove these shortcomings."*
Any priest or minister will immediately recognize here the setting of "a proper worshipful attitude" that is a requisite for prayer and ritual. We do not firmly or politely request favors from the deity, nor do we expect a decent response to a request we think would be just and fair unless *we **humbly** submit ourselves to the Lord, unworthy as we are, in the hope our pleas for mercy will not be dismissed or ignored.* It is to escape precisely this kind of groveling and self-debasement that many people flee from churches. It is in this step that we learn that AA sobriety is a supernatural miracle, not really the product of our own self-determination. Is it really character-building to believe that our well-being is subject to the whims of a rescuing deity?

A curious thing about the 12-steps is that not even a single word is said about how a substance abuser might arrive at a decision to not drink or use drugs. The idea of personal choice is absent. The program simply assumes that by becoming morally good, people will stay sober. Conversely, alcoholism is viewed very clearly as a moral failure, as separation from God, as a spiritual deficit to be remedied by a religious conversion.

Step 8: *"We made a list of all the persons we had harmed, and became willing to make amends to them all."*
A list? Became willing? Something's brewing here.
Step 9: *We made direct amends to such people wherever possible, except when to do so would injure them or others.*
"I feel so guilty. I can't live with myself. I need to help. Please respect me. Don't blame me for being bad. Help me feel better. Forgive me. I want to be good. I want to feel proud of myself."

Freud and others have written about the common defense mechanism, "undoing," where guilt-flooded persons seek to compensate for earlier misdeeds by symbolically or actually acting out scenarios that absolve the offense. To the extent that Steps 8 and 9 are to absolve persistent guilt about past alcoholic "sins," wouldn't self-forgiveness be more appropriate than dwelling on past mistakes and possibly opening old wounds? Aren't most people happy just to be rid of those who were once obnoxious drunks? Is it really constructive to exhume the past in this way? Do recipients of amends often appreciate surprises like this? Isn't the greatest gift of a substance abuser to society the mere fact of his or her sobriety? Aren't Steps 8 and 9 melodramatic and cloying? Are they really relevant to an appetite disorder? Are Steps 8 and 9 intended to help others or are they part of a ritual for conditional self-esteem?

Step 10: *"We continued to take personal inventory and when we were wrong promptly admitted it."*

Here we find out that AA is forever, ladle to grave. The program is interminable; members continue — and continue and continue and continue — year after year, decade after decade, to take searching and fearless moral inventory and they promptly admit it when they are wrong, unless, of course, the error is said to lie in the 12-step program. The idea of leaving the fold, leaving Mother Group, is anathema to AA. Members dwell on stories of those who "tried it on their own" only to drink again, and then, if they were fortunate enough (by the grace of God) to survive their inevitable alcoholic downfall, came crawling back to old Mother Group. Occasionally mention is made of so-and-so, who left ten years ago, and who was sober until last heard from but "he's still a dry drunk; he *can't* really be happy, we *know* he's really miserable...." The message of personal powerlessness is so strong that it becomes a self-fulfilling prophecy. Those who quit AA are likely to remember the grim pronouncements that those who leave the group are surely doomed. Then, in a moment of indecision, they succumb to the "inevitable," and take a drink of alcohol.

Doesn't almost everyone, except possibly some sociopathic or mentally ill persons, try to "be good?" Aren't people who try to recover from alcohol dependence *already* trying to "be good"? Are chemically dependent people so morally defective as to need constant indoctrination, constant and repeated FMI's (fearless moral inventories)? Does Step 10, with its insistence that life is a constant struggle to remain moral and sober, contribute to self-doubt rather than a healthy sense of assumed personal competence and goodness? Doesn't Step 10 really reflect the idea that life is only a stage for acting out the pervasive forces of good and evil?

Step 11: *We sought through prayer and meditation to improve our conscious contact with God as we understand Him, praying only for knowledge of His will and the power to carry that out.*

When AA finally loses its secular identity in court, as it seems likely to in time, this is the step that will probably be Exhibit A. As it stands, each member is expected to become an agent of God, praying for instructions from on high, and for the strength to carry out those instructions. AA adherents achieve a state of bliss, or inner peace, through meditation and prayer, a state they call "serenity," which is actually salvation through faith; this serenity is a major goal in the earthly lives of recovering substance abusers. Serenity, the peace which passeth all understanding, is regarded as a powerful hedge against alcoholic relapse. The phrase "...as we understand Him" is repeated, but by now it is clear that the deity in question is highly *specific*, One Who is interested in substance abusers and listens to them, One Who sends messages and advice to the faithful, and One Who expects worship, prayer, meditation, obedience and frequent meeting attendance as conditions to be met before special favors are granted and before character repairs are made. Wouldn't "...as AA understands Him" be more accurate? Isn't this intensely religious? Could any program short of a monastery be *more* religious than this?

Step 12: *"Having had a spiritual awakening as a result of these Steps, we tried to carry this message to others, and to practice these principles in all our affairs."*

Is a "spiritual awakening" different from religious conversion? If so, in what ways? If not, and the awakening occurred "as a result of these Steps," is not the 12-step program a religious doctrine of redemption and salvation? If 12th steppers try to "practice these principles in all our affairs," are they not practicing the religious life? Are many substance abusers really good candidates for this? If 12th steppers try to "carry this message to other alcoholics," aren't they proselytizing, or witnessing, for an evangelical faith? There is no mention here of trying to dissuade other alcoholic people from drinking alcohol, or to help alcoholics get whatever help they might choose, but only to "...carry *this* message," (the profoundly religious 12-step program of Alcoholics Anonymous) to others so that they might increase their faith in a Higher Power outside of themselves. After that, as part of their orientation, they are beseeched to refrain from alcohol.

If one completes the first eleven steps and then balks at this one, will he or she risk relapse? How does this step fit in with state-certified substance abuse counseling programs? Are states now participating in this step? Does this step ever create professional conflict of interest?

The above discussion of the AA spiritual healing program could continue, but this much should identify some of the issues that affect each American who seeks help with an addictive disorder. None of the above is really new. These questions have been asked for years, ever since success spoiled a good thing, ever since the helping professions gradually sold out to AA.

A recurring question is, "Wouldn't it be good if AA were to change, to 'lighten up on the God part,' to make concessions to the 'agnostics,' to recognize that everyone, regardless of religious faith or the lack thereof, deserves a chance to get better?" There have been some attempts to accommodate agnostics by segregating them into

122

informal groups that meet independently, but no alternative program is provided by AA national offices. There is no alternative literature and no plan for recovery except what interested persons might try to derive from the 12-steps. Some white out "God" and inject other abstracts, like "self" or "wisdom," but the result is always incoherent. Those who attend "We Agnostics" groups are accorded second-class membership in every respect, and one will likely feel "marginal" as an agnostic in AA after reading chapter 4, "We Agnostics," of "The Big Book."

Robert M., a recovered alcoholic from California, had attended AA for many years, but being a devout atheist, never came to believe in a rescuing deity. He achieved a durable sobriety his own way, using the AA group as a support and social outlet. He finally wrote *The Grapevine,* the internal newsletter of AA, stating that he believed that all the praying and religion during meetings were discouraging newcomers. He asked that his letter be published in the opinions column. Over the next three years, an escalating series of thirteen letters between Robert and various levels of the AA hierarchy were exchanged, hotly contesting whether or not the controversial 200-word letter should be published. It finally was, in an edited form. Robert was told that any change regarding the use of the Lord's Prayer in AA meetings would have to be voted on *by the entire membership.* So much for AA's capacity to change with regard to its theology.

An even more relevant question is *"Should* AA change?" This writer thinks not. It's fine the way it is for those who are inclined to believe. History has shown clearly that conservative religions flourish while liberal ones die out. The reason for this is that religions depend on a nucleus of "true believers" in an inflexible doctrine for inspiration, leadership, and finances, and to make up the rank and file. When the central doctrines are liberalized to accommodate outsiders, or malcontent insiders, the mainstream members feel betrayed and offended, and leave the fold. The outsiders and malcontents, being good liberals, weren't all that interested in causes in the first place and soon abandon ship with the rest. The organization then shrinks in strength and size to a mere residual of its former stature.

From all the foregoing it can be seen that the ideas and philosophies of RR and AA are mutually contradictory and irreconcilable. It would be inappropriate for one organization to try to support two conflicting philosophies. AA is good at what it does, and to change to accommodate internal dissent would erode its fundamental principles. Moreover, *The Small Book* is just as partisan as "The Big Book" in persuading the reader toward its viewpoint, and could never have been produced from within the current addiction care establishment.

Chapter 9

To the Family and Friends: Take Sides!

It is probably best to keep your distance from someone who drinks too much; by this I mean emotional distance as well as physical distance. If you are involved with an alcoholic person, it is very easy to get hurt, both emotionally and physically. If you are not careful, you could even get killed. Cemeteries are filled with people who got too involved with alcoholics. Few beings on earth are more dangerous than an angry drunk, or one who sits behind the wheel of an automobile. In order to take care of yourself, it will be necessary to take sides on some nitty-gritty issues. Briefly, here are some issues to take sides on. You can probably add more.

DO:

1. Remind yourself that you are a worthwhile person who deserves kind treatment from everyone.
2. Recognize that your first responsibility in life is to yourself, and that to help others in the family you must keep yourself in good emotional and physical shape.
3. If you are married to an alcohol or drug dependent person, make realistic plans for eventual separation and/or divorce, since the prognosis for alcohol and drug dependence is not good. Should your "favorite addict" recover, these plans can usually be dropped or reversed.
4. Have your own funds in a separate savings account, for leaving home and for other necessities. Save here and there, and deposit windfalls, unexpected income, etc.

5. If you are underage, confide in a trusted *adult* friend or relative and make plans with that person to move in if you need to. Tell your sober parent, if you have one, of these arrangements.

6. Go to meetings of Al-Anon or Ala-teen, even if you don't believe in a god. You can ignore the silliness, learn from the others there, and make some friends there, too.

7. Call the police when the alcoholic person threatens or becomes violent. Ask the police to take any guns away for safekeeping as often as needed. Remove and dispose of guns yourself if you feel they pose a threat. Remember that with new changes in the law, police are in a better position to arrest drunks during domestic flare-ups. Should this occur, it will serve as a deterrent against future violence. The police will also have information on domestic crisis services that can be of immense help. Remember that pain is therapeutic for alcoholics who find little reason to stop drinking and abusing others. Your self-protective actions may very well be painful to your special alcoholic.

8. Seek out an alcoholism specialist who will arrange an intervention with your alcoholic person. This may result in 12-step care.

9. Approach the alcoholic person when he or she is most sober and tell him or her that you think he or she is a hard-core, "bad" alcoholic and needs help desperately. By all means provide your loved one with a copy of *The Small Book*. Provide the phone number of an alcoholism specialist or AA. If he or she objects to AA based on past experience, ask if it would make any difference if the recovery program were non-religious. If so, urge him or her to read *The Small Book* and attempt a self-recovery. Get him or her to subscribe to *The Journal of Rational Recovery*, an informative periodical for AA refuseniks.

10. Warn the alcoholic of exactly what you will do, and by when, if the drinking does not completely stop.

11. If you live with an alcoholic, move out when you have had enough.

12. Regard yourself as an extremely worthwhile person and place number one priority on your own self-interest. Aim toward personal growth in spite of the present problems. Learn to think rationally at will by studying rational literature, by meditating on the Common Irrational Ideas and their antidotes, discussed later.

DON'T:

1. Drink alcohol with the alcoholic person.
2. Make alcohol purchases for the alcoholic person.
3. Argue with a drunk person, ever.
4. Ride with a drunk person, ever. Just say no.

5. Permit a drunk person to supervise children. Make other arrangements or do it yourself.
6. Value the opinions of a person who is frequently drunk.
7. Depend on a habitual drunk for anything, especially for love, no matter how you are related to that person.
8. Make excuses to others or "cover" for drunken behavior.
9. Expect that the alcoholic person will get better because of you.
10. Believe that you have anything directly or indirectly to do with the problem drinking or any of the preposterous drunken behavior. Even if you *told* the person to drink you would not be responsible for what she or he does.
11. Feel guilty when you decide to leave or end the relationship.
12. Diminish yourself by withdrawing from others, or by labeling yourself as "codependent," or by viewing yourself as sick because of your loved one's problems.

Are you codependent or SOdependent?

Let's use a hypothetical example that has become typical in recent years. In the example below, the expression "you" is used to give you a sense of being there. If you find yourself "there," you may have some options that are not usually considered.

Suppose that your husband, Sam, is a daily drinker who spends lots of money on drinks and is not being an ideal husband. He paid out $1,500 on a drunk driving fine recently and just started a new job that doesn't require a clean driving record. He is angry about his traffic court problem, and, if anything, he is drinking more than before he was stopped. He comes home from work late and usually drunk, so if you say anything about his behavior it is not only useless but also the start of another family conflict.

If Sam is like many others in his shoes, he was a drinker when you married him, and there was no particular time when he crossed over from good-time drinker to problem drinker. You remember how happy you used to be with Sam, but things are different now. Last year, after he was fired from another job (he claimed he quit because the boss was crazy), you persuaded him to attend a recovery group. You were hopeful that he would stop drinking and you had plans for the future that made sense. He started attending AA meetings, but wouldn't discuss what the meetings were like. Finally, he came home drunk late in the evening and said he hadn't been going to meetings for several weeks. Instead, he had been sitting at a bar talking with old friends and drinking lightly while the meetings went on. He explained that he was sure, now that he had attended AA, that he wasn't like other drunks, that maybe he did have a drinking problem but he would take care of it himself. You didn't believe that he would, because he had said similar things in the past, but you decided to "wait and see."

Sure enough, his drinking worsened, and now, a year later, the marital fights are more frequent, he is more remote from you and the children, and he is always drinking. You are depressed and angry at him for not taking proper care of his family responsibilities. You feel helpless to do anything and wonder if you are part of the reason he is drinking instead of enjoying family life. On TV, you see a talk show about women who are married to alcoholics. A woman who calls herself a "codependent" talks about how she was able to work through her "codependency issues" in a CODA group, and now her husband is in recovery along with her, but attending separate AA meetings. They are on the road to happiness, so you jot down an 800 number to find out about the "codependency" groups. You go to a meeting and find that the others there describe problems similar to yours, but you don't feel a part of the discussions. The group discussion is largely around admitting powerlessness and use of some Higher Power to solve practical problems.

One woman who senses you want to solve some pressing personal problems comes to you when the meeting is over and says, "I know you are having some tough times right now, but this program is for the long run. Get to know us and plan to keep coming back." You reply that you just want to find out if there is anything you can do to help Sam with his problem, and she says, "You will have to let go and let God. In this program, your life in none of your business. We learn to surrender control of others so that our Higher Power can take over for us, remove our character defects, and lead us to a better life. Most of us are married to addicts, but we are addicted ourselves and very sick with codependency. We help ourselves by helping others and leaving our own care to our Higher Powers."

Then you return home, uneasy and more confused than before. You think, "So, then, it *is* me. I am a codependent, and just as much a part of Sam's drinking as he is. They said at the meeting that the whole family is sick, that we are all codependent." You decide to talk this over with Sam, and you do."

When you level with Sam, he complains, "What? *You* went to a recovery meeting?" You explain more about the illness of codependence and the character defects that are ruining the family, and you ask what his AA meetings were like.

"The same crap you're telling me now," Sam answers. "Now you know why I won't go back to those asinine meetings. As far as I'm concerned, it's Sunday school." From the mouths of drunks comes occasional, albeit accidental, bits of wisdom.

I could continue this example with a happy ending, describing how you and Sam began to understand each other, laughed about the silliness of 12-step recovery in your lives, and how Sam decided nevertheless to abstain from alcohol. But it usually doesn't happen that way. Sam's Beast may have taken the advice given at meetings, "Take what you like and leave the rest." He may have, as millions do, taken the powerlessness of Step 1 and left the rest of the program, then remained addicted until a new level of illness developed. If that is the kind of situation you find yourself in, living with an unrepentant drunk and quite fearful of the future, then Rational Recovery may provide some direction that is based on sound mental health principles.

Another word game

In reality, you cannot "be" a "codependent." First of all, the word was made up within the last decade or so. Secondly, there is already a better word for the problem that affects spouses and family of addicts: *dependence*. Better yet is the expression *emotional* dependence. In the next example, you can read what a real woman has to say about codependency, based on her personal experience. Her name is Lois Trimpey, and she is my wife. We made it through the years of my alcohol dependence and through recovery, and we chose to remain together. At the time of this writing, she was an English teacher in a California high school. Today she is the associate director of Rational Recovery Systems.

"SOdependent No More"

Some people who coin new English words do so in jest, or as a form of literary license. They *always* show what they are doing, and they are usually creative, sometimes entertaining, and they operate within accepted norms of discourse. Others make up new words because there seems to be no useful word in the dictionary to express what they "really mean." Often these "neologists" (my word for those who make up words) have observed something unfamiliar but have not yet been able to correctly classify what they have seen. And sometimes people use jargon to mislead, as with middle managers who use stilted language ("negative profits," "neutral impact," etc.) to disguise reality. Only a very few of those who invent new expressions, such as scientists who discover a new element or an unclassified organism, are actually introducing new knowledge to others.

I do not know why the word "codependence" and its variants have been added to our language in the last decade, especially since the term, "dependence," is such a fine and descriptive one. Nevertheless, "codependence" is with us and it will remain so until it falls into disrepute and disuse. I, for one, hope that is soon, because large numbers of people are coming to think that they are afflicted with an illness or disease because they are well-acquainted or intimate with someone who is chemically dependent.

I understand the problem faced by friends and family of alcoholics and other substance abusers, having once been in the situation myself. At the time, I spoke to lay and professional people about the problem of having an alcohol dependent spouse. I have subsequently found the concept of codependency offensive and a violation of common sense.

I was told that because my husband was alcohol dependent ("an alcoholic") I was therefore "a codependent," and I would have to get help with my illness, called "codependency." Otherwise I would only contribute further to the problem. "Further?" I wondered. I was told that just as alcoholism is an illness, codependency also is. Group members also explained that it is a progressive disease that is beyond one's immediate control. It is a pattern of self-defeating and enabling behavior that occurs without thinking and is therefore habitual and obsessive, and I was told I could see a list of symptoms of codependency that would dispel any doubt that I was suffering a serious illness. Of a list of several hundred symptoms (what disease has so many symptoms?), I "hit" on a dozen or so in a very personal way. These I still recall, and I refer to the exhaustive list of symptoms in the enormously popular book, "Codependent No More" by M. Beattie:

- feel harried and pressured
- blame someone else for being in my present situation
- wish something good would happen
- believe things won't get better
- feel extremely anxious about problems and people
- abandon the daily routine because of being upset about something
- worry that other people will leave them
- stay in relationships that don't work
- believe other people are never there for them
- lie to protect or cover up for people they love

Many more on the long list also applied, and it seemed to me for a while that I may indeed have been afflicted with "something" and would need some help myself to come to terms with a worsening domestic problem — my spouse's drinking problem. I did attend Al-Anon, and there I met others, nearly all women, who also had drinking or sobered-up spouses. I was most impressed with their wisdom about not trying to control others and taking care of myself in the face of home problems I really couldn't solve. "Whose problem is it, anyway?" helped me see that there is more to life than a happy marriage, and "He'll quit when he's good and ready, and maybe not then," helped me remember that my first responsibility was to take care of myself,

130

since I really had little to offer in the way of getting my husband, Jack, to stop drinking. When they got to the God part, "Let go and let God," I knew that it was time to leave, which I did without bidding farewell. It was clear to me by then that this was a dependency club that would have me keep coming back forever if possible. But after leaving I recalled an uneasy feeling, as if I had not given the 12 steps a fair chance and perhaps the people at the meeting were right, that I had some program of self-destruct in me and that I was contributing in some subtle way to the problems at home. I felt as if I had some vague defect that others in the recovery group could see but which eluded my own awareness. I had not had that feeling before going to those few Al-Anon meetings.

I never had to find out any more about my codependency because things began to happen. Jack did stop drinking for reasons of his own and many immediate problems started to resolve. In spite of the remarkable changes for the better with the removal of alcohol from the home, I still felt that something was amiss, as if something bad was bound to happen. I worried that I might displease my newly sober husband, and I took it very personally when he was rude or made critical remarks about me. It finally struck me that during the hard times I had been so *dependent* on someone else in order to feel well and to live my own life, and now that my wishes were fulfilled I still had many of the same, original insecurities. I was still *so* dependent on Jack for his love, approval, and, yes, even his sobriety. And worse yet, I began to think that this was all because I had some chronic illness called "codependency," just as they said in the recovery group. That idea led to feelings of powerlessness, of being unable to cope without some outside support, of being vulnerable to something I didn't understand but was called "codependence."

As time passed, though, I learned more about chemical dependency and about myself. I learned that adults do not really need to be loved, and that my insecurities were caused by my emotional dependence on the acceptance and approval of my husband. Looking back, I think I would still do most of the things I did back then to help stave off disaster. My struggles were aimed at preserving the home for myself and my family. Here is an account of how I now think about my so-called symptoms of codependency:

• **feel harried and pressured** (You bet! Ever try living with a drunk?)

• **blame someone else for being in my present situation** (Well, it certainly isn't yours truly who was drinking up good money and getting wasted at the worst times!)

• **wish something good would happen** (Well?)

- **believe things won't get better** (After seven years of progressive alcohol dependence, why *should* they?)
- **feel extremely anxious about problems and people** (Yes, a lot is at stake when hubby drinks too much.)
- **abandon the daily routine because of being upset about something** (Marital conflict is not only unavoidable, but sometimes useful, and always draining.)
- **worry that other people will leave them** (Losses have always bothered me, and I hope they always do. One must *have* something to fear losing it.)
- **stay in relationships that don't work** (So? It finally *did* work!)
- **believe other people are never there for them** (It's lonely being married to a drunk, and there's really nothing others can do anyhow. Fortunately, I can be my own friend.)
- **lie to protect or cover up for people they love** (Why not? Seriously. It really helped *immensely* to lie intelligently. Didn't Anne Frank's keepers do it? Compulsive honesty is a vice in itself.)

My decisions to hide an ugly situation from others, to "cover" the problem, to feel very sad and depressed, to feel alone, to argue and fight with Jack, and even to deny to myself how bad things were — all of these things were reasonable ways to act in the face of what was happening then. I do wish that someone had pointed out to me, "Oh, Lois, you are *SOdependent* on Jack for your happiness. Maybe you'd better take care of yourself first, before worrying about everyone else's problems, so that in the event he ever gets better you'll be around and in shape to enjoy it."

More on Sodependence, by the spouse in question

I've been hesitant to speculate on why the "co-" was added to the word "dependence," noting only that the word has clearly been defaced with the addition of a benign prefix. I have also called this development "transpersonal graffiti," since the prefix obscures a word that strikes horror in the heart of any 12-stepper or New-ager: *independence*. (Transpersonalism is any system of thought, especially psychological thought, that asserts the existence of higher levels of material organization than the human being, and dimensions of existence beyond the individual organism or beyond normal consciousness that are to be sought as a way of solving life's problems or giving meaning to one's life.) Only recently, I reviewed once again the book, "Codependent No More" by Melody Beattie, and this time I was struck by another word distortion that had escaped my attention. In her long, matronly discussions on how "we" do this and that because of "our codependency," there is some suggestion of rational thought concerning self-worth and assertiveness. Never, of course, does the idea of emotional independence from the loving or rejecting opinions of others come to the surface, nor does she point out any way in which one may resist condemning oneself, blaming others, or feeling low and rejected. Some of the discourse is fairly rational, but she finally leads up to a discussion of what it is that eventually would replace "codependence" if one diligently practices the 12 step catechism. Would it be *independence* that the faithful would achieve as a result of their regular meeting attendance and moral inventories and turning their lives over to a Higher Power and then practicing these steps in all that they do? Well, almost. It is what she calls *un*dependence. I hadn't really noticed this on my initial reading last year.

What is this? Now it's *two* words that have been mutilated by newspeak gurus. And they are both among the most vital words in the English language. They are the words, incidentally, that drove our Founders into the great experiment that became America. "The Declaration of Undependence?" Or how about, "Give me undependence or give me death."

The codependency movement appears more and more to be a large group of emotionally dependent people seeking others to become the same way. *Caveat emptor,* i.e., "let the buyer beware," would normally be sufficient warning to those who seek transpersonal solutions to life's most difficult problems, but the matter is compounded by the service professions, all of which have made regrettable compromises to this movement of "Newdependence." It is a religious movement to be sure, yet it has taken on the forms of scientific discourse to lend intellectual respectability to its transpersonal agenda. As a recovery program it is dishonest because it calls people sick when they aren't, because it affirms dependence instead of independence, and because it meets a "need" of its own making.

Emotional dependence is a root cause of human disturbance caused by the ideas that (1) Adults absolutely *must* be loved, respected, and approved of in order to feel worthwhile, and (2) adults *need* someone or something greater than themselves upon which to rely in order to face the uncertainties of life. But we may often *choose* to be dependent on others *in practical ways* as a matter of convenience. For example, if I buy pork chops at the market, then I am dependent on the grocer for that item. I may choose to be independent of the grocer by raising hogs myself, but even then I am still dependent on farmers for the grain to feed the pig. If I am really serious about being independent in my quest for pork, then I might decide to shoot wild pigs, but still, I am dependent on the gunsmith for the gun I use in the hunt. As a last resort, I may tackle the wild hog and slay it barehanded, but is it really worth all the trouble to be independent? In this case, no, but as a general concept in rational living, *independence is preferable whenever possible and convenient.*

Independence in one's emotional life is far more important to enjoying life than practical independence. If our emotions depend on the opinions and whims of others, then we cannot act effectively in our own interests for fear of rejection and disapproval. If we are unwilling to risk failure, we will be unable to take the risks involved in achieving personal goals. Instead of being *so* dependent, it is preferable to become *less* dependent.

Let us learn what the codependency movement teaches us about the interactions between the sick and the well. But, as a matter of self-interest and personal growth, let us begin reading the word *codependence* as "sodependence," with the goal of being *so* (emotionally) dependent no more.

The family option: to be one or not to be one

"Family" is a word that has attained almost magical significance in our language, and perhaps in other languages as well. It is partly because we are so truly dependent as infants and children that we cherish idealized notions of family. Two of these are:

(1) The notion that families are intrinsically good, even sacred; that they must be made to survive and endure; and that it is invariably a bad or tragic thing when a family breaks apart or dissolves.

(2) The notion that our personal identities spring from family membership and family experiences, and that the events that occur in early family life are powerful determiners of our later adult selves.

These are two powerful sentiments that quite often go unchallenged in healthy families and seem therefore to have the stamp of truth. So unchallenged are our values on "family" that politicians strive for the "pro-family" image and many products use the word "family" on their labels and in their ads and promotions.

In reality, however, the worth of any given family rests on its merits, on its ability to nurture and sustain its members. To illustrate with a hypothetical example, suppose that the Pica family has a mother figure who has undergone a religious conversion, and her new deity requires extreme fasting for each member of her family. She now refuses to cook and angrily forbids eating except for bread and water on alternate days. She interprets the objections of the father and children as evil and refuses to accept any kind of help. Is this a healthy family? Not at all, either physically or mentally. Are its members, even the mother, benefiting from family membership? Hardly. Is this family normal? Of course not. Mrs. Pica is mentally ill, suffering an inner disturbance and spreading it to others, resulting in a disturbed family system.

The best solution would be for Mrs. Pica to get some help and return to normal, but that clearly might not happen. The next best solution? Obviously, dear old Mom has got to go, one way or the other; if Father's not in a position to raise young children, the family dissolves. Can the orphaned children be happy? Yes, most certainly, unless they are expected to be unhappy! As long as the children are under the supervision of at least one adequate (rational) adult, regardless of kinship, it will be difficult to *prevent* them from being reasonably happy and from growing into robust adulthood. Can Father be happy? Again, yes! That is, unless he expects to be unhappy, perhaps feeling guilty that he failed to keep the family together, or upsetting himself by thinking *how awful* it is that his children are without a "normal" family, or inventing other problems about which to stew. Can Mother be happy? Alas, no; she is sick and may very well die, and that is sad.

While alcoholism isn't a mental illness, the net result is often about the same. Emotional disturbance spreads through the family; financial security is destroyed, and there may be episodes of mayhem that are bizarre, frightening, and physically dangerous. As with our Pica family, the alcoholic family has only a few alternatives. The best solution is for the alcoholic member to get help and return to normal family responsibilities. The next best is for the family to break up, pushing the addict out of the picture as much as possible. Can the fractured family be happy without the alcoholic member?

You bet they can! In order to *avoid* being happy, members of alcoholic families, broken or not, would have to dwell constantly on past events, reliving them over and over; they would have to think that having lived in an alcoholic household "scars one forever," causing specific disturbances and problems in adulthood. They would have to believe that children always need two sober, natural parents to mature healthily, and that they themselves may have been responsible for the alcoholic member's drinking and should have been able to deter him or her from self-destruction. These values and others like them are common to our culture, but in actuality they are overly generalized falsehoods, as irrational as they can be.

Unfortunately, there is considerable popular support for these contentions, especially in the mushrooming "codependency" movement.

Suppose my "special alcoholic" stops drinking? What then?

Give your congratulations, appreciation, thanks, and best wishes for him or her. Then, get ready for a new set of problems.

Many people who go through the AA program become preoccupied with spiritual ideas and their personalities seem to change.

In their quest for God, recovering alcoholics sometimes ignore their loved ones, spend much of their time attending AA meetings or going to AA activities. Alcoholics who take the 12-step program seriously sometimes have a personality change that is bewildering to relatives and friends, with preoccupation with God, spiritualism, and preaching religious ideas to others. In time the recovering person often settles down, so that a predictable relationship is possible. You may find, though, that the one you care about is not as you imagined he or she would be without alcohol. Considerable irritability, aloofness, or "uptightness" may surface, and he or she may convey to you that there's something wrong with *you*, now that things are getting back to normal. The implication is that now it's *your* turn to get your act together.

Don't be surprised if the tables are turned this way, and, above all, don't become defensive or try to "argue to completion" with your former drunk. For about six months or longer after the drinking stops, his or her perceptions will not be especially sharp, and a lot of "old resentments" will come to the surface. Instead, take serious note of what is said about your behavior; write some of it down so that you can think it over later when alone. After all, he or she isn't drunk any more, and might even have some very good points to make about you. *You* aren't exactly a saint, are you?

Emotional Roller Coaster

You can help yourself immensely by coming to terms with some of your old feelings about life and about yourself. Of greatest importance to you is to get off the emotional roller coaster which could be called "The Saint's Descent." In our culture, we like to think that our intrinsic worth is somehow to be proven, that by adhering to certain standards of conduct and striving toward and attaining certain goals we can demonstrate to ourselves that we really are decent, worthwhile, "good" human beings. Conversely, it follows that if you do not succeed in your efforts, or if you fail entirely, you lose some of your "goodness" and become less worthwhile. Naturally, if you fail in some important way, your sense of personal worth can plummet; in that case you may not like yourself, and may even come to hate yourself.

For example, if you're taking a class and get a lower grade than you wished, you might feel like a failure and have an uncomfortable inner sensation of inferiority or worthlessness. Later, when you come home, your dog might bark happily at seeing you, and you'd feel a little better, reassured by the thought, "At least I'm worthwhile to someone." Then your spouse might enter the room and berate you for wasting money on classes when funds are short, and you take another fall. Feeling like a real turkey, you snap at your spouse and blame him or her for making you feel bad and interfering with your study habits in the first place. Then the phone rings and it's your neighbor calling to say that they all missed you so much at the party they threw last week while you were studying, and won't you please come tonight and bring that fantastic salad that's your specialty? Feeling real good at this point, you notice the overdue phone bill (threatening shutoff) lying on the counter, and suddenly you remember that the envelope containing the payment check is in the glove compartment because you forgot about it last week. So, now you feel like an idiot again, and so it goes. The point is that your sense of personal worth is *highly conditional,* and can vary widely during the course of a single day and also over longer periods. You may feel good about yourself on Monday through Thursday, but when "things go bad" on Friday, you might sink into a depression that will last throughout the whole next week. In an alcoholic household (which yours still is even though everyone has been sober for a while) you might feel depressed most of the time; you wonder what's wrong with you that you continue to feel bad even when the drinking has finally stopped. Sometimes the roller coaster gets stuck at a low point.

You have the option to (1) stay on the roller coaster, waiting for it to start up again, ever upward toward the high point when everything goes right and everyone admires you for everything you do, or (2) simply get off of the wild ride right now and walk on solid ground. This is where Rational Recovery can help the friends and family of the alcoholic, too.

The Doctrine of Variable Human Worth

The real culprit in the roller coaster ride, the idea that seems to make it impossible to get off and just enjoy life for what it is, is what we will call The Doctrine of Variable Human Worth. This is the pernicious idea that *in order to be a good, decent person, one must rate himself according to certain rules.* In this system of thought, the human ego is like a common stock, rising and falling according to outside events and the whims of fortune. This concept, which is vigorously promoted and widely accepted in American society, is at the root of most human disturbance. It is the direct cause of guilt, depression, anger, shyness, underachievement, procrastination, continuing addiction, and a wide range of self-defeating behavior. The Doctrine of Variable Human Worth makes one dependent on external conditions, especially the approval of respectable people and deities. It is as American as apple pie, and it is profoundly false and irrational. Another way of picturing the doctrine is to think of a vertical scale, as follows:

137

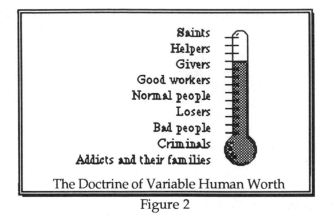

Saints
Helpers
Givers
Good workers
Normal people
Losers
Bad people
Criminals
Addicts and their families

The Doctrine of Variable Human Worth

Figure 2

If there were such a thing as pure evil (there probably isn't), this kind of thinking would certainly be a top contender for the title. Although few people would admit to having such a bigoted and jaded view of life, practically everyone thinks this way. In fact, it is unlikely that one can grow up in our society without getting moderately unhinged from this sick idea.

Let's examine the variable human worth idea a little closer, and find out just why it is so wrong, in spite of its tremendous popularity.

In the movie *Sophie's Choice,* a mother was forced by her sadistic Nazi captors to choose which of her two children should live; if she did not, both would die. In doing so, she discovered the great difficulties determining human worth. To rate one child worth saving implied the lesser worth to the other; this doctrine of variable human worth was a central belief of the Third Reich. The situation for poor Sophie was untenable.

It is true that in reality, people are assigned varying degrees of worth in any society because it is economically inescapable. In business corporations pay scales exist to differentiate the occupational worth of their members, and criminal codes define penalties according to some measure of one's worthlessness to society. These external measures of individual worth, however, are not the same as one's intrinsic worth, *or the value one places on himself or herself.* We are naturally gullible and inclined to accept the judgments made of us by others, so that when we are rejected, chastised, scolded, or criticized, we tend to conclude that, for the moment at least, we are somehow worth less than we otherwise might be, and that by making amends, or feeling guilty, or compensating by doing well in some other area we can regain our self-worth, self-respect, self-esteem, or whatever other term is used to describe the pervasive sense of personal well-being, or personal worth.

One may even feel somehow diminished or inferior in the presence of someone who is wealthy, highly competent, widely admired or famous, employed in an esteemed occupation, or a possessor of other signs of social rank. Shyness is in large part the fear of rejection by others, especially when they are perceived as being of higher status. Most important, guilt itself is a manifestation of low self-esteem.

The families of alcoholic persons are subject to massive doses of condemnation — first from the addict, then from themselves, and again from those in society whom they imagine would blame them for the turmoil in the home. Addicted persons invariably project anger and condemnation onto family members, blaming them for life's difficulties and for the results of addiction. It is vital that the alcoholic's family members, including the children, be able to defend themselves against the addict's accusations and condemnations. It is most helpful to understand clearly that the *approval* of a drunk or junkie is just as irrelevant as his or her rejections and condemnations. An habitually intoxicated person is *incompetent* in human relations, and it is a grave error to *depend* upon one for anything, especially love.

In the addict's eyes, you are less important than the addictive substance. Separating emotionally from an addict is considerably easier if you will simply recognize that *you do not absolutely need to be loved by anyone*, much less an habitually intoxicated person. This task may seem difficult at first, but the alternative — emotional dependence on an alcoholic — is far more difficult. Entrusting your personal well-being to an alcoholic is like accepting an automobile ride from a blind person. By struggling with the ideas listed below, and perhaps reading further into rational literature available from the Institute for Rational-Emotive Therapy, 45 E. 65th St., New York NY 10021, you may be able to grow out of your emotional dependence on others.

Common Irrational Ideas That Cause and Perpetuate Emotional Dependence in Alcoholic-type Homes

1. The idea that it is a dire necessity for an adult to be loved, approved of, or respected by others — instead of concentrating on one's own self-respect, on winning approval for practical purposes, and on loving others rather than being loved.

2. The idea that certain acts are awful and wicked, and people who perform such acts should be moralistically condemned and severely punished instead of the idea that some acts are inappropriate or antisocial, and people who perform such acts are behaving drunkenly, stupidly, ignorantly, or antisocially and would be better helped to change.

3. **The idea that it is horrible when things are not the way one would like them to be** instead of the idea that it is too bad, or unfortunate, that such hardships exist, and one would better try to change or control conditions so that they become more satisfactory. When that is not possible, the options are to accept the situation or leave it.

4. **The idea that human misery is externally caused and is somehow forced on one by other people and outside events** instead of the idea that human disturbance is caused by the view one takes of conditions and events.

5. **The idea that if something is dangerous or fearsome, one should be terribly upset about it** instead of the idea that one would do better to face it frankly and render it non-dangerous. When that isn't possible, one can accept the inevitable.

6. **The idea that it is easier to avoid than to face life's difficulties and self-responsibilities** instead of the idea that the so-called easy way is invariably much harder in the long run.

7. **The idea that one needs something other or stronger or greater than oneself upon which to rely** instead of the idea that it is far better to take the risks of thinking and acting independently.

8. **The idea that, in order to be a worthwhile human being, one must be thoroughly competent, intelligent, talented, and achieving** instead of the idea that doing is more important than doing well, and accepting oneself as a quite imperfect creature with human limitations and fallibilities is entirely possible.

9. **The idea that the past is an all-powerful determiner of my present behavior and should continue to be so indefinitely** instead of the idea that the past is non-existent and we have enormous control in the present over our self-defeating and self-destructive emotions if we choose to change the bigoted and unscientific hypotheses we use to create them. We presently feel the way we presently think, even though we may have learned to think irrationally during the distant past.

10 **The idea that human happiness can be achieved through inertia and inaction** instead of the idea that humans tend to be happiest when vitally absorbed in creative pursuits and devoted to people or projects outside of themselves.

11. **The idea that there is a perfect solution to life's problems, and we should endeavor, through obsessive searching, to find it** instead of the idea that life is full of frustration, probability, and chance, and despite this we can be reasonably happy, most of the time. Uncertainty is the spice of life, and I will do better to view life as an exciting self-experiment.

12. **The idea that because I am closely associated with an alcohol dependent person, I am therefore afflicted with codependency and had better submit to a spiritual healing program** instead of the idea that it's tough living with a drunk and I had better set about solving the many practical and long-range problems connected with that problem.

Finding a self-help group

By reading and rereading the ideas above, you may immediately notice their interconnections. This insight is the rational consciousness that helps one to function independently from someone who is incompetent in human relationships because of chemical dependence.

However, it is good to view the above core beliefs against the backdrop of cultural values in American society. So-called "codependents" are believers in social propaganda that not only affects them personally, as described in sections above, but also determines how our health care system attempts to help them. In most communities, there are numerous self-help and support groups for a wide assortment of personal problems. By self-help, we mean a task-oriented group of people who gather around a common problem with the purpose of overcoming that problem, and then leave the group when the problem is solved. Support groups are more social and focus on fellowship and a sense of belonging for people facing difficult circumstances. Support groups are a valuable social resource for people with specialized problems, because they are based on the tradition of people helping people. One serious drawback of support groups, however, is that they sometimes tend to foster dependency and quite often stray from the higher purposes of personal growth and self-reliance. Although special groups exist for people with stressful health problems (cancer, stroke, colostomy, blindness, etc.), other support groups exist for people who have suffered great losses or who have unusual personal problems (shortness, bereavement and grief, sons of bosses, spouses of prisoners, etc.). These valuable groups, which allow for sharing and learning strategies for coping, provide the comfort of recognition to people who are not regarded as sick or deficient but who feel alone in their personal struggles against adversity. They are generally spontaneous meetings of people with a common problem. There is usually someone who facilitates or leads in discussion, and the group develops its own norms and techniques for problem-solving. People confide their problems, share their sorrows, reach out to others, come and go as they please, and the general tone is, "Accentuate the positive."

Dependency groups

Unfortunately, self-help is a misnomer for what is offered in most communities to those who are closely associated with addicts or alcoholics. Some support groups, including the 12-step spiritual healing groups, go much further with the idea of support, in that they actively teach people that they *need* the support of the group in order to cope with the common identified problem. Over time, certain philosophies and practices of the group have been formulated into an incontestable creed; newcomers are obliged to "come to believe" as the support group does, even if it takes many years to "work the whole program" as set forth by their charismatic leader, Bill W., in his spiritual manifesto, *Alcoholics Anonymous,* reverently referred to by the membership as "The Big Book." Members become confident that their common beliefs comprise the "one true way" to deal with the presenting problem, if not for the enjoyment of life itself. Collectively, members of these groups enjoy a sense of having tapped into a ruling ideology and believe that all human beings might do well to become dependent on 12-step groups. These groups would better be called *dependency groups,* because the avenue to the desired goal always involves emotional dependence upon the group and upon its articles of faith. Newcomers who present specific life problems, i.e., "codependency," gambling, drinking, lusting, overeating, or overspending, are often quite surprised and disappointed to find that there is much, much more to getting better than learning better ways of thinking, acting and feeling. Invariably, the dependency group presumes to know what is best for the newcomer, even to the point of suggesting that the newcomer might regard the dependency group as "God." Many who come to these dependency groups are desperate for anything that will help, and so they accept the invitation to turn their entire lives over to the group in exchange for symptom relief. For them, relief is at hand, for now there is an entirely new preoccupation in life to supplant the original problem. Within the nurturing confines of the dependency group, life is much safer and more predictable. Submission, members report, "works."

Submission, for the rest of us, doesn't work because we are simply unable to submit. We are convinced that we can "see through" the concepts that make the dependency groups so popular. Try as we might, we cannot force ourselves to accept their articles of faith. For us, there is another system that is more consistent with the *nature* of our problem, the problem of being SOdependent on someone who is dependent on drugs or alcohol. If dependency is the central issue in SOdependence, then rational self-help, with its emphasis on personal independence, is very likely the most relevant solution.

etiquette \ 'et-i-ket \ n. (F. *etiquette,* lit, <u>a ticket:</u>) the forms
required by good breeding or prescribed by authority to be
observed in social or official life. **Syn** decorum.

—*Webster's Seventh New Collegiate Dictionary*

Chapter 10

Etiquette for Former Drunks and Junkies

As noted elsewhere in *The Small Book,* it is widely held that in
order to get better, alcoholics must somehow become better people, as if
to make up for past alcoholic sins, and to surrender oneself to notions of
morality based on selflessness, altruism, duty, godism, apology,
honesty, and humility. They are also expected to adopt a lifestyle
centered around programmed activities related to the pursuit of those
virtues. For some, these are good ideals to strive for, and the lifestyle is a
fine one about which to structure one's sobriety — provided, of course,
that one is sincerely interested in that kind of lifestyle and naturally
inclined to solve personal problems in such a manner. As one interested
in RR, your viewpoint is probably quite different from the traditional
one, and in some cases, just the opposite. It is because of your natural
preference for rational thinking that you became interested in RR in
the first place. You are to be commended — not discredited — for your
skepticism, critical judgement, and intellectual caution. These are the
strengths upon which your rational recovery is based.

Much of what the 12-step program regards as worrisome points
along the long, complex road to recovery, RR views as simple etiquette.
At this juncture, *The Small Book* will provide some common-sense
advice on the common issues faced by those enjoying newfound
sobriety. You are encouraged to use your own judgment when
dealing with sensitive issues and problems during recovery, and to
create original solutions to awkward situations concerning alcohol use
and your regrettable past. The rational viewpoints of *The Small Book*
provide a sound basis for doing so, without undue risk of failure and
with a cushion of self-forgiveness.

The most immediate issue of etiquette facing you, a newly-sober
person, has to do with your social identity, i.e., what you represent to

your family, friends (if any), potential friends, co-workers, bosses and potential bosses, and the community at large. What are you, what have you been up to for the last several years, and whose business is it? What will people think? Who really cares?

You will know that your rational insights are sinking in when you realize that these questions, and others like them, don't really matter when compared to the importance of staying sober. As one who has literally beat the odds against one of the harshest killers by refusing further use of alcohol, you are a seasoned soul who has probably seen more of life's hardships than most non-alcoholic persons. You may not have *felt* those hardships at the time, but looking back you can already see that the storm is passing, and you have survived, most likely in one piece. You have probably survived car crashes, jail, social fiascoes, beatings, sleeping while exposed to the elements, wrenching hangovers, falls, medical complications, wretched depressions, repeated humiliations, physical mutilations, social isolation, divorce(s), lawsuits and firings, and you may even have been shot. You've survived and you're sober; should you worry now what people will *think* of you? Should you be concerned about the *opinions of others?* If you are, then you are demonstrating the immense capacity of human beings to think crookedly, to persist in self-defeating nonsense just as the tide is turning in your favor, and to snatch defeat from the jaws of victory.

You can help yourself greatly by frequently reminding yourself that you do not really need to be loved, liked, accepted, admired, or approved of by other people or by the deities they describe. Moreover, you may find that very few people even care whether you are drunk or sober, or even if you are alive. These are *your* personal concerns, ones for which you are ultimately responsible. The first year of sobriety is a time for meeting the basic needs for food and shelter, regrouping, staying sober, and setting a new course in life. All else is etiquette. Because you care for yourself, and want more friends than enemies, more fun than boredom, more success than failure, you will favor good manners over bad. Because you are sober, good manners will come naturally, because *they are your ticket to the things you want in life.*

Let's consider the case of Steve, who found NHP sobriety preferable to spiritual healing because of its fundamental honesty and concern for the self. A year earlier Steve had alienated his next door neighbor by hurling ethnic insults as the neighbor and his family sat on the front porch. The next day, overcome with guilt, he drank to drown his pain. As time passed, he rationalized that they probably knew he was drunk and had forgiven him and he made no attempts to make amends. The matter rested until, after several months of NHP sobriety, he noticed that the neighbors were avoiding him like the plague. New waves of guilt flooded poor Steve; he recalled that the 12-

step program requires that one "...make amends to those we have harmed except when to do so would injure them or others." He had the urge to knock on their door and confess that he was drunk when he called them "dagos" last year. He wanted to ask their forgiveness, tell them that he has nothing against Italians, admit that he wouldn't blame them for blaming him, etc., etc. But he also imagined that the door would be slammed in his face and he'd be back to square one — guilty and probably angry on top of it all.

Steve was helped to see that, while the course of action he was considering was commendable, he'd be doing it for the wrong reasons. Of all the motivators of behavior, guilt is the least effective, the least productive, and one of the least rational. Even if he were to be forgiven by his neighbors, he would likely continue feeling guilty about his deplorable behavior because guilt is a philosophy, not a product of bad behavior. Accordingly, he would continue to have guilt as a symptom in other areas of his life, over other misdeeds, other transgressions, and other failings. Guilt knows no end.

When Steve had gained rational insight on guilt and realized that he could forgive himself for all of his alcoholic sins (as well as mistakes he would surely make in his sober life) and thus eradicate guilt from his adult life, he took a very different view of the incident with his Italian neighbors. The solution became obvious. "Why should I do *anything* about the neighbor?" he very rationally asked himself. "Is it to help me feel better about myself? Or is it to make this a better neighborhood for *me* to live in?" Having asked the right question, he got the right answer. The next day he did go to the neighbor, not so much to apologize for his stupid behavior and beg their forgiveness but to *explain* to them that, yes, he had been sick for a while because of alcohol, and to *reassure* them that now that he had quit drinking, he would be a trustworthy neighbor. He was asking nothing of the neighbor; he was simply *informing* them of something relevant to the life of the neighborhood. The reader is left to suppose what he may about the outcome of this episode. It would be nice if the parties became warm friends, but if they maintained a cool distance in the years to come, that's all right, too. Steve did his part both as perpetrator and diplomat. It was a simple matter of etiquette.

But, what about when the offended party is one's spouse or the children? The rational position here is to accept that some bad feelings in the family concerning your substance abuse may remain forever. In time you may offset much of this by showing that you are a trustworthy person, by staying sober and strong during hard times, by providing financial security, by putting money to its proper use, and by functioning as an effective parent, lover, and mate. On the other hand, your spouse may be disturbed by this reversal of an old pattern

145

(or disturbed for reasons unrelated to you) and undermine your efforts to reclaim your position in the family. Very often years of alcoholic disturbance in the family end with recovery from alcoholism only to be followed by new conflict and divorce. Some families stay together with the underlying hope that when so-and-so stops drinking, he or she will become a hero, a saint who will solve all of the family problems so that finally, everyone can be happy. In other marriages, the non-alcoholic spouse concludes, "I always thought Harry/Susan was a bastard/bitch because of booze/drugs. Now I can see he/she is just a *natural* bastard/bitch." Sobriety, NHP or otherwise, is not a cure-all for marital conflict but it sure helps.

In Rational Recovery, you will keep your options open, because you may not be *totally* committed to your marriage. Harsh as this sounds, it is true. Your greatest responsibility is to yourself, so you will not likely stay married if the quality of the marriage does not warrant staying in it. If this seems unromantic or callous, it would be a good idea to examine the marriage vows you originally took to see if you both still agree with the content. In doing this, you may discover that neither of you remember the vows or that you have different expectations of each other. Find out if there are limits to the commitment you each have for each other. Your mate may not agree to accept another drinking episode without at least a separation, or he or she may be so highly dependent on you that parting ways is unthinkable. You may feel quite uncomfortable with that degree of dependency, and some marital conflict may stem from inappropriate dependencies. Keep in mind that "love" means "like a lot" and that marriage is best between friends. If little good seems to come from your efforts to improve your marriage relationship, it may be time to exercise some options, as follows:

1. Cut and run. If you have had enough of your spouse, and there seems little possibility of change, there is no moral or legal imperative to remain married. Cut your losses and go elsewhere — sadly, perhaps, but guiltlessly. Sometimes sober alcoholics allow themselves to be taken advantage of in divorce court believing that because of their past alcoholic "sins" they deserve to be punished with a settlement that is grossly unfair. These cases illustrate why some say the phrase "pathological guilt" is redundant.

2. See a marriage counselor who understands RET. Plan on seeing several therapists if the first is not agreeable to both of you. Shopping for the right therapist is usually a matter of trial and error.

3. Separate, especially if you are having great conflict during your first two years of sobriety. Live away and visit on weekends. If you cannot move out, spend more time away from home. You and your spouse both need to learn that you are separate people who can function well without each other.

4. **Work it out.** This may mean marital fighting of the verbal kind. The best book on marital conflict this author has read is *The Intimate Enemy: Fighting Fair in Love and Marriage,* by G.S. Bach. It's about the etiquette of marital conflict. Any bookstore can get it. Here are some rational tips on working out the post-alcoholic marital blues.

Q: Should I apologize to my spouse for my alcoholism?

A: Of course, silly! To those who have not examined RR deeply enough it may seem that it would produce cold, unfeeling robots, devoid of human emotion. On the contrary, when you're emancipated by the knowledge of self-worth, you can take the risks of loving, caring for others, and, yes, apologizing to your spouse for past suffering related to your alcoholism. Even though you were very ill, you are still responsible for what happened during your drinking years, and apologies are certainly in order. If you tramp on someone's foot, isn't it good etiquette to say, "I'm very sorry"? For the alcoholic chaos you created, you are even sorrier, and it's imperative to tell your whole family of your sorrow and sadness over the fact that so much happiness was ruined because of your illness and your drunken, arrogant behavior. The key here is to let your family know that *you* know that they suffered because of your alcoholism, and that you understand the resentments they feel. Although you *hope* they'll forgive you and accept the past as past, it is unrealistic to *expect* to be forgiven. The resentment they continue to feel is usually a natural consequence of your past drunken behavior, and your job in this case is to *accept* that there are no perfect solutions to life's problems.

Q: Should I let it be known that I am an alcoholic?

A: Remember that no one is an alcoholic until he or she attends an AA meeting and starts calling him or herself one. There is no diagnosis called "alcoholism," so you may properly check "no" on any questionnaire asking, "Do you have a history of alcoholism?" It is self-defeating to stigmatize yourself with the term, "alcoholic," unless you are trying to impress someone with your humility. When you believe it would be in your personal interests, you may choose to disclose information about your past problems. Your medical history is a private matter that you can share with others as you wish.

In general, your problems are no one's business but yours. When you apply for a job, do not volunteer information about your previous addiction, unless specifically asked. Even then it may be in your interests to deny an alcohol problem unless it seems likely that it will come to the surface in due time. Your responsibility is get yourself on the payroll and stay there. Once employed, you may choose to mention casually that you quit drinking years ago because it was getting the better of you back then. It is practically impossible for anyone to prove that you are an alcoholic, and your medical and mental health records are normally very well protected. Not so with police records, but they only reflect convictions, not diagnoses. An employer who has come to know you personally is usually more accepting of a history of alcoholism than he would be when reviewing application forms.

This particular etiquette advice may disturb some moral perfectionists, particularly those who believe that alcoholics, as part of their interminable recoveries, are obliged to be perfectly honest. A rational person is likely to place a higher value on employment than on scrupulous honesty. On the other hand, with your closest relationships, deception would be most unwise, as well as unfair to someone who trusts you and whom you trust.

As a social matter, many consider it in poor taste to burden new or superficial acquaintances with personal matters such as your menstrual cycle, your lower back problems, the time you went bankrupt or went to prison, or your history of habitual drunkenness. You may already know someone who presents alcoholism as the central feature of his or her personality and the subject of most conversations. This suggests that the person assumes others would be interested in endless stories of "rehab insights" and alcoholic intrigue. It also presents an eccentric image to others, and your preoccupation with your own alcohol dependence will eventually tire people you would like to get to know better.

In your personal relationships, however, it is wise to disclose to your friends and significant others that you never drink because you cannot tolerate alcohol. You will benefit from doing this because you're setting up an inhibition against impulsive drinking by letting others know that you are a teetotaler. You would do well not to view these informed others as an external restraint, however, because you, not they, are responsible for your behavior. Some recovering alcoholics veer toward a subtle kind of dependency by telling others about their alcoholism, somehow expecting someone to intervene if the temptation to drink were to arise.

In deciding on what etiquette is best with self-disclosure, much depends on what you think you are. Are you something different now because you were once addicted? The current popular wisdom has it that, "I am intrinsically different from others because of my past addiction. Once an addict always an addict. Unless I continuously strain against my alcoholic nature, I will gravitate toward my alcoholic ways. I'm never really recovered from alcoholism, only *in the process* of recovering. I'm a psychological cripple, and mentally I'm in a wheelchair. I'm like a time bomb, waiting to be set off by slight deviations from the straight and narrow path of daily discipline." The picture is one of struggling, tortured souls who have, by the grace of

God, barely survived a personal holocaust, and are only a drink away from the threshold of death's door. Such drama, such suspense!

Granted, great apprehension is appropriate during the first months of recovery, because a struggle is taking place between the rational and irrational voices within one's cerebral cortex. But is it still a struggle after six months or a year? Is daily discipline still required after four or five years of NHP sobriety? While many former drunks choose to approach the sober life in this manner, it is hardly necessary for the rest of us to dwell on a past appetite disorder.

Why, if one was once addicted to a substance, should he still be regarded years later as an addict? Is it because to resume its use would lead to re-addiction? If something is addictive, then *anyone* who uses it will become addicted, or re-addicted. By that token, shouldn't we call *everyone* an addict? If one is not using an addictive substance, how can he be addicted? Why call him an addict, or an alcoholic? Is it because the formerly addicted are more likely to use in the future and need constant reminders against temptation? Surely there are better means to handle that situation than to promote an illusion that is so at odds with common sense.

If you insist on labeling yourself an addict when you are not presently addicted to a substance, you are conveying to yourself and others that you have some underlying functional disorder, some psychological or character defect, or some spiritual or metaphysical deficiency that heightens the risk of re-addiction and requires some corresponding treatment or care. Remember, ninety percent of the substance abusing Viet Nam veterans simply stopped using intoxicants upon returning home. It would be highly inaccurate to call those men who stopped using heroin addicts. If one stopped smoking years ago, are they still smokers? Not exactly.

Because there is practically no difference between previously addicted and potentially addicted human beings (other than the efficiency of re-addiction of the former), the treatment or care for the supposed underlying disease or disorder would have to be so broad and so ill-defined as to apply to *everyone*. This, interestingly, is precisely what has happened in the various spiritual recovery movements, especially in the "New Age" visions of addiction as a mere symptom of the universal diseases referred to as "codependency" and "the addictive process." The reasoning behind this kind of "steptalk" is obscure and related to the spiritual teachings of AA.

You can help yourself and also establish a basis for etiquette by sticking to the common definition of the word, "addiction," meaning *chemical dependency,* not compulsiveness. In this way, you can honestly say to anyone "I was once hooked, dependent on alcohol, but

I am *recovered* from that problem because I no longer drink. I don't drink anything now because alcohol would have a bad effect on me."

How to have fun at a drinking party

Recovering and recovered alcoholic people can have a ball at social functions where there is considerable drinking. The most obvious way is to stick with sober friends and be yourself, engage in cocktail talk without the cocktails, and nibble on the *hors d'oeuvres.* But you might also wish to observe the drinking behavior for your amusement. You can play "spot the alcoholic" with a sober friend, and lay early odds on whose social skills will deteriorate most rapidly. You may notice that those who go from the front door as they arrive straight to the bar or to the booze supply are also the front-runners later on. When they become loud and garrulous, watch the spouse to see of he or she reacts protectively, apologetically, controllingly, or with detachment. Playing "spot the alcoholic" is not only fun, but also provides inspiration for remaining sober as a stone for the rest of your life.

Further notes on etiquette

On rare occasions a host or acquaintance will persist in offering alcoholic refreshment after you have said no. If you feel that the person is being obtuse or manipulative, it's fair to say, "Please don't ask me to have a drink. I just said no and I mean it." If you are irked, you might indulge your annoyance by posing the question, "I'd like to know just *why* you want me to have a drink. Would you care to tell me?" Sometimes an aware friend or host will become protective and do such things as apologize for serving drinks to others, or even move liquor containers away from you, as if to prevent strange, unimaginable cravings from taking over. It's as if she expected your unconscious mind to seize your arm and make it grab at the alcohol. Be patient with these well-meaning friends. They too have been subjected to popular illusions and mythology about alcoholism. Simply explain, at an appropriate time, that as a recovered alcoholic you're really indifferent to the presence of alcohol and have no difficulty resisting it. You may even explain, if it is yet the case with you, that because of the time that has elapsed since drinking you actually prefer non-alcoholic drinks.

NHP Sobriety: Passage Without Rites

We have mentioned your social presence with regard to your history of alcohol dependence. As time passes, you will find it to be less and less important and therefore less relevant in your social dealings. Remember that recovery from alcoholism is only a phase of your life, about a year or so, when you are regrouping for your final assault on making life really fun. It's no fun to dwell on past sorrows, nor is it fun to hear someone else recount past miseries.

Does each anniversary of sobriety signify something more than the simple passage of time? In recovery clubs, members sometimes celebrate "birthdays," complete with refreshments and festivities, as rites of passage when the dates of members' original abstinences occur. Because of the focus on length of sobriety, the length of one's sobriety becomes part of one's identity, so that a hierarchy based on a number develops, i.e., "There's Joe, twenty years sober, and Mary over there, three years last month." In the thinking of many alcoholics, anniversaries are milestones that mark accomplishment, justify feelings of self-esteem, and become a basis for asserting new confidence in continued sobriety.

Fine for them, but there are difficulties in anniversary observance that are usually overlooked. Anniversary celebrations *discount* those who have less time since the last use of intoxicants. In one case, an RRS coordinator was denied access to a meeting room in a public building because the 12-stepping administrator believed that having "only" six months of sobriety was insufficient. Here, we see systematic discrimination based on the 12-step assumption that someone with less than a year of sobriety is only a "babe," and more likely to act irresponsibly or antisocially than someone who was never addicted. One might wonder what consequences might occur even if the meeting room applicant *did* relapse. Would he break all the windows? Write graffiti on the chalkboard? Or does it seem that newly sober people are ridden with character defects that make them poor risks? In this case, the backing of a local therapist and another RRS Coordinator with no history of substance abuse did not mitigate the suspicions of the administrator.

But there are several more general problems associated with focusing on length of sobriety. First, does being sober justify feelings of self-esteem? To a drinking alcoholic, it certainly may, especially if he is damning himself for his self-defeating behavior. "If I can just get sober for a while," he may think, "then I can get a little self-respect back into my life." He may attend a recovery club and actually meet people who have been sober for twenty years and are still focusing on that fact, and he may think, "Gee, that's a long time without a drink. I wonder if I can ever go that long?" Within the organization, the twenty-year-abstainer attains a kind of status, and his accomplishment is regarded with considerable admiration. "Gee," our newcomer might think, "that would sure feel good to have that kind of admiration, and if I did sober up and everybody could see how long I've been sober, I sure would feel good about myself. Even my Higher Power might be impressed, and that would be comforting." The difficulty here, of course, is that our newcomer is engaged in self-rating and other-rating, giving out

151

good and bad report cards based on performance — in this case, length of sobriety. To himself, he is giving very low grades in Human Worth and feeling rotten, and to the twenty-year-abstainer he is awarding very high grades, and admiring him, just as everyone else in the group is. Sober people, then, are admired, while relapsed people are less so, if at all. And sadly, sober people tend to take pride in their sobriety, while relapsed people tend to feel guilty about having erred.

Since habitual relapse is part of the definition of alcohol dependence, it would seem that one had better get off the roller coaster of self-worth early on. In Rational Recovery, an abstinence training program, members are helped to surrender ideas of varying self-worth in favor of unconditional self-acceptance. When applied, the result is usually a "leveling effect" in which others in one's social environment come to appear of equal status, regardless of performance, achievement, behavior, or length of sobriety. Consequently, relapsers in RR lose no sense of self-worth or status within the group when the principles of RET (rational-emotive therapy) are applied. Our newcomer may very well relapse after only a meeting or two, and feel very guilty — even hopeless — about ever getting better if he continues to believe that sobriety is a requirement for self-acceptance. But if he comes to understand that drunkenness has no bearing on his intrinsic (arbitrarily self-declared) worth, then, instead of guilt and despair, he will suffer only *regrets* over having relapsed. His willingness to continue in active recovery, therefore, will be enhanced.

A second difficulty in focusing on sobriety instead of effective living has to do with veteran abstainers who relapse. If our twenty-year-abstainer should resume drinking, what is one to think? For those who admired him for having abstained for so long, such as our newcomer, it would come as a blow. He, as well as other veteran abstainers, may think to themselves, "When can I *ever* have confidence that I won't relapse? Ever? Does that mean that recovery is a constant struggle to remain sober, and that I will continually have to guard against relapse every day for the rest of my life? Does that mean I must stay aboard this crowded lifeboat endlessly, pitching on the waves of temptation and working a catechism of submission that I don't really understand? Maybe this isn't for me after all. Maybe they're right, that we are all powerless over our addictions and that only a Higher Power can take over my controls and steer me from harm. If that's so, then maybe there isn't much hope for me, and maybe drinking is a reasonable alternative to all this. Twenty years is a long time without a drink, and he waited that long for what I can have right now — a drink!" Thus the widely hyped irrational idea that alcoholics are powerless over their addictions is reinforced in very convincing — and misleading — terms by focusing on length of sobriety.

A third difficulty with celebrating sobriety is that such occasions imply that not drinking is a terribly difficult task — like climbing the highest mountain. Those who have been NHP sober for a while know that abstaining is really quite easy, sometimes even from the start. The benefits of not drinking become evident in just a short time, months or even weeks, and as time passes, drinking comes to appear increasingly s-t-u-p-i-d. This is not to say that there are not many times of great temptation, when the Beast manipulates powerfully for another dose of alcohol. There are difficult moments at first, and one gains skill and mastery as time passes. But it is erroneous to believe that not doing something for a long time is terribly difficult, and it is also self-fulfilling to believe it is so. (Within the AA context, it is consistent to believe that abstaining is extremely hard, actually impossible, because at the 12-stepper's disposal is the greatest force in the universe, "God."

A fourth difficulty in focusing on sobriety when we have not drunk for a while is that it implies there is still something that distinguishes the formerly-addicted from the never-addicted. For example, if we see a football player on the field, he is assumed to be a "normal" person, living life in a self-determined way, pursuing fun and goals with gusto, dealing with problems as they come, etc. However, if we learn that he is "sober," he appears categorically different somehow from the next player whose appearance and behavior is essentially the same. When he passes to a receiver, after six years of "sobriety," we cannot help wonder what it feels like to be "sober" for that long. We may also wonder how much longer he will remain sober, or even to wonder if he's really been sober that long or just saying that. You see, the concepts of "sobriety" and "being sober" define people in a way that is not really substantial, and it adds a dimension that isn't really there in the first place. Would we say that someone who has never had any alcohol has been "sober all his life?" Was the President of the United States "sober" today? Are infants "sober?" Hardly. What does it mean to say, "My sobriety is the most important thing I have?" Is sobriety a goal in itself? In the rational context, sobriety is not an end in itself, but simply a *means* to the enjoyment of life. "Sober," then, is little more than another word for "normal," whatever that is for each of us. We generally do much better at living life when we are absorbed in life's enjoyments, struggles, and dramas, so to dwell on sobriety as a daily mantra is not only unnecessary when recovery is complete but also a self-involvement of dubious value. While there is no reason to eliminate the term "sober" from our vocabularies or even limit its use, this discussion simply addresses the implications of that word for the purpose of self-understanding.

A fifth difficulty with sobriety anniversary celebrations is that they have a bizarre quality when thought about objectively. These occasions for admiration seem to diminish the personal integrity of the celebrity in a not-too-subtle way. From an objective viewpoint, celebrants are conveying that the celebrity is acting out of character by not committing stupid and antisocial acts. To exaggerate for the sake of illustration, it's like having a party for someone because he hasn't killed anyone for three entire years or praising someone for refraining from armed robbery or wife abuse for a whole decade. Do we really admire people for behaving in common ways? If we do, aren't we really saying that we think that, underneath it all, they're crazy?

Your *Bar Misfit*

For alcoholics or others to express congratulations that one is not currently drinking toxic alcohol does little service and perpetuates several common irrational ideas that perpetuate the alcoholic relapse cycle. The goal of RR is to help "alcoholics" to get their alcoholism behind them, and to close that sorry chapter of their lives for good. We seek our own self-defined goals in a highly future-oriented way, so to regularly stare at the past, counting intervals of selfish non-drinking behavior, doesn't make sense. Instead of focusing on length of sobriety, members are encouraged to measure only the length of time in recovery. It is possible for one to continue too long in Rational Recovery, and that would not only be a waste of precious time (we only have one life), but it would also foster a kind of dependency on others that is inimical to rational living. From the experience of others, it is known that rational recovery is usually an intense struggle at first, and then there is a period for consolidating gains. After a lifetime of harboring the irrational philosophy of alcoholism, it takes a while to get a new, rational perspective on the problems of daily living. To spend a year in RR would be prudent, but there will be many who choose to resume normal, independent living earlier than that. Whenever one chooses to leave, whether it is after six months, nine months, or a year, it would seem fitting to observe a member's departure with an *encouraging* farewell.

Because the likelihood of one's ever being able to drink successfully is so slim as to be *assumed* virtually impossible, we may certainly view ourselves as being out of place in drinking establishments. Therefore, with no offense intended to the Jewish religion, the meeting of an RR member's passage from recovery group involvement to rational NHP sobriety can henceforth be called his or her *Bar Misfit!*

154

"We admitted that we were powerless over our clients' and patients' addictions, and we came to believe that only a Power greater than ourselves could restore them to sanity."

Chapter 11

To The Professionals: Take Sides!

The above "quotation" is a fitting epitaph for the twentieth century American health care system. Our descendants, who will be more fully informed about the nature of recovery from chemical dependency, may be perplexed at our present, unswerving commitment to spiritual healing in addiction care. Our ancestors believed that lightning rods interfered with divine will, and they warned of divine retribution for those who would protect their homes with the demonic devices. Progress is not entirely an illusion.

It is interesting that in the old days, before the elevation of science, the mentally ill were treated as reprobates, social misfits, and criminals, usually demon-possessed or spiritually unfulfilled. The social institutions that dealt with mentally disordered persons, including alcoholics, were the courts, jails, churches, and almshouses (locally- and church-financed board and care homes). About one hundred years ago, the idea of treating mental and behavioral disorders as illnesses gained acceptance over the prevailing mythology that human maladies were a sign of separation from God. The resulting *mental hygiene movement* spread worldwide as a mission of mercy to those who until then had been treated cruelly. This child of scientific thought held sway until the middle of this century, when it had brought America's state hospital network to its zenith. During that period scientific research led to great strides toward understanding the nature of mental illness and toward devising treatments to effect cures and alleviate suffering. Humane lifelong care for the mentally ill was seen as a human right, and the streets, jails and roadsides were nearly empty of mentally afflicted persons in need of supervision and care.

As we know, the 1960s were turbulent years, and one of the silent victims of the new conservatism that emerged in the 1970s was the burgeoning mental hygiene movement, along with its optimism for our most vulnerable people, the mentally ill. Today our streets, downtown hotels, prisons, and care homes are crowded with "deinstitutionalized" refugees from the state hospitals, most of which now stand empty. These unfortunates receive brief, superficial, revolving-door "care" at county-run clinics far too small to meet the real needs of the truly desperate. Neither the professions nor society claims further responsibility for these people — the "really tough cases" whose illnesses are chronic and whose real need is for asylum from the harshness of a world that even the robust find fraught with difficulty. "Privatization" has become the vulgar means by which unneeded health care is hawked at exorbitant cost to those who don't need it, while the poor and desperate are turned away from vital care. The treatment of alcohol dependence is either free during the early phases, or exorbitant when the individual has progressed to a point of desperation when the 12-step program must, according to an obscure logic, be administered to the patient in a hospital ward.

Increasingly, volunteerism is replacing professionalism, and it seems that each month another vice or diagnosis joins the word "Anonymous," while the jails and church basements fill with detoxers and other repentants who have come to seek a Higher Power to ease the pain of their desperation. In only twenty years we have veered back into the nineteenth century, and we may soon hear talk of demons and gods during clinical case conferences. Indeed, an erudite article in *The Gerontologist* (Feb., 1988) applies the arcane forms of scientific measurement and discourse to measure the benefits of religion to the elderly during times of diminishing health care budgets. In a recent *Newsweek* "My Turn" column, the writer cautions, "At the present moment, this religion is sweeping Hollywood. There are more than 2,000 AA meetings per week in Los Angeles, many jammed with people in the entertainment business. These are the people who write the scripts, direct the movies....What the 'creative talent' have on their minds is what they put into their work. If AA has put God on their minds, then it's fairly clear that God will soon appear on big and little screens." A 1990 article in the Palm Springs *Desert Sun* titled, "Counselors, Clerics Not Threatened by Religion of the Future," gushes praise on 12-stepism, while warning churches to get into the act, too. In that article, the 12-step rage is described by Marion Jacobs, director of the Califonia Self-Help Center at UCLA as being the result of (1) mental health cutbacks under Reagonomics, (2) concerted media promotion of 12-stepism. The re-Christianization of American mental health services appears well under way.

Twelfth-Steppers

A Constitutional crisis is brewing: our publicly-funded addiction care services are completely dominated by the secret society of spiritualists, Alcoholics Anonymous. Our addiction care agencies, clinics, and hospitals are staffed almost entirely by "recovering" addicts who themselves once sought relief from desperation in AA and made the 12-step spiritual healing program the basis for building a new life. These professional 12th steppers are exceedingly loyal to the program and feel part of an important social movement that will better the world. Twelfth-Steppers are never *recovered* from alcoholism, only *recovering,* so their survival seems to hinge daily on continuously "working the program" and recruiting others into it. Twelfth-Steppers love the program, revere its ideas, and they see in it deep, unfathomable wisdom. In effect, they worship the program, and consequently have a higher commitment to it than to the individuals who come seeking help. If ever there was a group of less objective practitioners, it would probably be found deep in the bowels of the Vatican.

Unproven assumptions, central beliefs

In the background of the 12-step creed is a general philosophy, actually a doctrine, based on Judeo-Christian theology and mixed with some useful information on addiction. In Chapter 1 you will find a list of some unproven assumptions that have been derived from the 12-step program, and in Chapter 5 you will find the specific central beliefs of the philosophy herein called alcoholism. As noted in Chapter 8, all of the assumptions and central beliefs of alcoholism reflect the philosophical underpinnings of American society, the so-called "traditional values that made this country great." Billions are poured annually into 12-step programs at all levels of care, and cost-effectiveness is only a peripheral issue in the ongoing administration of public funds. Our so-called war on drugs is more of a moral crusade, and the real losers are drunks and addicts everywhere. Change within the health care system will be exceedingly difficult because of the obvious vested interests in the present plan.

One of the ironic aspects of addiction care is that our monolithic treatment model has no accountability loop. Organizationally, AA is just like a church, in that its members share a common faith in unprovable doctrine and seek to obtain converts to the fold. Because the prime element in addiction care is belief in a mystical entity, any morbidity can be attributed to God's will, or to the supplicant's failure to have sufficient faith. None of us mere mortals, therefore, is accountable for AA's alarmingly low recovery rate: only about ten percent of newcomers remain abstinent after four years.

Research on treatment methods is further inhibited by a built-in blinder that prevents collection of vital data. Only a small fraction of those afflicted ever come to the attention of treatment facilities that actually collect scientific data on the nature of the problem and the strengths and weaknesses of various treatment approaches. These individuals are usually well advanced in their illness, and do not represent a cross section of the alcoholic population. A much better cross section appears every day at the thousands of AA meeting places across the land, but every effort is made *not* to obtain data on those individuals owing to AA's preoccupation with anonymity. (What other illness requires more than confidentiality?) Little is known, therefore, about the early coping efforts of alcoholic people, except as told retrospectively by those who later surface at treatment centers. The greatest block of missing information in the field of chemical dependency does not concern etiology, but the question of what happens to the ninety percent who try and quit AA. Do they all get sick and die, as AA predicts? Could they have been helped in other ways? Why did they quit? If some get better, how did they do it? The irony here is that the organization to which we have entrusted our millions of alcoholics and other substance abusers avoids the accountability we would expect from any other publicly-supported institution. Significantly, AA accomplishes this secrecy in the same way that other religions do, by claiming to be on a moral high ground, and by flouting mystical and altruistic concepts when it encounters serious inquiry. Consequently, the assumptions and questions listed above are largely untested and unanswered, and the most respectable journals in the field of addictionology are peppered with such comments as "there is little data available...." and, "the research is incomplete here...." and "not much is empirically known about...."

How we sold out

It would seem that we professionals have been dealt out of the chemical dependency scene; it is as if a groundswell of indigenous helpers has staked out the turf of addiction care and their old-time religion has proven so superior to professional methods that to practice as a professional one must be a personal convert to AA spiritualism. But we are not victims in this way. We have *sold out* on addicts because they are "hard to treat." When AA came upon the scene in the 1930s, not long after prohibition failed, America was still yearning for a "fix" on the original problem of alcohol dependence, then called alcoholism. We were a younger nation then, more innocent, more homogeneous, and more ignorant of human physiology, psychology, and behavior. It was love at first sight: AA fit the American ideal of hope for the afflicted while at the same time it immensely pleased the professions (most of all medicine and clergy, who were equally glad to surrender our reprobates to the Lord). After all, what does a doctor have to offer someone who insists on drinking himself into oblivion, and what clergy would not be thrilled at the idea of an army of Christian altruists witnessing for the Lord and providing the media with a steady stream of spiritually awakened former drunks? By the 1950s, AA had become a frequent feature in *Reader's Digest*, and AA was enshrined as a most revered social institution, reflecting traditional Judeo-Christian values —"the good, the true, and the beautiful,"— and redemption through faith. America had completed Steps 1 and 2. She was powerless, and only God could help. And God help anyone who said it wasn't so.

During the late 1970s the AA auxiliary group, Al-Anon, got a powerful boost when the term "codependency" began circulating. The term originally referred to the unique difficulties that families of alcoholics have, but within a few years, there was an explosion of public interest in the idea that codependency is quite common, associated with many "addictive" disorders, and in fact practically universal, so that there is not all that much difference between families with and without drunken members. To the untrained eye, this would suggest that "codependency" is a bogus concept, that "codependents" are simply normal people under stress from dealing with preposterous drunken behavior of a loved one. But with God all things are possible, and CD (chemical dependency) "theorists," drawing on every ounce of intuition (but no research), concluded that codependency is a *universal disease* which is triggered, or aggravated, by living with drunks, gamblers, shoplifters, lusters, overeaters, masturbators, or anyone else engaging in "addictive" behavior. (Note that we are also speaking of vices, matters of taste, bad habits, and compulsions in addition to chemical dependency.) This previously undetected "disease" is thought to be progressive, and responsible for a vast spectrum of "symptoms." We list only a few of the several hundred "symptoms of codependency":

1. Feel controlled by events and people.
2. Ignore personal problems.
3. Think they know best how people should behave.
4. Try to prove they're good enough to be loved.
5. Worry that others will leave them.
6. Get frustrated and angry.
7. Think other people make them feel angry.
8. Feel terribly anxious about problems and people.

As you can see, these "symptoms" are merely the stuff of life. We are all biologically inclined to be this way, to think crookedly and act self-defeatingly. The long lists of "symptoms" are actually lists of human characteristics. Some disease! And some cure is in store for those who submit to the codependency movement: Steps 1 through 12— for the rest of your life.

How do CD theorists view "professionals?" (Authors of codependency books often refer to members of the mental health establishment as "the professionals," seeming not to consider themselves such.) We professionals are codependents, of course. We have no idea that we are seriously ill and unless we are "treated" (by AA) for our codependency *we will continue transmitting the disease to our unsuspecting clients.*

Some professions, particularly social work and nursing, have made regrettable concessions to the pseudoscientific codependency movement. By publishing an article by Hall and Wray, "Codependency: Nurses Who Give Too Much," *The American Journal of Nursing* (November, 1989) seems to endorse a theory of psychopathology and personality development that, while certainly popular during the 1980's, is based on pseudoscientific thought and leads to outcomes that are less than ideal. The nursing profession gained its present high level of credibility by close adherence to scientific methodology. It is doubtful that the involvement of nursing organizations with codependency, which is too transparent to too many people, will benefit the profession in the long run. The following discussion of that article, excerpted from JRR, Vol. 2, Issue 3, shows how the nursing profession is becoming entangled with 12-stepism and the article can point to similar trends in the rest of the professions. The section on rational peer consultation is included here as a counterpoint to the proliferation of codependence support and therapy groups within the professions.

Nurses who are SOdependent

In "...Nurses Who Give Too Much", the authors correctly describe an occupational hazard of the nursing profession — that of the "messianic helper syndrome," i.e., when nurses become personally and emotionally involved in their professional duties, even to the point of self-defeat, burnout, and self-sacrifice. Indeed, it is well-known that very often those entering the helping professions are attracted by the obvious opportunities for messianic helping. But Hall and Wray leap to an unwarranted conclusion in the title of the article's second paragraph, "Codependent Behavior".

The first sentence reads, "A nurse who gives more of herself (or himself) than is essential for effective care of her patients (and of herself) is showing classical characteristics of codependency." This is an unprovable statement that is also palpably false because there many reasons why a nurse might choose to go beyond minimum requirements for the well-being of her patients and her own well-being. Overtime pay is one, and new graduates often anxiously overextend themselves as a continuation of graduate school self-motivation. Some nurses who have a narrower range of interests or view nursing as an expression of religious values simply enjoy the "trade" and will devote extraordinary amounts of time and effort to the service of others — even to the detriment of their own health and general fitness, and quite often without expecting extra monetary compensation. While these are not examples of ideals, does it add to our understanding or benefit them by calling them "sick" or "codependent?" Let us see.

Hall and Wray then give "symptoms" of codependency, which seems to be jargon that has attained currency. The pejorative term for one who attempts to meet the needs of others to the point of neglecting her own is "caretaker." Another label. Then this:

> ...As such, she (the caretaker) feels responsible for all aspects of another's life — even those that lie beyond her professional consideration. She's attracted to people who need her and she feels most secure when giving to them, but feels guilty when others attempt to give to her. She also feels sad because she gives so much yet receives so little in return.

The paragraphs that follow present other "classic symptoms of codependency" such as *perfectionism* (...her need to keep every aspect of her life under control, even when life is unhappy or unmanageable), *denial* (...refusing to acknowledge anything painful in her life, she ignores or represses all problems or difficulties), and *poor communication* (...she talks freely about others while holding back information about herself). Remember that this kind of discourse is intended to demonstrate the presence of a disease, "codependency," and not part of an astrological reading. *Anyone* reading these "symptoms" could easily conclude that he or she suffers from "codependency."

Hall and Wray assert that "The (caretaker's) needs for love, attention, and security have long gone unmet...," as if there are such needs in mature people, and an ensuing discussion attributes "perfectionism" to "...her need to keep every aspect of her life under control, even when her life is unhappy." Then they continue with,

"The *result* (emphasis added) of all that perfectionism, criticism, and abnegation is low self-esteem." For some readers this kind of pseudoscientific discourse may have the disarming ring of plausibility, but others will see that the authors have confused the symptom for the cause. Of course, perfectionism, with its self-blaming and abnegation, is a *symptom* of low self-esteem, not a cause. To make their medicine go down, Hall and Wray intubate the reader with the expression "denial," which is the assurance that if you do not agree with their point of view, you are wrong. Anything that contradicts the 12 step creed is "denial," as anyone who has sat in on a codependency meeting knows.

So, what do the authors propose that codependents do to become un-codependent? This vexing question is at the heart of this paper, and listed here is the answer provided by Hall and Wray: (1) Recognize the unhealthy behavior, and (2) determine to change it, (3) keep a journal of daily events, significant conversations, poetry, doodles, and drawing. Then, finally, the pitch, (4) ...recognize that she needs outside help...from a therapist or professional group experienced in working with *codependent personalities.* (emphasis added) Now we see that it is a psychiatric-sounding diagnosis, almost as if out of the DSM III-R. Then Hall and Wray specifically recommend any of the AA 12 step programs, and even suggest that the newcomer might want to start a group herself.

Using the more precise term, "irrational," to describe excessively indulgent nurses seems at first to be less kind than "codependent," but this article shows reasons why the nursing profession should weigh very carefully its acceptance of the latter term. Chief among these reasons is that the term "codependent" merely labels and offers no constructive direction on any given problem other than to join a 12 step dependency group. The effect of labeling oneself is to crystalize patterns of self-defeat into a powerful excuse to continue the same attitudes and behavior. It would be far better to strike the prefix, "co-", from codependence and recognize that all of the "symptoms" in question are of *emotional dependence,* (a normal stage of personality development in our culture). Most nurses who have troubles as described by Hall and Wray are really *so*-dependent — dependent on others for loving opinions, respect, acceptance, admiration, and approval, and dependent upon their own success, competence, and achievements to feel worthy of their next breath of O_2.

It is only fair to note here that Hall and Wray have an extraordinary sense of duty to vast numbers of yet-undiagnosed people who are not even aware that they have a problem. If there were a more "classic" example of the diagnostic non-entity than that demonstrated by codependency therapists themselves, it would be difficult to imagine.

The Rational Alternative:

What, then, might be better than the hybrid of Freudian psychology and old-time religion that has emerged as the new wave of codependency consciousness? Certainly there are traditions behind our professional identities that could provide guidance to those among us who prove to be only too human and become bogged down in the helping arena. Here are some dimensions of what we are professionally, as well as the philosophical roots that give us a claim to the public trust: *1. We are first of all scientific in our thinking and in our professional being. We accept knowledge that is objectively true, and we respect reason as the arbiter of professional decisions that affect our patients. It is our scientific credentials that stand behind our claim to the public trust. 2. We will sometimes place the welfare and safety of clients above our own during a tour of duty as a matter of professionalism. Unfortunately, that's part of the territory. At times this will mean a degree of risk or self-sacrifice, one determined by each individual nurse and as the situation warrants. 3. Our first responsibility remains to ourselves, so that we have the emotional, physical, and financial health to fulfill both our personal and professional roles.*

Working from these three axioms we can establish a close and friendly relationship between the nursing profession and yet another body of literature that addresses the central issues of personal and professional growth. In the rational-emotive therapy (RET) of Albert Ellis, Ph.D., we have an elegant alternative to the spiritual life as described in the 12-step program. Based firmly in the scientific tradition, it is both humanistic and secular; as such, it is well-suited as a frame of reference for professionals in the field who face complex and sometimes urgent decisions. For those of us who wish to continue our personal and professional growth but are not in the market for Higher Power therapy of AA, RET can provide the professions with simple, easily-understood tools. One such tool is Rational Peer Consultation, derived from RET and developed by Rational Recovery Systems (RRS), a national networking, consulting, and indirect services agency.

Rational Peer Consultation

In the place of the self-help recovery group, Rational Recovery Systems offers a plan for rational peer consultation (RPC) that emphasizes positive human attributes and maximizes personal and professional growth. Participation in RPC, always voluntary and by personal invitation, assumes all participants to be in good mental health (otherwise they would be in some form of disciplinary or probationary status), and capable of accepting critical opinions of their peers as rendered in the RPC style. RPC is a tool for conflict resolution as well as a way to identify and rapidly solve job-related performance problems.

Conditions for rational consultation with a peer.
Below are several common situations that occur almost daily in most hospitals, and which could be handled with a rational peer consultation.

> *You may notice that a co-worker is in a bad mood or has had a serious disappointment on the job, i.e., a patient died under her care unexpectedly, he may have had a poor performance evaluation and is feeling low, he may be going through a divorce, and so on. He is passive toward an unreasonable supervisor, she may have alcohol on her breath, he may have gotten angry at a demanding, recalcitrant client, she is overly involved with one particular family or patient, he always looks tired. Nothing is said when an unprofessional practice is endorsed by administration, a particular doctor is sexually aggressive toward nursing staff, several patients complain about one nurse's attitude.*

The RPC invitation:
Suppose that you observe the husband of a patient scolding a nurse named Jane because of the emergence of a new skin breakdown on his wife's buttocks. Jane becomes defensive to his accusations that she is neglectful and later she leaves the floor in tears. The Rational Consultant (you) may approach her in the staff lounge or at some other appropriate time and place (at lunch, at quitting time) and simply say, "Say, Jane, have you heard about RPC in the workplace? (If 'no', continue) Its a way for people to help each other on the job by talking about problems. It's based on a kind of logical, or rational, thinking that is used in some self-help groups that are becoming popular. I'd like to offer you a consultation when we can get a chance to get together — that is, if you're interested. I noticed how upset you were when the husband blamed you for his wife's decubitus. I have some ideas that might be really helpful to you in dealing with that kind of problem. Would you like to sit down with me (now?) for lunch tomorrow?" Here, the respondent will either accept or decline your offer. If the respondent accepts, give him or her a copy of the flyer, "RPC in the Workplace," to review before your consultation.
The RPC scenario:
Give the respondent the "RPC in the Workplace" sheet (below) and allow him or her to review it for a little while. On the back side is the "ABC's of RPC" sheet with the common irrational ideas that cause

problems at work. (Rational Consultation Spreadsheets may be ordered through Lotus Press.)

Rational Peer Consultation (RPC) in the Workplace: Common Irrational Ideas That Interfere with Professional Functioning

1. The idea that we have very little control over our emotions, which are externally caused and somehow forced on us by our past experiences, by other people, and by outside events instead of the rational idea that human emotions are caused by the *view* that one takes of conditions and events. In reality, our emotions and behavior are largely determined by our current thoughts, so we act the way we feel and *we feel the way we think.*

2. The idea that the past is an all-important determiner of our present behavior instead of the rational idea that the past no longer exists except as memory, and we may *change our minds* about the significance of earlier misfortunes or deprivations.

3. The idea that mature people, in order to feel worthwhile, need to be loved, respected, approved of, admired, or appreciated, instead of the rational idea that love and approval are usually *preferable* to rejection and they are *desirable* for practical reasons, but self-esteem is a matter separate from the opinions of others. Self-esteem cannot be earned or proven but is best declared as a matter of unconditional self-acceptance — as a birthright rather than as moral remuneration.

4. The idea that, in order to be a worthwhile human being, one must be thoroughly competent, intelligent, talented, and achieving instead of the idea that doing is more important than doing well, and one may fully accept oneself as a quite imperfect creature, with human limitations and fallibilities.

5. The idea that people who help other people are accordingly more worthwhile than those who do not help others instead of the rational idea that human helping is a convenient and natural activity for some people, while others have less aptitude or opportunity for helping; in either case, this need not be a measure of one's intrinsic worth.

6. Professional people are somehow responsible for the bad decisions and choices of their clientele, instead of the rational idea that the price of freedom is the freedom to fail, and the goal of professionals is simply to provide positive opportunities for their clientele. Patients who are noncompliant, clients who kill themselves, students who fail, people who commit crimes, alcoholics and addicts who drink or use, parents who abuse or neglect, and those who underachieve are exercising self-determination and may or may not learn from the consequences of their behavior; professionals are only a resource for clients to effect personal change.

7. The idea that in order to consider oneself a decent, caring, sensitive, compassionate, or loving person, one should become upset over other people's problems instead of the rational idea that professionalism is not a moral springboard, and a troubled person is in no way helped by someone who is also upset; to the contrary, a helper who is emotionally upset *reinforces* the pain the troubled person is experiencing.

8. The idea that professional people need or have reason to expect the appreciation and gratitude of those they help instead of the idea that we are paid in money instead of admiration. To expect clients to appreciate our services is to make us *dependent* on the client for our sense of well-being.

9. The idea that it is terrible, awful, or horrible when things are not the way one would like them to be instead of the idea that it is too bad, or unfortunate, that such hardships exist, and it would be better to try to change or control conditions so that they become more satisfactory. When that is not possible, the options are to accept the situation or leave it.

10. The idea that if a professional makes a mistake that adversely affects a client or patient, one should feel guilty and worth less as a human being instead of the rational idea that the practical consequences are sufficient penalties for error, and self-blame is superfluous and grandiose. To simply *regret* a damaging error and then take corrective and preventive action is more professional than to indulge in self-condemnation. To expect clients to invariably benefit from our services is to make us *dependent* on our clients for our sense of well-being.

11. Clients or patients should not behave poorly, antisocially, aggressively, or recalcitrantly, and they should be blamed for their actions and misdeeds instead of the rational idea that our clientele are usually under stress and we may *expect* their personal functioning to be far from ideal. To blame a client for poor behavior is to deny causality and makes us *dependent* on the client for our sense of well being.

12. The idea that professional people need the approval of their superiors for its own sake instead of the rational idea that in the world of work your superiors are not superior people but only vested with organizational authority. Approval of your superiors is simply a condition of continued employment, and a rating of your occupational worth (performance) is not a rating of your human worth.

The RPC need not last for more than a few minutes, and the purpose is to (1) identify an irrational idea on the RPC sheet that appears to affect the respondent's performance, (2) listen to the respondent's viewpoints on the incident, and (3) suggest that the corresponding rational idea may be a better concept to bring into play in the future.

For example, as consultant you might begin:

"This is an approach, Jane, that is being used in many professional settings as a way to improve staff morale and to help employees get more job satisfaction. Any professional person can be a rational consultant if the basic ideas are agreeable and make sense. One nice feature is that RPC doesn't *depend* on administration to solve problems; we do it ourselves, and when we take care of our own problems it's just better all around. RPC isn't an organization — it's just a lot of us who use this tool that was developed by Rational Recovery Systems. All that we in the RPC program do is link a work-related problem to one of the items in the sheet, and then try as best we can to understand the rational point of view. Then, if we have been helped, we offer the same information to others.

When that husband started scolding you and really running you down in front of everyone, I'm guessing that you started thinking, "Here, I've worked so hard with this patient, turning her frequently, charting diligently, and doing all the right things, and then I took a few days off for personal reasons. When I came back the skin problem was there and now everyone thinks I was responsible for the problem. This isn't fair, and I deserve some appreciation for the work I do. I tried hard, and now this!"

Jane: Yes, I *was* thinking something like that. I'm surprised you were aware of how much I had extended myself with Mrs. X. I tried to get a home-maker for Mr. X so he would have an easier time of it. While I was off, I even stopped by to feed their dog, so he could visit his daughter in San Francisco. Then, when he came in and saw that tiny decubitus and blew his stack like that I felt defeated, really cheated out of something.

Consultant: Like what?

Jane: Oh, we all want to do a good job, and I had visions of the X family at home after this long hospital stay, finally together and everything under control.

Consultant: I think that by spending some time really thinking about numbers 3 and 8 on the RPC sheet you can avoid this kind of hurt in the future. Would you say you were overextended in this case?

Jane: Now that we are talking about it, I would say yes. But it's an easy trap to fall into.

Consultant: You bet it is, if you believe those nutty ideas about proving that you are a good person because of helping others. Here, look at number three and see if it applies to you.

> 3. The idea that mature people, in order to feel worthwhile, need to be loved, respected, approved of, admired, or appreciated, instead of the rational idea that love and approval are usually preferable to rejection and they are desirable for practical reasons, but self-esteem is a matter separate from the opinions of others. Self-esteem cannot be earned or proven but is best declared as a matter of unconditional self-acceptance — as a birthright rather than as moral remuneration.

Jane: Boy, that really fits me to a tee. That goes back a long way in my past.
Consultant: Most everyone thinks that way from time to time; it's part of our culture. Being aware of it lets you do something about it.
Jane: Sounds like I need a shrink.
Consultant: I doubt that. These problems are so common, and anyone with your background can probably figure out how to put a stop to it. Several of the irrational ideas hang together; number 8 also seems to apply here:

> 8. The idea that professional people need, or have reason to expect, the appreciation and gratitude of those they help, instead of the idea that we are paid in money instead of admiration. To expect clients to appreciate our services is to make us *dependent* on the client for our sense of well-being.

Jane: You know, I feel better just thinking along these lines! This stuff really does make sense.
Consultant: See? You're already being your own therapist, and you don't have to start up any new dependencies to help yourself. That's how the RPC plan works. It's a do-it-yourself program.
Jane: I feel so much better because of you. I don't know how to thank you...
Consultant: Be careful you don't sell yourself short. All I have done is present some information to you. You have taken that information and used it on your own behalf to make yourself feel better. I do this because I get a kick out of it, and I have no special ability to make you feel better. If you think RPC is a good thing, then maybe you will want to pass it on, like I have to you.
Jane: You certainly do put a different spin on things. And I like it. I think I will get involved in RPC.

In summary, rational peer consultations have the following advantages over 12-step programs for professional people:

1. Participants are credited with having the strengths to quickly and independently resolve personal and performance problems.

2. Participation by management or administration in the solution of staff problems is unnecessary and avoidable.

3. The means of solving problems is consistent with the philosophical traditions of the profession.

A challenge

The 12-step movement has spread quickly to most communities, and in these days of the shrinking health care dollar, more and more mental health services are being replaced by spiritual healing. Codependency is the word that makes the 12-steps boundless, and if it qualifies as a diagnosis for third party payment, even more public funds will be diverted from their proper use.

What to do?

The key question is, "Is AA an adequate program for an entire general population?" If you think "yes," then you have already taken sides. The next step in addiction care is for there to be broad recognition that godism is useful only to *some* addicts, and that there are excellent alternatives for those who reject God-oriented spiritual healing. This is a formidable hurdle steeped in politics and prejudice. But the 1990s will call for professionals to *take sides* on this key question. Because you are a professional, I hope you will take sides on the key question above right now, if you haven't already. We are expecting clients to make major commitments on recovery, and it seems appropriate that we do the same.

From the beginning, RR has been the *counterpoint* to 12-stepism, disputing the venerable 12-steps almost point for point, and in essence redefining the nature of recovery from chemical dependence. More and more, Rational Recovery is attracting people who want out of 12-step programs and emancipating them from what they perceive as an anti-intellectual movement that represses honest inquiry and personal independence. These people, the "AA refuseniks" referred to in this book, are belatedly *taking sides* on some central issues that have always divided people throughout history. Rational Recovery is moving forward to make this choice of personal philosophy possible at the earliest time, so that the membership will increasingly consist of those who opted for the rational mode at the beginning of recovery.

The presence of Rational Recovery in any community has a direct bearing on each recovering person, regardless of which road to recovery is taken. The message to our addicted population is changing from, "Take the cure," to "Take sides." Thus, one of the most popular excuses for continued addiction, "I *tried* the cure and it's not for me," is preempted. RRS is changing the *character* of addiction care.

At a presentation of RR to a group of academics in southern California, a woman with many years of AA involvement commented (paraphrasing), "Rational Recovery was predicted fifteen years ago, when a group of key persons in AA met to discuss some organizational concerns. They said then that we were losing our focus on helping people to stop drinking and that too much importance was being placed on the program itself. They said that if we didn't get back to basics, some other group wold come along and do the job for us. Rational Recovery seems to fulfill that prediction."

Indeed, many in traditional programs have come to care more for the program than for the people seeking help, and I have found little evidence of self-initiated change within the 12-step movement. In fact, it appears to be becoming worse as time passes. RRS asserts that a substantial part of our national problem with substance abuse is our *fixation* on the teachings of the 12-step spiritual healing program of Alcoholics Anonymous *to the exclusion of other points of view*. Vince Fox, the Coordinator of RR-Indianapolis (who wrote a stunning article about chemical dependency in *Mensa Bulletin*) has pointed out that *communal AA* (the community-based self-help movement) has become entangled with public addiction care programs to such an extent that a new creature has emerged to capture all of America's addiction care resources — *institutional AA*. While the former is a truly American institution, institutional AA is not.

In the old days, before the "new menace" of alcohol and drug abuse, America had one mental health system. It is the one that we learned to trust as an extension of our scientifically-based (medical) health care system. Today, we have a second mental health system — institutional AA. Its roots are firmly in the church establishment and comes to us all dressed up in a doctor suit. It defines "sin" as "disease," and seeks ever more maladies for which its GAYUH (God-as-you-understand-Him) is the answer.

To expect sick people in publicly or third-party supported institutions to accept irrational beliefs as a condition of getting help with substance abuse is anti-therapeutic as well as un-American. We can do better; the article below, "A Reverse Bill of Rights" (reprinted from the July - August, 1990, issue of *The Journal of Rational Recovery*), encourages citizens to seek redress when they perceive that they have been discriminated against or had their civil rights violated in connection with addiction care. The Petition of Redress is aimed at *institutional* AA, wherever AA is the only program — "the one true way" — available to the consumer, or where clients are discriminated against because they disagree with the 12-step philosophy. It is odd that for once it is the seculars who are banging on the doors of public institutions, but here we are — holding, if you will notice, a winning hand.

A Reverse Bill of Rights for the Chemically Dependent

At the end of this section you will find a Petition of Redress that identifies several common ways in which the rights of chemically dependent persons are currently being abused. The eight items have been gleaned from the thousands of calls that RRS has received in recent months from people who have specific complaints about their treatment in chemical dependency programs. Although the common element in each item has to do with mandatory 12-step participation, the use of coercive tactics in recovery, or the lack of a viable alternative to spiritual healing, the Petition of Redress is not intended as an affront to Alcoholics Anonymous. Although it is quite likely that some people will choose to interpret the Petition of Redress as an attack on the integrity of AA, a careful reading will show that we are interested here only in social justice and planned, litigated change in the addiction care system. Some professional people may feel that the Petition of Redress is aiming at some of their own practices, ones that are common and widely accepted. If so, then they would do well to explore other avenues for their clientele who show clear resistance to the 12-step spiritual healing approach of Alcoholics Anonymous. Resistance to any form of therapy may be observed in the client's or patient's statements as well as in his or her failure to respond to a given form of therapy, i.e., recidivism. Rational Recovery is now in a position to offer an immediate alternative that is tailor made for AA refuseniks. The aim of RR is total abstinence from mind-altering substances and the controls to do so are found within each participant. RR projects may be started in existing addiction care agencies, clinics, hospitals, and also as freestanding projects in the community. Substance abuse councils, substance abuse advisory boards, civic groups, employment assistance programs and court-related agencies may provide leadership in initiating Rational Recovery programs. Through the direct involvement of local professionals and with the consultation and technical backup of Rational Recovery Systems, local projects may be implemented within a very short period of time in any community.

The following is a discussion of what may constitute a case.

I sought county mental health services for chemical dependency and was referred instead to a 12-step spiritual healing program of Alcoholics Anonymous. Many people reach out for help with personal problems expecting customary counseling approaches that are

171

associated with professional training. If they go to a community mental health center, however, they may be referred to a chemical dependency treatment program if it is found that they drink too much. In those chemical dependency programs, clients are usually introduced to the 12-step method, and sincere, 12-step-oriented therapists often interpret their objections to the spiritual teachings as "resistance to treatment." The problem, of course, may very well be that they are not candidates for spiritual healing in the first place and would do far better with a university-trained therapist at the mental health center that made the referral. When documented efforts to obtain conventional mental health services result in repeated referral back to a program that prompts one to seek God, it may be said that human services are being withheld from an eligible person, and he or she may rightfully sue the mental health center, the referring person, or the county of residence for redress.

While hospitalized for chemical dependency, my request for a scientifically-based, non-spiritual (rational) approach to my problem was denied to me by my physician. Many people return to expensive inpatient programs several times, only to be told that they are not "working the Program" correctly. In the field of medicine, it is agreed that when one therapy doesn't benefit the patient, it should be re-evaluated so that alternative forms of therapy may be instituted. Informed consent, including information on risk factors and alternative treatment approaches, is also a standard element in competent medical care. It is well-known that many people, probably a large majority, recover from chemical dependence outside of AA-oriented programs. With the advent of Rational Recovery, continuation of 12-step therapy beyond the wishes of the patient is unnecessary and anti-therapeutic. Patients in hospitals quite often express their wish for a rational alternative by stating clearly, "I don't understand anything about this program," or "I don't have a Higher Power and I don't want one," or "I can't get my Higher Power together," or "There must be something wrong with me that I keep relapsing over and over, even though I gave a real effort in the 12-step program." When these requests by patients in hospitals for something that is more relevant result in further exposure to 12-step therapy, it may be said that appropriate care is being withheld, and the patient may rightfully sue for redress. The defendant in such cases may be the attending physician, the health care institution, or both.

My benefits from a state or federal entitlement program (MediCare, Medicaid, Social Security, social welfare program, etc.) are or have been contingent on attending 12-step spiritual healing meetings. Clients of benefit programs are often directed to attend recovery meeting of AA by their caseworkers or case managers. If no alternative to 12-step spiritual healing is offered, then he or she may initiate legal proceedings against the social welfare agency. When a chemically dependent person is eligible for treatment at an inpatient or outpatient facility that is funded by state or federal third party programs, a choice between the spiritual and rational modes is also necessary to insure relevant care. Medicaid and Medicare and other third party underwriters are obliged to write regulations for participating agencies and institutions that specify minimum standards or conditions that will exist in those agencies and institutions, and when only 12-step therapy is offered, clients may sue those regulatory agencies for redress.

I am or have been required, as a condition of my military service or as a condition of receiving VA benefits, to attend 12-step spiritual healing meetings of Alcoholics Anonymous. One of the freedoms that soldiers and sailors defend is our freedom of conscience, so it is ironic that men and women who are willing to die for this freedom are expected to turn their lives over to God as a condition of remaining in the military. Nevertheless, many service men and women who drink too much or have had a run-in with an MP while intoxicated find themselves required to attend 12-step meetings of Alcoholics Anonymous or be discharged from duty, sometimes with a less than honorable discharge. Even though the lack of a viable alternative to AA in the military has occurred by default and is supported by military brass with the best of intentions, the United States Constitution promises redress when the government imposes palpably religious programs for those who are ill or violate civil or military law. Therefore, military personnel who are required to attend 12-step spiritual healing programs as a condition of avoiding disciplinary action may sue the United States government for redress.

As a result of violating the law, I have been sentenced by a court or remanded by a probation officer to attend spiritual healing meetings of Alcoholics Anonymous. The spiritual teachings of Alcoholics Anonymous are palpably religious, as reading the associated literature, observing the meetings, and polling uncounted thousands of people who have rejected the program (because of its religiosity) will show. Whether AA 12-stepism fits the technical definition of a "religion" is a moot point as long as substantial numbers *perceive* it to be "religious." When convicted persons are sentenced to spiritual healing sessions, they are, in their own sincere judgement, receiving religious instruction as a result of violating the law. The United States Constitution contains phrases in its First Amendment that specifically forbid any laws that would require any citizen to worship God, ask God to remove character defects, or proselytize for God, as is now happening in traffic and other courts everywhere in the nation. Even though sentencing problem drinkers to AA has occurred by default of and through inaction by the helping professions, and even though judges execute those sentences in good faith and in accordance with accepted professional standards, the civil rights of convicted offenders are violated when they are sentenced to what they as a class perceive to be religious instruction as a result of violating the law. Those sentenced persons may therefore appeal their convictions and sentences and sue the government entity of which that court is a part, for redress.

I have been denied employment or educational opportunity because of my disagreement with the 12-steps of Alcoholics Anonymous. Because of the loyalty and determined efforts of its long-term members, Alcoholics Anonymous has come to dominate American addiction care. Its quasi-religious 12-step program is appealing to a select group of people who recover from chemical dependence and then take up responsible positions in all of our social systems, public and private. There, they conscientiously open doors to the spiritual 12-step movement, as they are directed to in the twelfth step of the 12-step program. Many individuals in the academic, corrections, and health care communities have in effect forsaken the scientific and legal credentials upon which they lay claim to the public trust, promoting the articles of faith contained in the 12-step spiritual healing program of Alcoholics Anonymous rather than functioning in a balanced, objective manner. Consequently, the employment selection practices in the health care industry, public and private, and the admission procedures in institutions of higher learning strongly favor the selection of persons who are members of Alcoholics Anonymous or who are in agreement with the spiritual teachings of the 12-step program. This widespread bias, far more than the success or the special relevance of the 12-step program to chemical dependence, has been the direct cause of AA's virtual monopoly of addiction care. Alcoholics Anonymous should not be criticized for being what it is — a faith-based, expansionist, spiritual movement that intends to change the world. Instead, corrective action would best take place within the social institutions that have allowed this radical shift in social philosophy to take place. It is a tradition in America to address long-standing policies of discrimination based on race, religion, or national origin through affirmative action whereby minority applicants for employment or educational opportunity are granted preference until the effects of past discrimination are nullified. Therefore, applicants who believe they have been denied employment in public or private health care or applicants who believe they have been denied educational opportunity in state or federally supported or state or federally certified institutions of learning because of their disagreement with the 12-step spiritual healing program of Alcoholics Anonymous may rightfully sue those institutions or government entities for redress.

I was recruited into the religious sect, Alcoholics Anonymous, by force of fear while I was mentally impaired due to the use of mind-altering drugs. One of the most serious shortcomings of Alcoholics Anonymous is that it is broadly unsupervised. With programmatic supervision from the mental health professions it is most unlikely that certain deceptive and abusive practices would have evolved to become standard practice in 12-step recovery groups. To briefly mention a few:

1. "If you stop attending 12-step spiritual healing meetings, you will relapse and risk death." This message, a central ingredient of present day 12-stepism, undercuts the natural strengths and independence of recovering people so that they may continue attending meetings endlessly out of unwarranted fear, and it is also a powerful anti-therapeutic suggestion that actually incites many to return to the use of mind altering substances. Research abounds showing that the majority of those who recover from chemical dependency do so outside of 12-step spiritual healing programs.

2. "Anything can be your Higher Power — even the doorknob or a tree." While this may be useful for a neophyte who is motivated to pursue the spiritual life, this technique is actually a means for coercing God-belief among nonbelievers at a time of special vulnerability — when they are desperate from the excessive use of mind-altering chemicals and when they are defenseless against aggressive spiritual proselytizing. This unethical practice is carried on in most if not all communities under the assumption that belief in a Higher Power, especially a Supreme Being, is a necessary condition for recovery from chemical dependence. It is widely known that this is not so. Newcomers who are implored to "Fake it (God-belief) until you make it," are not building on a foundation of self-understanding but rather on a plan of self-betrayal, and they are consequently quite prone to relapse.

The internal practices of AA are protected under the United States Constitution, and therefore not a concern of this Petition of Redress unless deceptive, unethical, or coercive practices occur under the hospitality or auspices of publicly supported health care institutions or involve paid personnel who supervise or oversee such activities. Therefore, clients or patients of publicly supported health care institutions who believe that they have been taken advantage of while mentally impaired from the use of mind-altering substances may rightfully sue that institution, naming employees of that institution who witnessed or participated in the abuses as witnesses, for redress.

I was denied information about or prohibited from attending meetings of Rational Recovery by persons employed by or agencies funded by my health insurance carrier, the federal government, or the state, county or city of my residence.

175

Rational Recovery, a national program available in most areas, can be very quickly instituted in hospitals, clinics, agencies, court programs, and in communities. RR, based on sound principles of mental health, is a lifetime abstinence program, tailor-made for those who find 12-step spiritual healing programs unacceptable or unhelpful. When it can be shown that a client or patient has been prevented or deterred from attending Rational Recovery meetings, he or she may rightfully sue the responsible parties for redress. The two-track system (AA/RR) is a market-based approach to addiction care in which the consumer is not only in control, but also the ultimate winner.

If you believe that you have encountered situations as described above, and are willing to be a plaintiff in a case that may go to court, please fill out the petition and return it to RRS, along with a written account of your story. Remember that individual court cases often take long periods of time to reach adjudication and require your time and energy. In most cases the desired outcome will be a change in the system rather than monetary awards, but it is also entirely possible that plaintiffs could seek compensation for actual or punitive damages.

RRS has been advised by its legal counsel that class action suits will be far more efficient with regard to time and convenience. If your story seems to fit any of the above examples, send a summary of your experience to RRS as soon as possible and we will see if there is any clustering of complaints in areas where a class action suit can be instituted. In this scenario, it takes about four or five (the more the better) individuals with the same complaint to form a class. A class action suit will take little of your time, and you will probably not have to appear in court. A judge may then, weighing the merits of the complaint, sign a mandate or writ of prohibition to force service delivery systems to include a rational alternative to spiritual healing in addiction care programs.

Petition of Redress

To: American Civil Liberties Union
From:
Name_____Address:_____

City_____State_____Zip_____Tel:_____

Dear ACLU,

I believe that my civil rights have been violated in the following way(s):
_____I sought county *mental health* services for chemical dependence and was referred instead to a 12-step *spiritual healing* program of Alcoholics Anonymous.

_____While hospitalized for chemical dependence, my request(s) for a scientifically-based, non-spiritual (rational) approach to my problem was denied to me by my physician.

_____My benefits from a state or federal entitlement program (MediCare, Medicaid, Social Security, social welfare program, etc.) are or have been contingent on attending 12-step spiritual healing meetings.

_____I am or have been required, as a condition of my military service or as a condition of receiving VA benefits, to attend 12-step spiritual healing meetings of Alcoholics Anonymous.

_____As a result of violating the law, I have been sentenced by a court or remanded by a probation officer to attend spiritual healing meetings of Alcoholics Anonymous.

_____I have been denied employment or educational opportunity because of my disagreement with the 12-steps of Alcoholics Anonymous.

_____I was recruited into the religious sect, Alcoholics Anonymous, by force of fear while I was mentally impaired due to the use of mind-altering drugs.

_____I was denied information about or prohibited from attending meetings of Rational Recovery by persons employed by or agencies funded by my health insurance carrier, the federal government, or the state, county or city of my residence.

I have written a brief explanation of this formal complaint on separate paper. In the event of court proceedings, I appoint Jack Trimpey, LCSW, Director of Rational Recovery Systems, or his designate, to provide expert testimony.
Signed:_____, Date_____

Please forward this petition to RRS at the above address and it will be forwarded to the ACLU in your area, along with a copy to ACLU national offices.

Figure 3

177

Rational Recovery Systems
Box 800, Lotus CA 95651
916) 621-4374; voice or fax: (916) 621-2667

To Whom it May Concern:

I am in need of addiction care from your agency or as a requirement of your organization or institution. I have personally evaluated and examined the services that are being offered to me, and I have reached the following conclusions:

___The 12-step program is in disagreement with my religious principles

___The 12-step program is religious and therefore not relevant to my problem

___The 12-step program is the same as previous unsuccessful treatment I have had

___The 12-step program is impossible for me to understand, accept or make use of

Moreover, I have requested that a rational mode of recovery be provided for me, and I have been told the following:

___There is no other alternative to the 12-step approach

___The 12-step approach is the only approach that works

___I cannot get better from chemical dependency in a rational mode of recovery

___My request for a rational alternative is part of my disease of chemical dependency

___There is room for all degrees of disbelief in the 12-step approach

___I am not sincere in my desire to stop drinking or using drugs

___I will get sicker, or relapse, or die if I don't accept the 12-step approach

___I have been subjected to humiliation and group pressure to accept the 12-step approach

If I don't continue with your 12-step program, I will be punished in the following ways:

___I will be dismissed from your facility or agency with no referral elsewhere

___My bill for your services will not be paid by my health insurance carrier

___I will be sent to jail

___I will receive a harsher sentence

___My benefits will be terminated

___My employment will be terminated

___I will be discharged from military service

___I will be expelled from a school or university

___My professional license will be suspended

___I will be in violation of probationary status

The above statements I have made constitute a violation of my civil rights, and I hereby demand that you cease and desist from requiring me to participate in any way in a 12-step program, and refer me to an agency that does provide a rational mode of recovery from chemical dependence. Furthermore, if you do not honor this request, I may seek legal recourse including a class action or individual lawsuit against your agency, organization, or institution, with the assistance of Rational Recovery Systems, private legal counsel, and/or The American Civil Liberties Union.

Signed:_____, Date:_____

Witness:_____, Date:_____

Figure 4

The following recommendations, if accepted by professionals in health care and other key persons in public life, will bring us closer to the day when everyone, regardless of their religious beliefs (or the lack of them) will have an equal chance to recover from chemical dependency.

1. Put yourself in the place of a chemically dependent person. Are you a candidate for faith healing? Are you in the market for a Higher Power? Do you personally like the idea of attending recovery meetings for the rest of your adult years? After reading the chapter, *Discussion of the 12-steps*, would you find those ideas relevant to *your* personal problems? Perhaps you agree with them, but do you understand that many of us have no capacity to think that way, and that we will die if that's all there is for us in the way of help? If you wouldn't find the AA steps relevant, then you're being severely discriminated against, since it is your tax dollar and your health insurance premiums that are being used to perpetuate our monolithic addiction care system — this to the tune of billions annually, and with sad recovery statistics.

2. Initiate conversations with professionals, administrators, and other public officials, pointing out the inequities in the AA-dominated system. Accept the current psychiatric nomenclature that rejects "alcoholism" in favor of "alcohol dependence" and "alcohol abuse." Use the term "NHP sobriety" when speaking about alcohol dependence. Comment that an entire branch of medicine has been given over to divine intervention. Write a note to the editor of your local newspaper. Mention *The Small Book* to mental health professionals, especially administrators. Ask mental health administrators what kind of services besides AA there are for alcoholic agnostics, atheists, disbelievers, and humanists in general. If there are none, call your legislator and suggest that he or she contact Rational Recovery Systems. Talk to your municipal judges about RR; suggest that they be among the first in the field of corrections to honor the United States Constitution by offering offenders a choice between rational and spiritual recovery programs. Don't hesitate to point out to a judge that sentencing or otherwise coercing someone into AA is *de facto* government-enforced religious instruction.

3. Start writing differential diagnoses into your clients' and patients' charts! The health care system, despite its prejudice and sluggishness, is sensitive to professional issues, but it can only respond to hard data. If a dying surgical patient desperately needed a specific operation performed only on Mars, it would be prudent to record that information in his chart, even though there's no chance of getting him there on time. "Refer to non-spiritual recovery program; pt. not a good candidate for other procedures," might not produce the desired results, but the community search might prove interesting and eventually productive.

179

4. Become an RR Coordinator or Advisor, helping an RR program get started in your clinic or organization, or start one yourself. Let it be known that you will treat AA refuseniks one-to-one or in a Rational Recovery group. Be assured that what you have to offer, based on your education and experience, is *infinitely* better than AA for those who are not candidates for spiritual healing. Remember that your community is teeming with alcoholics who are motivated to get better, but who are not candidates for spiritual healing.

RGD's

For several years, RRS has made reference to "kicking the recovery habit." Thousands of people now call RRS every year; most of them have a recent history of chemical dependency, and nearly all of them have recently been involved in a 12-step spiritual healing program. Here we will explore the ironical outcomes of addiction care — when people seeking help find that the solution has become part of the problem, sometimes making things worse.

It appears that there are *recovery group disorders* that are directly related to previous experience in addiction care. People coming to RR are often depressed, angry, confused, or relapsing, even though they usually have made a sincere effort to apply the spiritual teachings of AA. They present in a typical, familiar fashion, so that subtypes of the recovery group disorder are recognizable as distinct from one another. Several are listed below, along with descriptive information:

Relapsing type: These people have "come to believe" in AA Step 1, but are unable or unwilling to accept the Higher Power concept of Step 2. "I can't stop drinking/using;" they say, "I keep going back to it." They tend to accept the idea of powerlessness without seeing its necessary relationship to the rescuing deity of AA. Others report great frustration with the spiritual teachings of AA, and with the negativism at meetings where people tell sordid stories of alcoholic excess. "I rarely feel like having a drink except after an AA meeting. All they talk about is booze and " "I hate going to meetings, but every time I stop going I start drinking again. Then I go back for a while, and it starts all over again." Some report feeling "cursed," i.e., "Everyone said I would drink again if I didn't work the program. I guess they were right — I'm powerless over alcohol. I don't go along with the higher power stuff, so I guess I'm pretty hopeless." The relapsing type often has an escalating record of failure at work and in the community. They grow impatient with repeated failure to comprehend spiritual teachings, or to comprehend the AA principle of taking action to consume one's energies and to divert one's thinking from drinking. They usually accept quite literally that there is some inner deficiency that interferes with their ability to abstain from intoxicants, rather than to seek means for self-control.

Depressed type: They complain, "I'm not growing any more. Life seems stagnant. The meetings are so much the same — the same people, the same stories, the same rituals. Is this all there is?" The response of the 12-step group is usually, "You get out of you program what you put into it; stop your stinking thinking and become people-centered rather than self-centered. Be grateful you're in the program!" Naturally, people suffering from a recovery group disorder, depressed type, may be suffering from a genuine mood disorder and could benefit from psychiatric care, but in most cases these platitudes serve to intensify the sense of guilt and inadequacy from failure in the program.

Anxious type: (also, recovery group dependence disorder) "If I miss two meetings in a row, I start feeling nervous, like something bad will happen. Then I feel this great need to get to a meeting as soon as possible, like I can't make it another minute. When I get to the meeting, I wonder what it was all about." These people make a clear superstitious connection between meeting attendance and protection from adversity. Usually labeled, "codependent," these people find the idea of endless meeting attendance a dreadful prospect, yet they feel compelled to attend meetings.

Angry type: Naturally, people who are coerced into attending 12-step meetings are likely to be angry at the circumstances that led them to be there, and it is understandable that they would generalize this anger to persons present in the same room. People who have been hospitalized as a result of an "intervention," people who have been sentenced to AA attendance by a court, people whose professional license is threatened unless they cooperate with the 12-step agenda, and others whose therapist is cooperating with an employer to force long-term compliance with the 12-step regime, may all suffer from this kind of recovery group disorder. Their anger is understandable but unproductive, i.e, "They're a bunch of goddamn zombies! Every time I open my mouth, they said I am in denial. I can't stand their religious trip. They're just pumping God on sick people — making them worse! I finally stormed out and told them to 'shove it!'" Even though these people recognize that there is something seriously wrong, they rarely conclude that they had better seek out other rational means to achieve their goals, including self-inspired sobriety. Instead, they sit angrily, rooted in place by feelings of powerlessness, and feeling victimized by people they are not fond of in the first place. When they finally do leave the group or program, they are ripe for relapse.

Guilty type: These individuals are keenly aware that they are out of step with the 12-steps, but they also see most others in the group smiling radiantly as they tell of spiritual awakenings and serenity. "I feel guilty that I cannot accept or understand the 12-step program. I tried, but I didn't try hard enough. I should feel grateful for the privilege of being in the recovery group, but I didn't like it at all. I never could take advantage of opportunities. Now I'll never get well. I guess I'm a hopeless dry drunk." In order to avoid taking personal responsibility, they sometimes offer cosmic explanations for everyday events and decisions, i.e., "It's karma."

Worthless type: Closely related to RGD, guilty type, this condition is more self-involved, and we see more self-blame, self-loathing, and self-condemnation, i.e., "I am defective in a way that only others can see. I'm an alcoholic, al right, and a *bad* one. I failed to remain sober in AA, and that proves I'll never get better. Everyone else seemed to get the program except me. I guess I'm pretty dense to fail AA."

Paranoid type: People with paranoid orientation are likely to interpret outreach efforts of AA members as intrusive and threatening. The expectation that one divulge sensitive personal information about one's past moral or ethical behavior presents unique problems to people who then leave the group against the group's advice. Efforts to bring back discontinued members are often seen as coupled with the idea that they are the central subject of discussion at current meetings, and the sense of "being talked about" may become acute. Some feel that they are under a kind of surveillance, and there seems to be a good kernel of truth when they get calls from people who are trying to help themselves by helping others. Some typical reports by RR newcomers are: "I get calls at night from anonymous people saying, 'This is your conscience. We miss you at the meetings.'" "I met a group member in a cafe, and she asked, 'Did you relapse?'" "When I quit going to meetings, the people at work stopped talking to me."

Helpless type: "I am incompetent to live life on my own terms." "I stopped going to meetings after three years, and I still don't drink, but I feel like I can't get my life in gear. I have been blessed with several miracles, but I still can't get ahead. I haven't found serenity, but on the other hand I don't plan to start going to meetings again. My life is a big rut. You know me — I'm just a hopeless alcoholic." These people seem more prone than others to seek other transpersonal solutions to life's problems, such as pyramid power, crystals, channeling, exotic meditation, and other remedies that involve charismatic leadership, require little in the way of independent action or thought personal effort, and therefore offer little risk of failure. They may have multiple 12-step memberships (ACOA, CODA, Sexers Anonymous, etc.) and may supplement their 12-step "work" with church attendance, inner child work, long-term 12-step-oriented psychotherapy. Their inquiry to RRS is usually highly tentative, i.e., "I don't want to say anything bad about AA, but I'm having some trouble with some of the ideas in the program."

Confused type: Many people inquiring about RRS have problems with critical thought process. They have gotten hung up intellectually on philosophical "catch-22's" that are embodied in steptalk, i.e., "I can't trust my own thinking or my own decisions. No one can know anything for sure. My thinking is my disease. I doubt the 12 steps, but I doubt that I doubt. Must I not be skeptical of my skepticism. Oh, what *can* I believe? If I trust God, am I making him up? Am I tricking myself? If there is a God and I don't accept Him, then I am sunk. If there isn't a God, then life sucks. Oh, woe is me! Why, why, why can't I know anything for sure?" Their attitudes toward the spiritual recovery program is characterized by great ambivalence, much in the same way as people growing out of the religions of their childhoods experience the crises of faith. We had better not underestimate the extent of despairing of people who suffer this kind of recovery group disorder, because they are prone to act out their intense, inner conflicts in self-destructive ways. They are usually angry at the recovery group milieu, which they view as a kind of inquisition that offers no escape.

Differential diagnosis in chemical dependency:

Proper treatment is an expression of proper differential diagnosis. The diagnosis of addiction itself is sometimes a challenging, multi-faceted task. We obtain the client's subjective complaints, observe his or her behavior, take a relevant history, sometimes obtain the observations of friends and family, and, from this initial database, we arrive at a diagnostic category. Differential diagnosis, however, is the quest for additional information that will help in the selection of the best treatment procedures and modalities for that condition. Some of these include age, other concurrent diagnoses, allergies, cultural and ethnic considerations, religious implications, gender, client's motivations, history of previous treatment outcomes, chronicity and lethality issues.

In the chemical dependency field, however, differential diagnosis is a moot point, because practically speaking there is only one treatment available, the 12-step spiritual healing plan of AA. When the diagnosis of chemical dependency is established, further refinement of the diagnosis is superfluous, because the treatment will be largely the same, even though there are many spiritual healing programs at different levels of care from which to choose.

For example, an alcoholic amputee would best be sent to an AA program in a one-story building; an alcoholic veteran might do well in an AA program in a Veteran's Administration setting; an insured, depressed alcoholic in his thirties or forties might profit from a private inpatient spiritual healing program; a homeless or vagrant alcoholic person could be directed to a residential care AA program; a violent drunk would best be sent to a jail where 12th-steppers will visit him is his cell; and a well-fed, employed, still married alcoholic person might best be referred to an outpatient clinic to see a professional AA sponsor or join a community-based AA group in a church basement or community center.

Unfortunately, about half of those who enter AA spiritual healing programs quit within thirty days, and half of those thirty-day survivors quit and presumably relapse during the next eleven months. Many of these refuseniks are repelled by the religious content, object to the social milieu, or find the the 12-steps unhelpful, irrelevant, or difficult. The purpose of a differential diagnosis is to identify traits that would seem to clearly predict failure in spiritual healing, regardless of the setting.

"Do you believe in God?"

We who are professionals ask about everything else, so why should we not see if our chemically dependent clients have backgrounds that are conducive to the spiritual healing approach? At the present, professionals seem to assume that all alcoholics have an existing belief in God or will be able to construct or discover a rescuing deity around which to build a new and better life. A good differential diagnosis will help to determine whether these assumptions are so. There are two ways to tell if a chemically dependent person is a candidate for spiritual healing: (1) a history of recidivism in spiritual healing programs, and (2) the client's answers to our questions.

When making a referral for addiction care (or any other health problem, for that matter), it is vital and proper to inform the client of the treatment proposed before asking him or her to consent to it. A copy of the 12-steps of Alcoholics Anonymous should be presented to the client, and he should be frankly asked, "What do you think of this way of handling your problems with alcohol? Is there anything about it that you find hard to understand? Do you disagree with any of the ideas here?" If the client expresses no objections, but has previous unsuccessful experiences with AA, it is fair to ask, "Why did you leave AA the last time? Was there something you didn't like? Were you able to use the Higher Power concept?" To these questions, many addicts will confess their faith in God and assert their willingness to pursue a spiritual awakening as a way of remaining sober. But others will let it be known that they don't want to seek spiritual goals, that they do not even know what the word *spiritual* means (nor do they want to) and that the idea of a rescuing deity for alcoholics is silly. Some may say they have no belief in God, others may say they believe in some kind of a cosmic being but choose not to drag that into these problems, and still others may say that all the religious stuff in AA bothers them. It has long been a tradition to interpret these kinds of statements as resistance to treatment, as a sign of poor motivation, or of passive aggression.

These assertions of doubt and skepticism, however, are the basic strengths upon which to build a sober life! Rather than suggesting that the client may "come around" to the AA viewpoint, you should *commend him or her for exercising good critical judgement,* and refer him or her to a professional person in your community who is competent in cognitive-behavioral methods, especially RET. If the chemically dependent client is uninsured or cannot pay for a private therapist, you may call the local community mental health center and request that you be given a call when the client is accepted for care. Discuss the client in the context of *The Small Book,* and if the clinic says it offers nothing besides AA-oriented care, ask to speak to the agency director. Tell the director that your client is not a candidate for AA because of the program's religious content. Do not accept assurances that AA is not a religious program or that there is room for all degrees of disbelief in AA. Ask if the director has read the 12-steps him or herself. If you are among those who would not take the AA program seriously if you yourself had some compulsive problem, tell the director so; ask that a rational alternative to AA be a priority in next year's budget, and that all prospective clients for addiction care be offered a choice between those programs. Ask the director how your client's needs will be met.

Methods

Let's say that you are planning to treat substance abusers in your own practice. As stated elsewhere, RR differs from AA in both principle and practice. There is no need to emulate AA in any way, although there is some overlap of some empirically validated concepts and practices. If you have no special training in the treatment of chemical dependency, that may be an advantage for you, because there will be less for you to unlearn. Foremost among the agreements with AA is the RR contention that abstinence is the most reasonable goal once a period of addiction has occurred. There are persistent reports in health care magazines that many people can return to social drinking, and there is little doubt that magazines carrying this banner may sell well. Rather than debate this tired issue, it would be better to use the question as a diagnostic one, and assume that if a problem drinker or substance abuser ever returns to real moderation, then he was not an addict or "alcoholic" in the first place. RR does not support people in their efforts to drink "moderately", because the chances of success are so slim, because the danger of further harm is so great, because the beverage has little intrinsic value, because the nagging desire of alcohol-troubled people to drink "moderately" or use drugs "recreationally" is in itself a symptom of chemical dependency, and because abstinence is so much easier than struggling against an unruly appetite for alcohol. If a client persists in proposing moderation as a goal, you may consider the "30 x 2 wager" described in the chapter titled "The Essence of Rational Recovery."

One key to treating substance abusers is to establish in the client's mind a clear causal link between the intoxicant and pain. Though simple enough, this is usually a difficult task, because substance abusers associate intoxicants with most of life's pleasures. The frequent question, "Suppose you had not been drinking (using) then; would that have happened?" is utilitarian, and strengthens the client's understanding. When signs of improvement are reported, such as making a new friend, or getting a job, or avoiding a conflict, or having a license renewed, or just feeling better, reinforcement is in order. You may ask, "Could this have happened if you were still drinking?

Another key element in the rational mode of recovery is The Big Plan, i.e., a commitment or desire to never use or drink again. Never. The Big Plan is not a substitute for the short-term strategies that are so important during the early phases of withdrawal and recovery. RR is quite "here and now" oriented and the one-day-at-a-time approach has great merit as a way of conceptualizing early progress. But, one-day-at-a-time wears thin before long, and often becomes a way of *creating* a daily struggle when there is no justification for it. Moreover, plans for relapse — such as "When I get off probation" or "If I should find I was terminally ill," or "If I might be drafted into the military," — can be cleverly hidden in the "one-day-at-a-time" platitude.

A good questioning technique is, "So what stops you from planning to never drink (use) again?" Here, you may encounter major resistance accompanied by anxiety, for the client's addictive voice, the Beast of RR, will intrude with many reasons why one *must* not decide now to never drink again. Chief among these is the idea that, I can't predict the future, so how can I say never?" Of course, anyone can plan or vow anything, and intend fully to carry that plan out even though there is no guarantee of success. But the addictive thinking will usually envision failure as a catastrophic event that can be avoided by staying sober "One day at a time," or even "One hour at a time." You can help your client by introducing the concept of rational self-acceptance, wherein one may regard him or herself as a worthwhile person even though a relapse has occurred.

The goal of RR is to close the book on the issue of chemical dependency within a reasonable period of time, sometime during the second and third semesters of NHP sobriety. Few persons are inclined to devote a lifetime to recovery, as AA dropout statistics suggest. Judging from RR experience, one or two clinical contacts per week are sufficient, even during the early phases of detoxification, provided that the therapist and client account for how time is to be spent between contacts. Contacts can taper off after about six to eight months to once weekly or biweekly, as agreed upon by both parties. The presence of an RR group in your community can accelerate your client's emancipation. Therapy can be terminated earlier if necessary, because of personal circumstances or because of the client's desire to "go it alone." Early termination should not be construed to mean that anyone has failed. Every effort should be made to fortify the client's confidence that achieving a durable sobriety is entirely possible even though additional therapy would be desirable. Termination before three or four months is ill-advised because of the time needed to incorporate and synthesize the gains realized from sobriety.

The clinical strategy in RR is twofold; to (1) to prevent relapses, and (2) to enhance self-esteem and long-range hedonism. The approach is iconoclastic, inducing the client to gain insight into his own self-downing and self-defeating philosophies and replacing them with rational ones that are collectively opposed to chemical dependency. Many resistant clients will express fascination when asked if they have ever considered alcoholism a philosophy rather than a disease. The role of the therapist is counter-propagandist, so some sessions may take on an argumentative quality; care must therefore be taken to avoid alienation of the client with the irrational idea that he or she is a stupid person for having irrational ideas. By focusing on the idea that adults do not need love for its own sake, or the idea that emotions are caused by one's own conscious thinking, the client can be led to broader insights. The therapist gently, even tenderly, can show the client that he or she *could not help* coming to think in such a slipshod way, because we all live in the same nutty, pathogenic society, and virtually everyone comes to think irrationally during their early years. Our irrational tendencies lie in our human nature, but they are bolstered by cultural values which teach one to approve of himself *only conditionally,* and often only with the consent of a supernatural deity. The irrational beliefs that comprise the philosophy of alcoholism and perpetuate the relapse cycle are listed and elaborated upon in the chapter "The Essence of Rational Recovery," and will provide impetus for an endless series of interviews.

The chapter "Voices" will illuminate another aspect of rational addiction care that is unique, and part of each interview should be spent exploring the spontaneous and intrusive cognitions that nag at the substance abuser and lead to relapse. The client needs to be reassured that the voice is nothing more than psychological craving, and that all addicts experience this. When a client denies hearing any voices but still reports strong desires to drink or expose himself to

187

drinking opportunities, you may, by working backward from the desire, infer that there *almost certainly must* be a voice, even if it's only a quiet whisper, because we feel the way we think, and the feeling of wanting a drink cannot be a physical craving after the first week of sobriety. Ask him to *listen more carefully* the next time he or she feels like having a drink, and he/she will certainly finally hear it, perhaps as a whisper, or another strange voice, or even in his own voice. When the client can identify the psychological craving as a conscious thought, it can then be split off from the rational self, mercilessly attacked through aggressive reasoning alone, and finally subdued. It is useful to have the client personify the addictive voice, with visual imagery if necessary, to give it attributes that are ego-alien. The character Smaug in Tolkien's *The Hobbit* will provide a sample of imagery, as will the odd creatures portrayed in the book, *Gnomes.*

In Rational Recovery your client will learn from you that guilt is an emotion of childhood which, if it weren't for the disorienting effects of our pathogenic culture, could usually be resolved in the transition from adolescence to adulthood. In children, guilt is the feeling of "badness" stemming from actual or perceived parental rejection. It is a natural product of parents' authoritative role in disciplining the child. When scolded, the child cannot differentiate his behavior from himself, and feels rejected and condemned. But guilt is an inappropriate emotion among adults who, by virtue of their neocortical maturity, have the capacity to perceive themselves as fallible yet worthwhile, and to reject the opinions of others when they imply personal worthlessness. In RR you will show the client that to think lovingly of one's self at all times is in no way pathological, and that the resulting sense of personal goodness or self-worth is not an earned privilege; rather, it is a birthright that may be exercised arbitrarily and authoritatively simply because (1) there is no good reason to refrain from doing so, (2) because it feels better, (3) because guilt has little, if any, beneficial effects for anyone, and (4) guilt actually contributes to the alcoholic drinking cycle, as shown elsewhere in *The Small Book.*

Alcoholic clients will often ventilate freely about past alcoholic sins, confessing them to you over and over as if there is some inherent benefit in telling someone else about past mistakes. Getting something off one's chest usually means that by confessing or admitting some error, the guilt (worthless feelings) resulting from the misdeed is somehow neutralized. This cycle of error and confession does absolutely nothing to correct the guilt-producing philosophy, nor does it lend itself very well to constructive intervention in the pattern of maladaptive behavior. Instead, we are confronted with a well-rehearsed, compulsive confessor who is probably reflecting cultural values about confession and guilt. A good rational intervention is to halt the client just before he or she is about to tell you about "something terrible" he or she did long ago. Ask your client if there is any reason for you to know what is about to be told. If there isn't, you can explain that confessing mistakes is of little value unless the client forgives himself. Confession need not be to any other person, but simply to oneself, and one can recognize error, even serious error, without feeling guilty in the first place. One might feel sad, sorry, regretful, or even remorseful, but to feel guilty, i.e., worthless, is only to commit another error. In this case, then, you might ask the client if the confession might be kept to him- or herself and regard it as none of anyone's business. Then ask the client to simply forgive him- or herself right then and there without having to disclose the misdeed to anyone. Suggest that the mistake became so only in retrospect, when the poor outcome became apparent; at the time, the behavior seemed like the best thing to do. Mistakes, you may add, are usually the result of not having magical abilities to predict the future. You may also wish to inject a little therapeutic humor by drawing out the idea that your client is blaming himself for not having precognition (ESP). If this is done in a highly supportive way, and the client helped to generalize, a new level of emotional independence may be achieved.

If after reading this chapter you are interested in expanding your practice to include the large population of substance abusers, there is an excellent clinical manual, *Rational-Emotive Therapy With Alcoholics and Substance Abusers,* (Ellis, McInerney, DiGiuseppi, and Yeager) available from the Institute for Rational-Emotive Therapy (IRET), 45 E. 65th St., New York NY 10021. It provides a wealth of current information about the treatment of substance abuse disorders within the RET paradigm. Those providing care for substance abusers "should" have that book on their bookshelves.

Although it does not seem to require special training in chemical dependency to work effectively with substance abusers, it is important that you be an active, directive therapist with a cognitive-behavioral orientation. Training seminars on RET are available through IRET in many American cities every year, and if you would like to join the ten thousand RET therapists around the world, you may wish to take a training junket to New York.

The following article appeared in November - December, 1989, issue of *The Journal of Rational Recovery.* The Vestibule Inpatient Program (VIP) is a model for institutional change that can be adapted to any agency. It requires that health care administrators acknowledge the existence of distinct *subtypes* of chemically dependent people, and then assume responsibility for internal program planning that will avoid assigning patients to the wrong program by matching them to the correct program.

The Two-track (AA/RR) Vestibule Inpatient Program (VIP) for Hospital-Based Chemical Dependency Units

by Jack Trimpey, LCSW, RRS Director,
and Forrest Martin, M.D., RRS Medical Director

Abstract - In recognition of individual differences in philosophical orientation of patients in a general population, hospital based CD units "match" patients to highly contrasted therapeutic approaches ("tracks") based on differential diagnosis. Administrative rationale for the two-track vestibule inpatient program (VIP) is provided along with clinical guidelines for running cognitive-behavioral therapy groups. The VIP is incorporated into a community-based two-track system with outpatient follow-up provided in both AA and RR meetings for the first year following discharge.

Background:

While the 12-step program of Alcoholics Anonymous (AA) has been found to be useful in the hospital setting for initiating the process of recovery from chemical dependency, recovery statistics have shown that the majority of patients continue their addictions during the year following discharge. Theoretical advances in the last several years have drawn to light that client receptivity to the central concepts of the 12-step program is predictive of treatment outcome. Ideally, patients with a secular or humanistic orientation would select institutions where non-spiritual methods are employed, as a matter of personal preference or with the advice of a referring professional, but during the early 1990's practically all American inpatient care is based on the 12-steps of AA. The two-track Vestibule Inpatient Program (VIP) is a means for any 12-step inpatient program to immediately diversify its theoretical basis for addiction care and to clinically accommodate those patients who give early indicators that the 12-step program will not lead to a satisfactory outcome.

Program Summary:

Transition to the two-track VIP is accomplished through systematic staff development with administrative support and encouragement. On-site consultation with qualified RRS consultants is highly recommended in order to benefit from inservice training in clinical methods. The materials presented here include:

(1) Administrative matters and concerns

(2) Philosophical and conceptual backdrop for VIP

(3) Common problems in the VIP

(4) Orientation of the patient to the hospital unit and the VIP

(5) Guidelines for differential diagnosis of alcohol dependence (DSM III-R 303.90) and alcohol abuse (DSM III-R 305.00), including sample interview format and dialogs

(6) Schedule of daily activities and the program calendar

(7) Suggestions for Rational Milieu Therapy

(8) Clinical protocol for management of the daily Rational Recovery group sessions. Didactic learning and the group process.

(9) The required readings — *Rational Recovery from Alcoholism: The Small Book,* by Jack Trimpey, LCSW, Director, RRS; and *Rational-Emotive Therapy With Alcoholics and Other Substance Abusers,* by Albert Ellis, Ph.D., John F. McInerney, Ph.D., Raymond DiGuiseppi, Ph.D., and Raymond Yeager, Ph.D., of the Institute for Rational-Emotive Therapy, New York.

Conceptual backdrop for VIP

Mankind has been divided throughout history by ideology, and this continues today in pluralistic American society. One of the most salient of these divisions is the one over metaphysics, supernaturalism, and spiritual entities, i.e., "God." Addicts themselves probably represent a cross-section of the general population in their viewpoints on such matters as politics, religion, philosophy, psychology, education, economics, and even chemical dependency. Indeed, values and perceptions concerning all of the above vary widely from country to country and from culture to culture. While the physiology of addiction may be fairly uniform between social and ethnic groups, the ideological factors are not. For a program to be successful, it must be perceived as being *relevant* by the client.

Because of the diversity of clients who come to a typical hospital CD unit, it will be impossible for reasons of time and money to have programs catering to each cultural and ethnic group, i,e., one for Catholics, one for Protestants, one for Blacks, one for Hispanics, one for Eskimos, one for Jews. AA has already shown that one program fits all for a population of spiritually-oriented or spiritually receptive clients; however, AA does not help those who find the 12-steps unhelpful. Many clients who have fixed, humanistic values will have specific objections to 12-step requirements such as the Higher Power, group dependency, personal confession, fearless moral inventories, and lifelong recovery. Others offer no objections but by their recidivism demonstrate the need for another, probably contrasting, approach. The vast majority of these refuseniks and recidivists will be good candidates for Rational Recovery, an application of the system of self-help and psychotherapy devised in the 1950's by eminent psychologist Albert Ellis, Ph.D. The system is called rational-emotive therapy (RET), and it is taught to students of the helping professions in most universities. Based on the scientific method, it is ideal for those with inquiring, skeptical attitudes, and it has been shown to provide potent guidance for persons seeking personal change. For decades, experts in the field of chemical dependency have recognized the high degree of relevance of RET to addiction care, so that today many 12-step recovery programs already offer RET or one of its cognitive-behavioral variants as an adjunct to their spiritually-oriented programs. RRS, in its VIP, presents RET as a *comprehensive* alternative to traditional programming. Between AA and RR, both of which are comprehensive plans for leading a sober life and each of which represents the opposite side of one of the most fundamental divisions of mankind, we can probably cover about 99% of the waterfront.

Administrative matters

Until recently bed occupancy supported continued growth of inpatient care for addictions. In addition to an overall tightening of health care dollars in recent years, new outcome studies have contributed to the occupancy problem by raising questions about the cost-effectiveness of inpatient versus outpatient programming. Doomsayers predict the collapse of the hospital-based inpatient concept while the hospital industry continues with traditional marketing approaches in which the spiritual healing model is the *sine qua non* of hospital-based practice. Market saturation and fewer third party dollars seem to explain low occupancy.

While the market for present services may be saturated and insurers may be reluctant to authorize inpatient service when outpatient care would seem to them to suffice, marginal programs based on humanistic values are targeting persons who are resistant to the 12-step approach. Rational Recovery Systems, started in 1986, is a coalition of qualified professionals who advocate for individuals with fixed humanistic values and who therefore are poor candidates for traditional spiritual healing services. Local RR groups have professional backup for the purpose of screening newcomers for special problems (psychotic conditions, mood disorders, suicide risk, etc.) and make referrals to medical and other resources when indicated. Among its many advisors are Albert Ellis, Ph.D., Forrest Martin, M.D., Emmett Velten, Ph.D., Philip Tate, Ph.D., Robert N. Dain, Ph.D., Hank Robb, Ph.D., Guy Lamunyon, MSRN, CDAC, Joseph Gerstein, M.D., and

Alan Marlatt, Ph.D., all of whom are fully supportive and active in the movement toward the two-party service system. RRS has freestanding projects in numerous American cities and several in Australia. An inpatient program based on Rational Recovery has opened at Canyon Springs Hospital in Palm Springs, California, not far from the Betty Ford Center. RR-Residential programs in California are showing good abstinence rates. Outpatient clinics like The Effort, Inc, of Sacramento, CA, offer RR as part of their general program. RR-Sacramento gets about two self-referrals per day when a small ad runs in a small alternative newspaper. By all indications, there is a substantial market for a recovery program that contrasts with traditional recovery imagery.

But administrators face a dilemma when they contemplate innovation by breaking from traditional patterns. They have reason to fear that they will lose credibility with established referral sources because there is such loyalty to the 12-step program of AA in the field of chemical dependency. Among the more orthodox AA believers it is held that anything other than the 12-step approach is not only inferior but also harmful. Disbelief in a higher power and refusal or failure to work a program of moral betterment is regarded as *part of the illness* of alcoholism, so nontheistic treatment plans are seen by some of these individuals as not only inefficient but also pathogenic. In a few cases, key people feel that if they were to give way to another recovery plan that did not fulfill the spiritual needs of others they would fall from grace with their own personal deities and lose the resolve to remain sober themselves. Such is the adhesive quality of 12-step recovery among some of the recovered, that the Higher Power *itself* seems to argue for strict adherence to traditional programming.

As a way to explore multimodal inpatient care, RRS encourages direct communication among managers and administrators who are contemplating the RRS:VIP. This document will make a good agenda item at any meeting of managers or administrators, whether or not an RRS representative is present. When the discussion opens, you will likely find that you all have a common concern for the many clients who go away with complaints about the 12-step program and then continue their addictions. Most managers have an inner sense that there are many possible ways to fill an inpatient treatment day, and that AA is only one of them. By talking with your peers you may get a clearer sense that there is plenty of leeway for innovation along the lines of RRS:VIP. In fact, you may come away hoping to be among the first to address a vast, untapped market of agnostics, humanists, atheists, freethinkers, Buddhists, Jews, and liberal and nominal Christians who have been staying away from traditional 12-step recovery programs in droves!

Getting started in RRS:VIP will require an initial survey of the clinical staff to determine the degree of readiness for and commitment to organizational change. The perceptions of your clinical staff are critical to the success of VIP, but experience has shown that uniform or unanimous support among the staff is not necessary. To the contrary, you will be looking for the predictable spectrum of opinions from "liberal" (pro-RR) to "conservative" (anti-RR), and then assigning responsibility for RR to those who show a natural inclination to work outside of the traditional 12-step paradigm.

Some administrators may view multimodal inpatient care as a way to preempt perceptions that their institutions skirt or even violate equal opportunity employment practices. It is not a well-kept secret that practically all clinicians in the field of chemical dependency themselves have a history of chemical dependency and also attribute their personal sobrieties to the 12-step spiritual healing program of Alcoholics Anonymous. Traditional hiring practices, whether by default or design, are selective of applicants who show evidence of accepting the steps and traditions of AA, many of which have theological content. Some agencies have designed application forms with questions about specific "steps," for example, "What do you think about the Higher Power idea?" Other pre-employment inquiries have to do with the extent of recent AA meeting and organizational involvement. The VIP incorporates ideological spread in its design, and you will have ample evidence, as shown in your hiring practices and in the program itself, that there is little consensus on theology or philosophy within your staff.

Occasionally tension can develop between staff members with divergent clinical orientations. Focusing on management priorities rather than on immediate conflict will give a larger context for internal problems of this sort; by consistently supporting both parties you can avoid escalating conflict with an eventual loser. Some staff may defensively note that *The Small Book* presents an aggressive critique of the 12-steps and also portrays AA as having overstepped its role in addiction care and even of being detrimental to some recovering alcoholics. Staff may become alarmed that RR seems to undermine the very faith that is required in 12-step recovery, that RR directs one toward self-centered sobriety, and that RR views the issue of "control" in a clearly opposite way. Staff members may perceive that RR is in effect strengthening character defects rather than treating them. At this juncture, you or your clinical director may suggest that they review Chapter 4 of "The Big Book" and put themselves in the place of a humanist who values his disbelief just as highly as others may love God. If they will do this, they will find that there is *mutual* antagonism between "The Big Book" and *The Small Book*. Moreover, you may remind your dissenting staff that whatever conflict now exists between theistic and humanistic alcoholics was started by Bill W. in 1936, and this is one institution that will no longer *exclude* those who sincerely want to stop drinking but have little use for the 12 theological steps of AA.

Common problems in VIP:

We may anticipate some early difficulties in transition from homogeneous 12-step programming, as we would in any planful change. Some of this centers around how AA and RR interface ideologically and socially. The following issues may surface among staff or within the patient population. They are perceptions that are natural, understandable, and ultimately desirable in the process of program development. Although most mature organizations will have the depth of supervision to manage transitional problems listed below, skilled RRS consultants may prove to be well worth the investment. They can help overcome the idea that AA is the only thing that works, that it is timeless and proven, while RR is new, unproven, and troublesome.

Within the fellowship of AA there is consensus that there are many paths to recovery, and many who are loyal to AA admit that their own recoveries were atypical, that they bent the meaning of the steps to suit their own fixed values. If AA is to work through attraction and not coercion then the presence of an alternative would not seem to pose a special problem.

Because of the virtual monopoly of the 12-step Minnesota Model in hospital settings it has become the standard of the industry. Therefore, research statistics largely reflect measures performed on outcomes of the 12-step approach. Even though there has been little against which to compare 12-step recovery statistics, it is widely assumed that statistics prove the effectiveness of that approach when applied to the general population. For example, if a report shows that 24% of those discharged after completing a 28 day program are sober after one year, we tend to think of the 12-step approach as being successful at that level in the population that the hospital serves. Recidivism of 76%, as in this case, would seem to be an acceptable figure, since few programs exceed a 24% one-year abstinence rate. But if we interpret the hypothetical but not unrealistic figures above to simply mean that only 24% of the patients were receptive enough to the 12-steps to achieve a one-year sobriety, then we are left with an unknown percentage who may have been fine candidates for RR. If Valiant is correct in his observation that "Some treatment is better than no treatment," then we may easily extrapolate that, "Treatment that is perceived as relevant by the patient is better than treatment that is perceived as irrelevant." To use a loose analogy to the hospital CD unit, think of a blood bank. If type AA blood is the only type given to all patients and 24% survive, how many more could be treated successfully by adding type RR blood to the inventory? If either blood type helps more patients than the other, can we then say that one kind of blood is *better* than the other? If so, for whom?

Ideological contempt

It is true that the differences between AA and RR outnumber the similarities, but the similarities *outweigh* the differences. As the differences become apparent, it may be helpful for the clinical director to emphasize the following viewpoints that are common to both AA and RR: (a) alcohol dependent persons may suffer a genetically transmitted, life-threatening condition that predisposes one to excessive alcohol use, (b) the goal of treatment is to be reasonably happy and successful in life without psychoactive intoxicants, (c) group meetings centering around the goal of abstinence are ideally suited for arresting the progression of alcohol dependence, (c) the only qualification for participation in the program is a sincere desire to stop drinking and remain sober.

Both AA and RR vigorously and unashamedly argue for their respective viewpoints in things philosophical, but neither would intentionally place the importance of their own ideology above the individual lives that are at stake in addiction recovery. When proponents of each approach recognize the value of the other to those who choose that route to recovery, we are all placing a transcendent value on the principle of self-determination on the road to abstinence.

As a program manager, your role in VIP is to recognize the value of *taking sides* on the ideological controversy between AA and RR, both among your patients and among your staff. In this way, both groups can act consistently with their central values, rather than attempt to hide (deny) honest opinions. In your leadership role, you are also now more or less forced, in reading this article, to take sides. Here is the key question that will shape the future of your program, depending which side you come down on. "Is the 12 step approach of AA an adequate program for the general population?" We at RRS are not trying to make your job easier. We are trying to get more out of you.

The VIP is an advanced concept in addiction care in that management is aspiring to a higher principle than contained in any clinical methodology. The unifying concept is the value we place on helping clients abstain from drinking alcohol or using drugs and then grow in sobriety. The following section discusses a highly sensitive issue that will call on your managerial skills.

Failure to accept a higher power is part of the illness of alcoholism

There are two common versions of this viewpoint, first that disbelief in mystical beings or higher authority is a symptomatic character defect of drunkenness and, second, that this character defect is part of the *cause* of alcoholism. At any rate, acceptance of a Higher Power is traditionally viewed as intrinsically therapeutic and therefore a necessary therapeutic task.

While this may be true for many who aspire to sobriety, others with fixed humanistic values will find a thoroughly secular, cognitive-behavioral approach more palatable and digestible. When humanists, agnostics, atheists, Buddhists, and members of other groups of people are told that their central values are symptoms of a terminal illness, their chances for remaining in treatment or benefiting from it are correspondingly reduced.

There are some authors who can make a convincing argument that devout belief in supernatural entities is a form of mental illness; indeed, a number of such books — well-written ones at that — do exist. But this is an extreme point of view, and one that can incite conflict between believers and disbelievers. No one likes to be diagnosed as "sick" because of what he or she believes or doesn't believe.

With the VIP, patients in the vestibule are surveyed with attention to their philosophical orientation and then assigned to the track that is more relevant, usually the one of the patient's own choosing. By taking this very active role in treatment planning, the patient is validated and empowered on the journey to recovery from chemical dependency.

Orientation of the Patient to VIP:

The purpose of the Vestibule is to give each patient an exposure to both programs as a way of insuring informed consent to care and to enhance commitment to recovery through participation in treatment planning. "Vestibule" refers to a status that is assigned to each patient at time of admission. While the patient is "in the vestibule," he is unassigned (and uncommitted) to either recovery track, but he or she is free to make a selection of program as early as the second day. The patient will be provided reading material from both programs, at least including personal copies of *Alcoholics Anonymous* ("The Big Book"), and *Rational Recovery from Alcoholism: The Small Book.*

On the first day the patient will meet with his/her therapist to discuss treatment planning, as is the common practice. This first session, however, will focus on differential diagnosis, as described in detail in the next section. During each day in the vestibule the patient shall attend at least one meeting each of AA and RR.

A Sample First Day Orientation Interview of a 28-year-old Vestibule Patient

T: Hi, Tim. I'm Sandra, a counselor here at the center. I may be your counselor as long as you are here, but that will be decided later, by you and by me. Tell me a little about yourself and why you're here at the hospital.

C: Well, I guess I'm here to sober up. I've been in so much trouble with everyone; I guess this is a last resort.

T: You came to a hospital to sober up? Pretty expensive hangover...

C: You know, like I drink too much and I've got to get stopped. I guess I'm an alcoholic or something.

T: Something? Like what?

C: Like nothing. I am an alcoholic; at least I got that much from AA.

T: It sounds like you've got the right idea — about quitting drinking. But, how long have you known that you're an alcoholic?

C: I think I've always known it, at least after I graduated from high school and got heavy into the booze. I've been in four programs so far and here I am again.

T: Is anything different this time?

C: I feel like I'm at the end of my rope. I don't last for more than a month after leaving a program, and then it takes about six months or a year to get sick enough to start another program.

T: Have you ever felt this bad before?

C: That's the trouble. I always feel like I've never felt this bad before when I check into a hospital program. It seems like I don't ever hit bottom; or maybe I just stay there and don't know the difference.

T: What have you learned so far from your recovery programs?

C: I'm not sure what you mean by "learned," but I have tried hard to work the program. I go to the meetings and it seems to make sense but then all of a sudden I decide to have a drink and I don't know why. Usually I drink before I call a sponsor or get to a meeting and then I just drop out and stay drunk. I just can't help myself, and I have trouble with the Higher Power thing. I guess I believe in God, but my Higher Power disappears every time I need it. I've tried and tried but I can't get the Higher Power thing straight.

T: Maybe you need something *besides* a Higher Power to stay sober.

C: Besides? I haven't heard of that before.

T: Yes, many people can learn to stay sober without depending on God or something outside themselves. AA is a program for people who accept a Higher Power and make that the center of their lives. But there's another approach that is available here at _____ Hospital called Rational Recovery. They call it RR and instead of "The Big Book," they have one called *The Small Book*. Because this is your first day here, you aren't yet in either program. For the next day or so, you will

198

be checking out both programs by reading from both "The Big Book" and *The Small Book.* and by attending group sessions for both AA and RR. When you feel ready, decide which track you want to be in and let me know.

NEXT DAY:

T: You have one more day to select your program, Tim...

C: Forget it! I'll make my decision now! I read *The Small Book* and attended one RR meeting, and now I *know* where I belong. If RR had been available to me five years ago, I would probably be five years sober right now. That RR stuff really makes sense! This is the first time I have ever felt like I am really *in* recovery!

Differential Diagnosis in Chemical Dependency:

Proper treatment is an expression of proper differential diagnosis. The diagnosis of addiction itself is sometimes a challenging, multi-faceted task. We obtain the client's subjective complaints, observe his or her behavior, take a relevant history, sometimes obtain the observations of friends and family, and, from this initial database, we arrive at a diagnostic category. Differential diagnosis, however, is the quest for additional information that will help in the selection of the best treatment procedures for that condition. Some of these include age, other concurrent diagnoses, allergies, cultural and ethnic considerations, religious implications, gender, client's motivations, history of previous treatment outcomes, chronicity and lethality issues, and so on.

The purpose of a differential diagnosis is to identify traits that would seem to clearly predict failure in 12-step spiritual healing, regardless of the setting, as well as traits that would present serious obstacles to cognitive behavioral therapy as in Rational Recovery. There are two ways to tell if a chemically dependent person is a candidate for a given therapeutic approach: (1) a history of recidivism in that approach, and (2) the client's answers to our questions. There is no reason why we should not ask a patient if he or she believes in God, especially when this element represents one of the central differences between AA and RR.

It is vital and proper to inform the client of the treatment proposed before asking him or her to consent to it. A copy of the 12-steps of Alcoholics Anonymous may be presented to the client, and he may be frankly asked, "What do you think of this way of handling your problems with alcohol? Is there anything about it that you find hard to understand? Do you disagree with any of the ideas here?" If the client expresses no objections, but has previous unsuccessful experiences with AA, it is fair to ask, "Why did you leave AA the last time? Was there something you didn't like? Were you able to use the Higher

Power concept?" To these questions, many addicts will confess their faith in God and assert their willingness to pursue a spiritual awakening as a way of remaining sober. But others will let it be known that they don't want to seek spiritual goals, that they do not even know what the word *spiritual* means (nor do they want to) and that the idea of a rescuing deity for alcoholics is silly. Some may say they have no belief in God, others may say they believe in some kind of a cosmic being but choose not to drag that into these problems, and still others may say that all the religious stuff in AA bothers them. It has long been a tradition to interpret these kinds of statements as resistance to treatment, as a sign of poor motivation, of passive aggression, or an expression of one's desire to drink alcohol.

In the VIP, the client is regarded as a Very Important Person with very important opinions. Assertions of doubt and skepticism are the basic strengths upon which RR builds a sober life. Rather than suggesting that the client had better "come around" to the theistic AA viewpoint, VIP treatment staff *commend* 12-step-resistant clients for exercising critical judgement and advise them that they are well-suited for RR, wherein they will be encouraged to turn that critical energy inward on specific ideas and beliefs that are causing and perpetuating chemical dependency.

Clinical Protocol for the Daily RR Group Sessions

I. The therapist shall have a working knowledge of rational-emotive therapy, preferably gained from university training in cognitive-behavioral methods, through the Institute for Rational-Emotive Therapy (IRET), or through RRS-sponsored consultation or inservice training. When no staff person is qualified in the above ways, the RR therapist may be recruited from the community for part-time or full-time responsibilities. RRS and IRET may be of assistance in identifying or recommending such personnel. Paraprofessional counselors may conduct some, but not all, daily sessions in conjunction with qualified supervision as above.

II. A group session will be held twice each day, one in the morning for sixty minutes and one in the afternoon or evening for ninety minutes. The AM session will contain specific information about RET provided in didactic fashion by the therapist. These sessions will focus on an issue selected by the therapist and there will be opportunity for patient participation with illustrations, specific exercises, questions and answers. The PM meeting, which is longer is unstructured and spontaneous with the therapist interjecting lines of rational thought and managing the group therapeutic process. The RR therapist will meet with each patient individually at least once during the hospital stay, but more frequently as clinically indicated.

200

III. The following patient/therapist dialog illustrates one of the central therapeutic interventions in Rational Recovery. It is as fundamental to a rational recovery from substance abuse as the "higher power" concept is to the 12-step program. Shown below is the introduction of the "Beast" concept. The patient's early progress and uplifted feelings are typical in RR.

T: So, who's been thinking about drinking?

P: My name is John and I'm and alcoholic...

T: John, would it be OK if we think of you as a person who is alcohol dependent?

P: What's the difference? I mean I really *am* an alcoholic, aren't I? How else could I get into this hospital? Besides, in AA you've *got* to say you're an alcoholic or you're in denial.

T: It's a label. I don't see how you can be an alcoholic when you're really a human being. If you had a broken leg, would you say, "Hi, I'm John, and I'm a fracture?"

P: No, but I might say I'm an amputee.

T: What would that say about you?

P: It would say that I have a leg missing.

T: Who would care? And wouldn't it be pretty obvious anyhow?

P: We say we are "alcoholic" to mean that we can't drink, no matter what.

T: And you'd say you are an "amputee" to say you can't walk?

P: Wait a minute. I *know* I'm an alcoholic! It took years for me to finally admit it. Now you say I'm not. I came here for help with my alcoholism, and you seem to be saying I'm not even an alcoholic.

T: What I think isn't as important as what you think, John. You've been telling yourself you're an alcoholic for years, and for years you've been coming through this program about every twelve months. Something's not working for you, and that's why you've been assigned to the RR track this time. Tell me, what does it mean to be an alcoholic, except that you can't handle alcohol.

P: It means there are times when no human power can stop me from drinking. At those times I'm just powerless over alcohol and I drink, and then I continue to drink until I'm way down, like I am now.

T: So, if no human power can stop you from drinking, what is there to stop you?

P: That's where I have the problem. The higher power. Mine comes and goes. I think I have it, and then I don't. I've got to get my Higher Power together so I can get on with my life. I can't go on this way; it's too painful to...

T: Tell us more about the higher power.

P: Well, the second step, after you admit that you're powerless over alcohol, is to start believing that a higher power, something greater that the individual person, can give the strength to stay sober. (pause)

T: And...

P: And I can't get it together. To tell the truth, I don't believe in God — I mean I can *pretend* to believe in something out there that's interested in me — but then a voice comes on and says, "Aw, come on, John. It's phony. You're making it up and you know it isn't real". And then it's over and I'm all by myself again and then I get real depressed and really get a desire to get drunk. I have tried to meditate and even pray to get into the higher power but all the time I seem to know that when I think I'm getting in touch with some entity or power I'm just making it up myself, so then there *isn't* any higher power. It's just me. You don't know the trouble I've gone to, reading the "Big Book" and the Bible and praying and going to the step meetings and everything. I want it, but I just can't get it. I'm ready to give up.

T: Good.

P: What? Good that I feel like giving up? Oh, you mean surrender. Like to a higher power.

T: No. I mean giving up on the higher power stuff.

P: But if I'm an alcoholic and powerless, something has to be there.

T: It's you! *Just* you, John. AA is fine for some folks, John, but you've shown that it isn't for you. And you say it here. You don't believe in a higher power because you can't. So we're going to put you in the driver's seat. You can get sober with no higher power. Just you. And it's not that hard, either. Here's how it goes.

There isn't any medical disease called alcoholism. An alcoholic is just a person who *thinks* a certain way. But we do know that you are alcohol dependent, which only means that you depend on alcohol in order to cope with anxiety, frustration, boredom and the old feeling of "just wanting a drink". When you drink you feel you need more and more and then your judgement goes bad and you drink until you're way down. That's the condition of alcohol dependence, and although there isn't a lab test available now, it looks like your body is alcohol dependent. Calling your alcohol dependence a disease doesn't mean you are powerless, or in need of external controls or moral betterment. The status of "disease" simply recognizes that you have a serious *medical condition* with implications (etiology, demography, pathology, diagnosis, therapy) that can be understood from a scientific, physiological viewpoint. That is a far cry from your version of "the disease of alcoholism." When you're not drinking, John, you're not much different from people without a drinking problem. You have the same feelings, the same frustrations, and the same desires as anyone else. Lots of people want what they can't have, but you have a special

202

problem because you believe you are powerless and can't say no to booze.

P: That's the biggest single problem in my life. I think all of my troubles start with that.

T: That's right! You think! And that's how you can get better. By thinking!

P: But that's supposed to be the cause of my trouble, that I want to think too much and figure things out and be in control of everything — including my drinking.

T: It might seem a little late to be saying this, John, but you've been right about a lot of things all along. You've been right to think as you do, and to doubt as you do, and to want to be in control of your life. But it's time now for you to see why you relapse over and over, so you can stay as sober as you want.

P: If I could do that I'd be better.

T: Right. And here's how it is. You think, up in your head, right?

P: Right. I think, therefore I am. Descartes...

T: And what do you think about your drinking alcohol?

P: No way. It's death.

T: But, do you always think this way?

P: Well, not really. Sometimes I think I'd like to drink. And it seems like a good idea at the time. I don't know what comes over me.

T: Nothing comes over you, John. It's just you, thinking another thought — a stupid thought. Sometimes you think drinking is a bad idea, like now, and sometimes you think drinking is a good idea, like just before you relapse. Right?

P: Right, but so?

T: So, we can see that after all these years of rehab and all the programs you are still quite ambivalent about drinking. In other words, you have two opposite ideas about drinking at the same time — all the time.

P: Mmm... Well, maybe you can say that. I guess I do think about drinking in different ways at different times.

T: Fine. Now, when you think anything, what do you hear, up in your head.

P: Hear? You mean my thoughts?

T: Of course. What do you hear?

P: I hear my own voice, thinking.

T: Yes, even as we talk right here, you are talking to yourself up in your head, making comments to yourself, and when you talk, you are really thinking out loud.

P: I follow you.

T: So when you think about drinking, like it would be a bad idea to drink alcohol, you hear your own voice saying, "No way; it's death".

P: But when I'm home with nothing to do, the same voice says, "You need a drink, John. It's time to go have a few".

T: And here you have it! That is the voice that destroys you every time, John, the voice that tells you to drink. And that is not the same voice that is the sane you, the voice that tries to keep you out of trouble, and the voice that wants good things in life. The voice that tells you to have a drink is the voice of your appetite for alcohol, and it's a powerful voice in your case because you're alcohol dependent. It's a biologically-driven voice that wants booze all the time and waits for any opportunity to get you to go get booze, and it doesn't give a damn what happens as long as it gets booze. This voice, John, has a primitive, animal quality, and for that reason we often call it by a name, so we can learn to recognize it and get it under control. We call it the Beast voice, because it is so powerful and cunning at times.

P: You mean it's my thinking that's been getting me into trouble?

T: Exactly, and this is exactly the point of everything we've been talking about. When you get this straight you will have very little trouble resisting the impulse to drink. From now on, you will have a very different task than before, and that is learning to think about what you think. Your Beast voice is with you all the time, but you also have another voice, a rational one, that wants you to abstain from alcohol and get on with a better life. By working hard in this group and then sticking with the outpatient RR group for a while, you may be able to close the book on your so-called alcoholism. We will be helping you to make your rational voice, the voice of *you*, the stronger one, so that it can overpower the Beast when it rears its ugly, thirsty head. From, now on, any time you think of drinking alcohol, you will know that you are dealing with something that is dangerous and *not really you* — a Beast that can ruin and even end your life. Do you see this?

P: Yes. I can see it well, and all of a sudden I feel like I have some hope of getting better.

The Role of the Family in VIP

In contrast with traditional approaches, family members are not viewed as afflicted with some illness or adjustment disorder stemming from having a chemically dependent family member. Because they may have purposely or unwittingly enabled the addict to use or drink prior to hospitalization, family counseling sessions may address these issues. The idea that the family is "codependent," however, does not apply in the rational context. Instead, families who are emotionally entangled with their chemically dependent relative are viewed as being *so dependent* that they are unable to function in their own or anyone else's best interests. Accordingly, they are helped through direct one-to-one RET counseling to start thinking, emoting, and acting more independently of their alcoholic spouses or relatives.

Suggestions for Rational Milieu Therapy

Rational-Emotive Therapy With Alcoholics and Other Substance Abusers, by Albert Ellis, Ph.D., et.al., includes a chapter on RET in the therapeutic community that provides some excellent examples of RET in structured residential programs. Generally, the hospital milieu is regarded as consisting of many consecutive activating events ("A's") that lead to the emotional consequences and behavioral consequences ("eC's" and "bC's"). These C's become the grist for endless therapeutic interventions by alert staff members who can help the patient identify the specific beliefs ("B's") that are causing dysfunctional emotions and behavior. Staff can learn to help the patient to dispute (D) the iB's that are causing emotions such as anger, guilt, and depression (eC's) with the understanding that those emotions are high risk factors that predispose one to relapse (bC). The more immediately a rational intervention is made when a patient is upset or acting self-defeatingly the more therapeutic it will be.

Examples:

The patient is withdrawn, quiet and passive (bC) on the unit. Upon questioning she may reveal shyness and anxiety (eC) about talking to strangers. The staff person may suggest that she is now sober but when intoxicated may be the life of the party. Her irrational belief (iB) is probably that she needs love and approval to feel worthwhile and therefore fears rejection. The staff person may ask why she is frightened of the opinions of strangers and encourage her to take the risk of rejection. If the patient is unable the staff person may notify the RR therapist of this dysfunctional ward behavior, for further consideration in the daily RR group session.

Advertising to humanist alcoholics and addicts

It is known that many chemically dependent people resist entering hospital-based care because they do not care for traditional programming. This is especially true of persons who whom previous inpatient care was unsuccessful, and who now are candidates for further inpatient treatment. Reaching these consumers is difficult because program content is rarely an element in commercial advertising of health care services; medical advertising focuses on "before and after" rather than on the treatment itself.

However, the treatment of chemical dependency is less technical than, say, treatment of affective or psychotic conditions, and the consuming public is quite aware of the content of most alcoholism treatment programs, i.e., 12-step therapy, as endlessly depicted in media. In this respect, advertising for the rational alternative differs from traditional approaches also, and can be done in a straightforward, yet tasteful and appropriate, fashion. The following messages will get the point across without raising ideas of faddishness or suggesting that traditional programs are deficient.

- When all else fails, we try something different — different and effective!
- We would never skin a cat, but we know there are different ways to do it. Smith Hospital has a two-track inpatient program. If one doesn't fit you, then the other one will.
- America has a two-party system — why shouldn't a recovery program offer a choice?
- Are alcoholics really powerless? It doesn't really matter at Smith Hospital. We help them stay sober either way.
- (Picture of distressed man or woman.) "I've tried and tried, but I just can't get it together". Smith Hospital has a new recovery program just for you. It's really different.
- Custom-made Sobriety. We know that people are different. That's why Smith Hospital has two very different alcoholism recovery programs. We are leaders in the field. You are the winner.
- (Picture of a bartender mixing a drink in a shaker, with customer slumped over the bar, obviously drunk)) Q: What do you get when you mix the old and the new? A: An even better recovery program. Smith Hospital builds on traditional excellence by adding something new — the option of Rational Recovery
- (picture of a hand grasping a liquor bottle) HOLD IT! If you've been holding off doing something about your drinking problem because you've already been through some treatment, think again. Smith Hospital now offers Rational Recovery in addition to its excellent 12-step program. It's like starting over.

Your community relations department and other media personnel can undoubtedly do much better than the above examples, and they will immediately grasp that introducing RR to the community is an exciting professional adventure.

Chapter 12

Some Common Objections to Rational Recovery

AA has a tradition of not venturing critical opinions about other approaches and organizations, of remaining neutral on all issues and presenting a positive alternative for alcoholics who want help. You, on the other hand, seem to do a lot of AA bashing. You talk about AA almost as much as you do about your own alternative, RR. Wouldn't it be better to just describe RR as you see it and leave AA out of it?

People who are interested in RR have almost invariably been to AA and are discouraged in their attempts to overcome chemical dependence. Rational Recovery is more than an alternative to AA — it is the *counterpoint*. AA's "losers" are our winners. In order to reach our segment of the population, it is necessary to discuss current practices in the field of chemical dependence. AA has been all that is in practice, and perhaps it is a burden of their success that in order for one to critique current practices it is necessary for critics to focus on 12-stepism. If I were promoting a three-pronged widget when everyone was accustomed to a two-pronged widget, I would first point out the problems and limitations inherent with the current device. *The Small Book* is titled to be immediately associated with "The Big Book" of Alcoholics Anonymous. It is vital that alcoholics who are considering getting help know that there is more than one way to skin a cat and — just as there are differences among people — there are different ways to achieve a durable sobriety. Rational-emotive therapy (RET) is an irrationality-bashing approach to mental health, and members of RR attack irrationalities in themselves and others as a matter of survival. In our discussion of the 12-steps, we can see that Rational Recovery is not so much another creed, or set of prescribed beliefs, but rather a way of thinking, or reasoning, as opposed to believing. For people starting out on the road to recovery, there are choices to be made, and it is best that they be made as early as possible.

RR and AA say about the opposite thing on many central questions in the same way that the Republicans and Democrats disagree. The message of RRS is, "Take sides!" The choice is between "To overcome my compulsive drinking problem, I will choose to become more faithful to a rescuing deity, God, and more dependent on a recovery group," on one hand, and "I will do better by becoming more rational and independent of others," on the other. There is too much at stake to be in the middle of the road on recovery issues. There is a great need for healthy competition between the ideologies of AA and RR, so that those in need can shop and compare, and so that when one reaches an impasse in one program there is a better alternative than the corner bar. Since "The Big Book" includes an entire derisive chapter about "agnostics" as a way to argue its case for faithfulness to God, *The Small Book* makes frequent mention of the irrationalities contained in the widely accepted AA model. That seems fair enough.

In the disciplines of theology, humanity is divided into the elect and the reprobate, those worthy of special advantages in this and/or other lives, and those who are less worthy and condemned to suffer misfortune. The elect are those who endorse or have faith in God and follow His instructions; they are eligible for supernatural aid in daily living, including character repairs, enhanced intuitions, and infusions of fine moods. The reprobates are those who refuse to believe in God or carry out His instructions; they are subject to the laws of probability and chance, which are said to run counter to the interests of human happiness. The expected result for atheists, agnostics, and other reprobates, according to theology, is suffering and death. Although it is said that God is an "equal opportunity" deity — anyone can believe in him and qualify for benefits — many find it impossible to do so by reason of never having heard of God, or by reason of intellectual disability, such as when one is *unable* to believe in God. People with this "disability" (such as this author) are "spiritually deficient" and firmly convinced that they can *see through* theology; they tend to require that their beliefs be as closely aligned with objective reality as possible. Other than as a word naming a type of ethnic music, the word "spiritual" has no meaning to them. When the word "spiritual" is explained to them by others, these spiritually deficient people often say, "Oh, you mean happy and fascinated with life!"

But perhaps this objection is really an objection to irreverence toward God, cautioning that a non-theistic or humanistic approach should "tone it down" so as to avoid being tasteless or offending those who do believe. If so, we had better acknowledge that there are millions who cannot be helped by AA precisely because they can *see through* the religiosity therein. This book is written specifically for them, just as the "Big Book" is aimed at those who are in the market for spiritual healing. *The Small Book* is an affirmation for AA refuseniks, and it is a vindication for those who have had their personal objections to religiosity discounted at AA meetings. It is also their guide to recovery from a life-threatening condition. By obtaining appropriate help, they may learn that abstaining from intoxicants is far less difficult than it is commonly made out to be.

The Higher Power controversy has more to do with semantics than theology. There are lots of humanists, atheists, and agnostics who find help in AA. The "Higher Power" is your gut instinct, your voice within, your intuition, your inner self, anything you want it to be.
If the Higher Power has more to do with semantics than with theology, as you say, then for God's sake, *why don't you get rid of it?* It is the chief reason that the majority of people leave your program, continue their addictions, and cause great harm to others and themselves. Of course, you *can't* get rid of it, because it's there, and the best you can do is apologize for it or explain the God part away. I sincerely hope that you will recognize that there is no longer a need (except possibly a personal one of your own) to provide HP-resistant clients a special education that translates the palpably religious into something vaguely secular and just as vaguely helpful.

RR is unproven, and it has no recovery statistics to prove it's any good. It's just a new theory you've made up, and it's irresponsible. It'll just make recovering AA members start doubting and some of them will begin to drink again.
If *The Small Book* is all that it takes to cause a recovering person to have a downfall, we should be *doubly* glad to have it in print. If a recovering alcoholic has serious doubts about AA after a lengthy immersion in it, then he or she is probably in the wrong program, and RR would probably be preferable to continuing on such thin ice.

RR is not new; it is another application of rational-emotive therapy (RET), developed by Albert Ellis, Ph.D. RET is a cognitive-behavioral (thinking) approach to self-help that is naturally and ideally suited to the problems of addiction. Cumulative evidence collected on RET over the last twenty-five years confirms that it is at least one of the best ways to bring about desired personal change, especially in the case of compulsive and mood disorders. A longitudinal study by the National Institute for Mental Health in 1985 found that the cognitive-behavioral approach is just as effective as antidepressant medication in the primary treatment of depressive disorders in adults. Rational Recovery is in itself a research model because data on participants is routinely gathered for later analysis. Most substance abusers are quite satisfied with confidentiality and are willing to share their experiences with researchers.

The "Horse Race" Error
Some people would like to see comparative statistics showing how well RR stacks up against AA. That is usually the case when people

ask, "Do you have any recovery statistics?" The assumption here is that,"If there is one approach that will do better than the other for a general population, then that program is superior and is the best one for anyone to use". In other words, "I want the fastest horse". Public officials also make this error when they say that AA has helped more people than any other method, or make even more embarrassing or bizarre statements like the one given by the executive vice-president of the Betty Ford Center on 7/23/90 to the Desert Sun newspaper in Palm Springs, "If you do not participate in a 12-step program, your chance of staying clean and sober is zero percent". This man feels as if he is mounted on Superhorse, or perhaps on the only horse in the universe.

The fallacy here can be seen in comparing recovery programs to life-sustaining, human blood. Could we pose the question, "What is the best type of human blood?" Of course, provided the answer is, "For whom?" Thousands of people will confirm that AA is a wonderful program that hits the mark for them, but even more will reject that approach. The latter represent a huge subtype of substance abuser that requires a rational mode of recovery as much as any patient requires a transfusion of his or her own blood type.

For these reasons, RRS does not engage in comparative statistics as a way of showing that RR is as good or better than other approaches. When we state numbers showing poor performance of 12-step programs, it is for the purpose of identifying the desperate need that RR-type people have for a change of programs. Some may also leave RR and continue with AA, as their judgements suggest.

Not only is the 12-step program inadequately researched after fifty years of widespread use, but in and of itself it is an impediment to scientific inquiry. The few figures available indicate that AA produces dismal recovery rates, with 50 percent of new members quitting (relapsing) within 30 days, 75 percent within one year, and 90 percent within four years. If there had been a two-party service delivery system in recent years (AA/RR), so that people could gravitate toward their *treatment of choice*, the overall recovery rate would likely have been far better. At present, the alternative to AA most everywhere is still the corner bar.

AA in its present monopoly accepts everyone, regardless of viewpoint. One size fits all, as some mistakenly say. RR, for now caters to persons who already reject AA, so the RR participants are not a random sample of chemically dependent people. AA carries an unfair burden in trying to be all things to all people. With RR finally in place, increasing numbers of AA newcomers will be there as a matter of choice and will not have to go through "denial hazing" in order to gain status in the group. With a two-party service delivery system in place, it would seem that recovery statistics will *improve* for AA, because fewer people will enter the 12-step program who are poor candidates for spiritual healing in the first place. This is one of the intrinsic beauties of pluralism. Both RR and AA can have their share of failure and success stories. Many chemically dependent people will not be helped by either approach; substance abuse is a serious, life-threatening condition.

At the end of *The Small Book* is a Confidential Registry (Appendix A), inviting readers to participate in a descriptive study of their positive and negative recovery experiences. Registrants are not anonymous, but they *are* held in the highest confidence, just as they would be in any other professional health care program.

It's unfair to suggest that anyone can get better through RR with only *The Small Book*. It takes more than reading a book to get better from alcoholism. There is no network of RR groups, and AA is everywhere.

Because there is such a heavy emphasis in RR on independence, some people may find *The Small Book* an adequate reference with which to establish sobriety. Let's not discount the strengths that some people, however many, may have. RRS receives calls from people who live in wilderness and other remote areas where there are no people to form a recovery group. Should we assume that these people are doomed to endless self-sousing? RRS also receives many letters and Confidential Questionnaires from people who got better only after quitting AA. But realistically, most substance abusers will probably do *better* with a recovery group.

There actually is a resource in virtually every community for alcoholics who object to AA spiritual healing. I am speaking of the university-trained psychologists, social workers, nurses, physicians, and counselors who have an understanding or working knowledge of RET. With publication of *The Small Book*, professionals are notified that provision of direct care for alcoholism is not only within their expertise, but also an emerging professional responsibility. Alcohol dependent persons or their friends or family can help by recommending or giving a copy of *The Small Book* to professionals they trust. Many professionals in agencies or private practice will accept alcoholic clients, and some may act as Advisors to RR groups, free of charge, in addition to providing individual rational-emotive therapy consultations.

Another obvious resource is Alcoholics Anonymous, where one may go for specific reasons even though one may not accept the guiding principles of the 12-step program. You can learn much vital information about abstaining from alcohol, and AA provides a social outlet with people who don't drink. When you hear all the talk about powerlessness, be careful you don't come to accept that part unless you really believe that a rescuing deity will come to your aid. And, finally, when you're ready to leave the group, leave, regardless of predictions of dire consequences. You may very well relapse, but it won't be because you're powerless. It will be because you very stupidly decided to drink or use drugs again. Then, you may recover once again, selfishly, guiltlessly, and probably very quickly.

By concentrating on the addict's irrational thinking, you're just playing into the trap of believing that the alcoholic can be in control, and needs only to try to figure things out to get better. The addict's best thinking got him where he is — in big trouble! RR is just more "stinkin' thinkin'" and you're actually encouraging the very cause of addictive behavior and lifestyle.

The addict's thinking didn't entirely cause the addiction, but it does *sustain* it. Alcohol plus many biological and social conditions did that. Recovery, however, is exceedingly difficult if the addict is vulnerable to frequent mood swings and thinks these variations of emotion are being caused by external events or other people. Not realizing that he is already controlling his own emotions with his angry demands that reality "shape up," he will struggle for control over others, as a way of protecting himself against further negative emotions — emotions he is already causing himself. RR teaches the chemically dependent people that they are already in control and can effect enormous changes in how they emote and behave in the future. Rational people, for example, can easily avoid guilt altogether, as a matter of principle, and they can minimize other negative emotions by cautiously monitoring and modulating their negative evaluations of virtually any discomfort, frustration or disappointment that may occur. Recovery, then, is within the grasp of any addict who will discover within himself the irrational ideas that hold him captive to the illusion of external control. He can then, literally, *think himself sober.*

The expression, "stinkin' thinkin'" stems from the contempt with which many in 12-step programs regard the human intellect. Faith and reason are diametrically opposed to each other, and each forms the philosophical basis for AA and RR, respectively. The intellect distinguishes humans from lower creatures more than any other attribute. To paraphrase Robert Ingersoll, the American patriot who championed reason over faith last century, "reason is sometimes a flickering, feeble light, blown by the winds of emotion and tested by the darkness of fear, but it's the only light there is. If we can just make our way by holding that flame ahead, placing one foot before the other, then each step will land on solid ground and our progress will lead us toward higher and higher planes". We are all capable of believing and feeling that we are worthy, decent people simply because we are human and capable of making that assertion. Guilt is just the opposite belief, that we are unworthy, tainted, evil, in need of redemption through submission to penance or a higher authority. When one of us comes to "see through" theology as little more than a human-worth rating scheme with the effect of perpetual dependency, we are then ready to become the final authorities on the question of our individual worth. Thus, we may become self-liberated from the opinions, approval, acceptance, and yes, sometimes even the love of others. What a pleasant irony it is that the less we need the love and approval of others, the more it tends to come our way!

You are correct, that the alcoholic's best thinking got him into where he is, if you mean "in need of help". *But look at the mess his thinking is in!*

But look at what a mess he'll become as a so-called "rational thinker". Won't the sober NHP addict become a cold, unfeeling, remote kind of person, with no depth, no compassion, no sensitivity, no real appreciation of life?

If you were to become less angry, less guilty, and love the living thing you are, would you become that kind of person? To the contrary, you would be considerably more free to vitally engage yourself in human affairs, especially since the stakes involved in rejection or failure have been greatly lowered. Since your rational self-esteem is a constant, independent from the love and approval of others, you will finally be able to concentrate on loving rather than being loved, and on caring rather than being cared for. The sweetness of loving and caring comes not from the moral thrill of demonstrating such noble attitudes, but from the intrinsic "kick" inherent in those involvements. Rational people understand that the only good is human happiness, and that one fine way to gain happiness is by helping others to be happy too.

Remember that the word "emotive" in rational-emotive therapy is there for a good reason. In RR, we learn to have *more* emotions than before — and more of the emotions we really *want* to have! When we discover how to reduce or eliminate the ugly feelings that blot out human happiness, we find exactly the *opposite* qualities you have listed in this objection.

Everyone knows that recovering alcoholics must lead a life of spiritual growth or face the increasing probability of relapsing. Being non-spiritual, RR sounds like a quick fix, one that will likely deteriorate with time. One's life loses meaning when it has no connection to higher truths.

It may interest some to speak of "rational spirituality," but that would be irrational. In truth, "rational spirituality" is an oxymoron, the joining of two words that contradict each other. However, there is a corresponding zone of experience for both "rational" and "spiritual" people which, if properly understood, can create a sense of unity among former drunks and addicts of different persuasions. I am speaking of a subjective sense of well-being — the feeling that life, in spite of its difficulties, is essentially good and therefore worth living vigorously, even with excitement and fascination. To borrow a term from psychiatry, "euthymia" describes a person meaningfully engaged in life, pursuing self-defined goals, and gaining satisfaction from his or her own efforts. Please remember that rational thinking *by definition* leads one to self-gratification, toward the achievement of all the good things and personal pleasures that are possible in one's lifetime. These pleasures include intellectual adventure, voluntary love relationships, political intrigue, social frolicking, sexual strivings, cultural and artistic indulgences, and philosophical musings. While the addict weasels out his daily short-range hedonism, the sober NHP person concentrates his energy on long-range hedonism, or pleasure fulfillment.

Ultimately, however, one's beliefs about spirits, God, and religion in general are matters that are separate from Rational Recovery. Some of our professional Advisors are themselves religious, in the sense that they believe in God or Jesus and attend worship services and belong to churches. Although these people are theists, they remark that RET is so self-forgiving and other-forgiving that RR is quite congruent with their personal brands of religion. So RR is not interested in having people give up any of their religious beliefs; it's just none of our business what people believe about gods and saints. The only exception here, of course, is when one is *depending* on a rescuing deity in order to remain sober. If that is one's preference, then AA is an ideal program. A common remark in RR meetings is, "Please check your religion at the door. It'll be there when you leave".

I have a desire to stop drinking, but I'm also a member of NORML (National Organization for the Reform of Marijuana Laws). I believe that pot should be legalized and, if it were, I would have no qualms about smoking it. Does this disqualify me from starting up an RR program?

The idea that, in order for a person to be a credible or productive human being, one must have a long period of abstinence from drugs or alcohol is another overgeneralization from 12-step ideology. It is based on the idea that if you use or even abuse chemicals you are "diseased". While substance users and abusers may sometimes be *less* credible and *less* productive than they would be clean and sober, that does not discount their other strengths and potential contributions they may make. Some RRS Coordinators, like you, have started up an

214

RR group as a creative way of getting proper care for their addictions. One such Coordinator in Maryland was denied the use of an agency-based meeting room for RR meetings because he had *only* six months of abstinence.

As for your desire to use marijuana in the future, it sounds as if you don't feel well enough to be satisfied drug-free, and are therefore polydrug dependent. This may be caused by your current use of the central nervous system depressant, alcohol. Be that as it may, RR encourages members to make decisions for themselves and not others. Substance abusers who currently drink or use drugs are welcome in RR, for as long as they choose to involve themselves. RR is an abstinence program, and although it is possible that you may continue to use chemicals with few ill effects, the program doesn't *support* the goal of moderate drug or alcohol *dependence*. We regard abstinence as a better bet, much easier than continued efforts to moderate, and one that feels better. The human body seems to run best on its own chemicals unless there is some chemical imbalance that indicates the need for prescribed medication.

It sounds so coarse to say that rational people are hedonists, interested only in pleasure. Isn't self-centeredness the chief character defect that AA helps alcoholics overcome?

Yes it is. Pity! We are indeed self-centered and selfish. In fact, those of us who are sober NHP are so selfish that we stubbornly refuse to drink, even when our internalized addict voices beg and beg for alcohol or drugs. We remember how intellectually dead we were when we were drunk, and we remember well how withdrawn from politics and human affairs we had become. We remember the pointlessness of sex and the flatness of music and art that our use of drugs brought to us, and most of all we remember the awkward numbness with which we drenched ourselves just to be able to say hello to strangers. Because we have but one short life to live we want to cram as much fun and pleasure into it as possible. With alcohol, our pleasure quickly and without fail dissolves to pain. Greedy, however, we are not, for the following reasons: (1) Greed breeds retaliation in others, and what rational person wants that? (2) Excesses of any kind tend to drain one's health, something else no rational person wants. (3) Greed establishes itself as a norm in our immediate social sphere, and what rational person wants to live in that kind of environment? We call our selfishness "enlightened self-interest," and we understand that we each have a responsibility to ourselves that exceeds all others. Although we get a kick out of helping others, we are not altruistic. The good some of us may perform for others springs from our human nature. We have no overriding sense of duty, nothing to prove.

Rational Recovery seems to focus mainly on the alcoholic. What about the family? Aren't they sick, too? If the codependents don't change, won't the alcoholic be forced to return to addiction?

It would be nice if the term "codependent" were dropped immediately from the vocabulary of professional people (or perhaps replaced with yet another neologism, "comiserant"). The term "codependency" has yet to be properly defined, and even its origin is in doubt. By dropping the prefix, co- we are left with the more familiar term dependency, which, in its many forms, is the chief villain in chemical dependency. Originally, codependency just referred to the fact that it's tough living with a drunk. It's tough because a family is a balanced system, and when one member is "out of it," the rest suffer alienation, anxiety, rejection, and sometimes fear of violence or abandonment. Al-Anon emerged to meet family members' needs, which it did nicely for a while, but later, in the 1980s, the codependency craze caught on, and so did the idea that codependency is a *progressive disease* that is aggravated by living with an alcoholic, a disease that needs treatment as provided by the thousands of Adult Children of Alcoholics (ACOA) groups and codependency groups that have sprung up all over the nation. The premise here is that virtually everybody suffers this disease, but adults who had an alcoholic parent can trace their present disturbances to their unhappy childhoods — a distinctly irrational idea. By joining an ACOA group, one can come to grips with one's "codependency" and presumably get more good out of life, but there is much wheel-spinning and time-wasting as members recount endless examples of childhood deprivations. The problems addressed in these auxiliary 12-step groups are just the same as anyone else's and the solutions are remarkably the same for all of us, ACOA or not. Oddly enough, the expression, *"adult children* of alcoholics" may very well frame the problem in a highly constructive way, if the reader's sense of irony is intact.

What do the codependency groups offer those who believe their adult lives are being ruined by a history of familial alcoholism? You guessed it. Membership in a codependency group is essentially the same as membership in any other AA group, except that now more groups are run by "professional" 12th-steppers who teach ACOA's and so-called codependents how to "work the program". Since the symptoms of codependency number in the hundreds, just about anyone can be considered a codependent. The "treatment" is to trust in God, pray to God for character repairs, do a fearless moral inventory, confess, make amends to people you may have offended, make another fearless moral inventory, pray, meditate — and so on for the rest of your life.

RR was originally not greatly involved with the families of alcoholics, taking the position that rational sobriety does not depend on families to improve or change. If the drunk becomes sober, there is a gradual and natural return to health; the family members then have an opportunity to work out their problems on their own, like any other family, or to seek professional help. We should not underestimate the capacities of people to help themselves, and it is rash to assume that because there is a recent history of chemical dependency the family is still sick and in need of outside help.

The idea that if the family does not change, the alcoholic person will be forced to return to the use of alcohol, is precisely the kind of dependency thinking that RR seeks to correct. The addict has been saying all along, "They drive me to drink. The world has to shape up for me." For us professionals to buy into that idea by painting the substance abuser's family sick is to enter into an *addictive agreement* with the alcoholic, more or less encouraging powerlessness, dependency, and helplessness. One person who attended ACOA meetings remarks, "They (ACOAs) blame their bad feelings on others and wear victimhood like a badge. It was like Whiner's Anonymous."

But in the last few years, the codependency movement has grown on the momentum of its alarmist message, so that many people are seeking a way out of uncomfortable dependencies on groups like CODA and ACOA. Because there is now sufficient interest from those people, along with many others who desire a potent self-help program for a wide variety of problems in daily living, RRS is introducing SODependence Awareness (SODA) groups, following somewhat the pattern of the chemical dependency groups.

AA has helped more people than anything else. Isn't RR a throwback to the time before AA, when people tried to control their drinking through willpower?

If we go back in history, we will find that people have been learning to abstain from harmful substances for thousands of years, largely through their wits and determination, and with severe social injunctions against irresponsible drinking or drug use. Over the centuries, far more people have probably helped themselves independently than through recovery programs. Before all the disease hype of the last few decades, stopping or reducing the use of intoxicants was seen as an unremarkable thing — just common sense and hardly worth the use of good parchment to record. Human beings have a remarkable capacity to survive through self-control — especially when they are aware of those capacities.

"Willpower" is an incomplete description of RR. We combine our desire (will) to have a better life and our native intelligence. Together, *free will* and intelligence are entirely sufficient to bring about major personal change and lifetime abstinence from intoxicants.

In 1935 the field of psychology was in its infancy and there was no such thing as rational or cognitive therapy. Freud dominated current thinking and his psychoanalytic approach has little utility for alcoholism or anything else. Albert Ellis was originally of that school but broke from it to set up a separate school of psychology. His seminal work came to fruition in the 1960's and has inspired broad changes in clinical thought ever since. Those changes have been fraught with difficulty because of the inherent contradiction of traditional values that are based on theology. Initially unwelcome by his colleagues, Dr. Ellis has attained eminence and was chosen for the 1971 Humanist of the Year Award by the American Humanist Association in addition to his many other distinctions. Rational Recovery has descended from his major contribution to the field of psychology, rational-emotive therapy.

AA has descended from an ancient tradition of worship in which man is seen as essentially helpless and in need of revealed knowledge and supernatural aid. In 1935 AA was in the right place at the right time. As a lay movement in a virtual vacuum it grew into a quasi-religious movement that today monopolizes institutional addiction care. But people are getting better from substance abuse outside AA as well. Discouraging relapse statistics for those in AA programs point to the need for a sharply contrasting alternative. Now RR is joining in with AA to serve our diverse population of alcohol dependent people.

You seem to be suggesting that alcoholics can go on "autopilot" and develop a casual attitude toward their life-threatening condition. Isn't that inviting disaster? Aren't the cemeteries filled with alcoholics who smugly thought they were finally on top of their addictive process?

Considering that the majority of those who try AA reject it out of hand because of its spiritualism and unbending demands for perpetual dependency, it would seem that alcoholics die in largest numbers when there is no acceptable care available to them. If one deeply believes that he is incapable of resisting the desire to drink, as he is told over and over in spiritual healing programs, the prophecy can be self-fulfilling.

Let us consider someone who is severely allergic to milk products but also extremely fond of milkshakes. He might feel ambivalent about indulging in that treat, but the central lesson for him would be, "If I want to feel well and live a longer time, milkshakes aren't for me". His appetite could lead him to experiment with drinking tiny milkshakes, but with painful experience he would likely sacrifice short-range pleasure for the longer-term goal of fun, health and survival. He will *never forget* that for him milkshakes are poison. Being human, though, he *might* one day get depressed and self-destructively have a milkshake. If he survives the allergic reaction he would be wise to get relevant help so that he is not vulnerable to self-destructive moods.

But can an *alcoholic* get his alcoholism behind him and get on with a normal life? Or is he living on a narrow ledge of sanity awaiting to be swept off by a whim into the abyss below? Must he, even after years of sobriety, constantly remind himself of the terrors of addiction and structure his personal and social life around the avoidance of alcohol?

As one who has faced this prospect, I can report that addiction, including the consequence of death, appeared to be a reasonable alternative to a life defined this way. When the requirements of the universal spiritual healing program were made clear to me, I knew that, drunk or sober, I would have to die if my only help would come from a Higher Power. Addiction and death seemed a reasonable alternative to committing my remaining years to an organization of persons engaged in an endless struggle to remain sober.

Of course alcoholics can learn the simple lesson to abstain, and then make the decision stick, year after year, without constant vigilance, daily ritual, prayer, or viewing themselves as somehow handicapped in life. People do it every day, yet they are even more anonymous than Alcoholics Anonymous. Though these self-inspired abstainers are not paid attention in the media, they are probably the true heroes of the human struggle against addiction. They show that ordinary people, given the opportunity, are quite capable of learning and remembering a simple lesson — if you can't handle the booze, knock it off.

Rational Recovery, a vehicle for self-inspired, no-higher-power sobriety, is the thinking man's solution to the drinking man's problem. The personal changes brought about in RR are about as deep as one can go, for they address the fundamental rules of life, and the basic assumptions about human nature. The phases of Rational Recovery are (1) recognition of alcohol dependence, (2) decision that the consequences of that dependency are unacceptable, (3) withdrawal, (4) stabilization and relapse management (a period of adapting to life without alcohol — about six to twelve months — when new learning is critical), (5) consolidation of gains and relapse management (reaping the benefits of sobriety — social, financial, emotional, intellectual, physical, sexual, vocational, etc.), another year or so, and, finally (6) autopilot, or the time when you have a reasonable expectation that you are the master of your alcoholic (irrational) voices and further use of alcohol seems a remote possibility. Now it's time for your *Bar Misfit!* You're on your own and you know how you got there. There's no point in looking back; the struggle is over.

The principles of rational-emotive therapy, when finally internalized, are an *excellent* autopilot for NHP sobriety!

Chapter 13

Your Local RR Group

If you recognize that every social system that has anything to do with addiction care in America has spiritual healing as its central ingredient, then the implications of the name Rational Recovery *Systems* (RRS) will be clear. Rational Recovery Systems, an integrated auxiliary of the American Humanist Association, Amherst, NY, is a national networking, consulting and indirect services agency that provides free services to chemically dependent persons. Groups that address the problem of "fatness," or the psychological syndrome that causes and perpetuates overweight, overeating, and other eating disorders, are also forming in many cities, using the book, *Fatness: The Small Book*, by Lois Trimpey. The third RRS self-help program is SODependence Awareness (SODA) groups. SODA groups will accommodate a wide variety of persons with problems in daily living.

The long-range goal is to introduce the two-track service system into the self-help movement and then into the addiction care industry. This means that addiction care agencies, *especially publicly-supported ones*, will be increasingly obliged to simultaneously offer two programs that have conflicting ideologies — two separate tracks. Addicts and others seeking self-improvement will be accorded *informed consent to care*, as is the case in other branches of health care. Philosophical (religious) preference will be incorporated into differential diagnosis of substance abusers. In order to have social change so that rational alternatives can be offered to substance abusers, it will be necessary for helping professionals and other key persons to take sides on the issue of pluralism and act accordingly.

Recognizing that the needs of secular-minded addicts cannot be met by traditional spiritual healing programs, RRS assigns responsibility for development and implementation of self-sustaining rational recovery programs to the professional community at large. These include health care administrators, judges, attorneys, social workers, doctors, nurses, counselors, psychologists, teachers, and many others who provide public and private social and health care services. There is more to RRS than recovery groups, and those who work in the social service and health care systems can assist RR by *opening doors* for the rational alternative. To be an RR Coordinator or Advisor, you need only subscribe to *The Journal of Rational Recovery* (JRR) and communicate the kind of support you can give in a letter. Your support as a Coordinator or Advisor can be to contribute articles to JRR, give subscriptions of *JRR* to key persons in your community, or provide skilled consultation to Rational Recovery Systems as you are able. Some professional members who are qualified become RR Advisors, linked directly to local RR groups. Advisors are resource persons who are known to the local RR group by name and by telephone number. It is well-known that many substance abusers also have other conditions that require special care. Sometimes the second problem is the primary problem, as in the case of depressive illnesses or thought or behavioral disorders. Professionals can identify serious psychiatric problems such as these and save the client lots of time and suffering by promptly referring to a psychiatrist, or to a physician for evaluation of a known or suspected medical problem.

An RRS Advisor need not attend many of the twice-weekly RR meetings. The chief purposes for Advisors attending meetings are to provide occasional rational input to the group and to survey the group for unusual problems that may indicate a higher level of care. Advisors do not act as therapists or counselors to the RR group, although they are free to introduce information that is relevant to the group discussion. The chief activity at RR meetings is discussion; "cross-talk" (the interrupting of or responding to others that is forbidden in traditional 12-step meetings) is required in RR meetings. Group members refer to rational literature, learn to think rationally, and each becomes a rational counselor to himself and to others. Those attending RR meetings are not "clients" of anyone, but simply participants in an open discussion meeting.

The RR group Advisors volunteer their services to their communities during an epidemic of untreated addictive illness as an expression of their humanistic values. The rational treatment of alcoholism is free of charge, according to the self-help tradition in America.

As a consulting agency, RRS works along with any RRS Coordinator or Advisor who wants to start a recovery group anywhere. A drinking alcoholic, a doctor, a family member, or a senator can contact RRS by phone or letter and receive direct support and advice on how to proceed. This service is also without charge. Training seminars through the Institute for Rational-Emotive Therapy and RRS may be scheduled on a regional basis for RRS Coordinators, Advisors and interested professionals; for these, nominal fees may be charged for the costs of trainers, facilities, speakers, refreshments, etc.

RRS thrives on the challenge of destroying the *monopoly* of spiritual healing in addiction care and offering a highly credible and effective avenue to alcoholics and other substance abusers who sincerely want to get their chemical dependence behind them. The growth of RR since 1985 has been slow, but during 1990 our growth has been explosive due to favorable media attention. RRS is getting a solid base of experience in community development and stands as a leader in the field of self-help.

How can I help?

There are three ways you can help RRS. The first is to subscribe to *JRR*. Second, assist RRS by subscribing for someone else. It could be someone you know who continues to drink, or a family member, or it could be your doctor, an agency administrator, your assemblyman, the mayor, or anyone. The subscriber will be given your name as the giver. No "anonymous" gifts of TSB or *JRR* will be sent.

Third, and most important, you can get the ball rolling in your community for a Rational Recovery project. With outside support from RRS, it shouldn't be too difficult to have a group up and running in a short time. It will involve doing the following, after you have notified RRS by phone or mail of your intent to start up:

(1) Insert ads in the local newspaper(s). Get a reporter to write a story using RRS press materials. Seek free or low cost media.

(2) If you are not employed in the health or addiction care system, recruit an RR Advisor. Personally visit the local mental health clinic and alcoholism treatment centers. Call ahead and ask to see the agency director or the alcohol services program chief. You will be representing RRS, pointing out that many alcoholics are unserved because of the religious nature of, and dependence requirements of, AA. Offer to help get a local group started. If you are not a trained professional in addiction care, you will be asking the agency administrator to help identify someone there or in the community who would be interested in becoming an RR advisor. If the agency sees fit to reimburse the professional for the time spent on RRS activities, so much the better. That is as it should be, for the agency is supported by taxes paid in part by those who cannot or could not use the religious AA approach. If that isn't possible, ask the administrator to use personal channels of communication to recruit a volunteer advisor who will immediately get in touch with RRS by phone or mail. RRS will then provide consultation to the Advisor, and he or she may then ask for your further cooperation in developing a local RRS project. Always point out that you know there are those who will volunteer their time because that's the way many people are — they will pitch in and help when they

know more people will die if nothing is done. Stress that professionals are volunteering in other communities for this reason. If the administrator says there is already the means for serving atheists, secular humanists, Buddhists, agnostics, and others who will not avail themselves of AA, point out that AA, despite its disclaimers, cannot adequately serve them, *and that the community deserves a separate, recognized, rational alternative to spiritual healing.*

(3) You may report back to RRS and depending on the results of the first contacts a plan will be made to proceed or seek results through other agencies or channels. RRS program development is tactful, yet forceful, and we will gain a reputation for tenacity and success.

There are several factors working against RR acceptance and they are worth considering here:

(1) To support an alternative to AA is to suggest that there are some inherent weaknesses in AA. That amounts to blasphemy, for at the center of AA is God as described in the Bible. God has no inherent weaknesses. Nor do His recovery programs. In politics, blasphemy is the kiss of death, and most administrators, legislators, and elected officials know this. The more closely an "alternative" resembles AA, the more initial acceptance there will probably be within the health care establishment. RRS does not resemble AA except as an abstinence program. Some secular alternative groups that are lay led promote ideas of dependency and inherent character weakness, and do not take serious issue with the central ideas of alcoholism. They may achieve some grudging support from within the present addiction care system and be allowed to operate within the orbit of AA. It is quite important that substance abusers and professionals alike *take sides* on these basic questions. RRS occupies quite a different universe from that of AA, and is as much a professional education project as it is a grassroots lay movement.

(2) The American health care system has, in effect, taken the second of the 12-steps, which states, *"We accept that only a Higher Power can restore our patients and clients to sanity"*. AA is in; all others are out. AA and its legions of faithful who work at these recovery centers intend to keep it that way. Many health care professionals seem to have little insight into the deeply religious nature of the AA spiritual healing program. Others seem not to care. At stake are billions of dollars spent on the dissemination of spiritual teachings, especially in hospital settings.

(3) The public is not aware that all alcoholics, regardless of their religious beliefs or lack of them, are pressured into godism as part of their recovery. Nor is it generally known that an entire branch of medicine, addictionology, has been given over to a religious movement that practices faith healing and believes in divine intervention. Many

people imagine that challenges to AA are a threat to those who are dependent on the 12-steps for sobriety. Anyone so threatened would also be wise to insist on a viable alternative to spiritual healing.

(4) Many people who express agreement with you when you explain the goals of RR will later capitulate. They are fearful of retaliation by defenders of 12-stepism. Some may have good reason to fear for their jobs if they are found guilty of "the RR heresy," but most are simply conditioned to keep their mouths shut and "go with the flow".

These are powerful deterrents to any rational alternative, sure enough, but Rational Recovery has made great strides toward its goal of achieving parity with Alcoholics Anonymous. Based on the comprehensive system of rational-emotive therapy devised by Albert Ellis, RR is the *counterpoint* to the 12-steps, and will very likely emerge as the balancing factor in the recovery equation.

As you can see, RRS is a set of systems, i.e., a network of community self-help groups, a system of self-help — rational-emotive therapy, the system of professional discipline organizations, the health care system, the legal system, the family system, and the many services that RRS provides — all working together. Come aboard and work with us for a larger society of sober, rational people.

Orientation notes for Coordinators and Advisors

Your role as an RR Coordinator is to open doors for the rational alternative in your home community. In effect, you are selling a product — a social product — using known marketing techniques. Our market is the chemically dependent people who find existing addiction care programs difficult, unhelpful, or otherwise unsatisfactory. Some may come to RR as a first resort, but most will already have participated in a 12 step program of some kind. Our purpose is to first vindicate those persons who have rejected the 12 steps, and then to offer a potent means to remain sober that affirms positive human traits. The heart of RRS is the freestanding local RR group. It is an autonomous, lay-led, study and discussion group that seeks abstinent sobriety through the rational-emotive self-help method of Albert Ellis, Ph.D.

Each RR group will ideally have some qualified professional person to insure the stability of the project and to manage special problems that may develop within the group. Projects may develop, however, around one or more coordinators — activists like you who choose to work for social change. The Advisor may attend only a few meetings, and does not act in the capacity of group therapist. RR groups observe traditional values on confidentiality ("What's said here stays here") but members are free to identify themselves in public and in the media as members or associated with RR.

Anyone with a chemical dependency problem may attend RR group meetings, and the length of involvement for each member is self-determined. It should be recognized by those in attendance that recovery from alcohol dependence is a long-term project and that one's chances of continued sobriety are enhanced by continuing for upwards of a year. Persons who want to continue their involvements with RR past the first year of continuous sobriety are encouraged to refer to themselves as "recovered" and to accept some program responsibilities as agreed with the RR Advisor.

Public Relations:

To get the word out, start with your immediate sphere of influence — friends, relatives, neighbors, colleagues, acquaintances — as it seems appropriate. Then, thinking of concentric circles, see how many of them know of someone who also is interested in chemical dependency, either as a group member or as a community supporter. Be on the lookout for key people in this secondary circle, such as mayors, doctors, businessmen who may share space for a meeting room, psychologists, nurses, social workers, large employers, legislators, judges, attorneys, librarians, and the list can go on. Then, ask your contact to give that key person a call on the telephone and (1) discuss the great need for a local Rational Recovery project, (2) get some indication of commitment from the key person, and (3) make some specific arrangement for you to be in touch by phone with the key person. When you later talk with the key person, tell of your organizing efforts and ask for assistance in as direct terms as possible. For example, to a judge, explain the need for an alternative based on personal choice at the time of sentencing; to a doctor explain the need for his or her colleagues to know of a non-religious recovery program for chemical dependency; to a psychologist, nurse, or social worker explain your need for local project Advisors; to a city council member explain the need for social change so that local clinics and hospitals offer their patients a nonreligious alternative; to a librarian explain the need for information to the public that there is a highly contrasted alternative to AA; to legislators explain that public addiction programs discriminate against non-Christians and offenders are being sentenced to religious instruction; to teachers explain that many kids are turned off to AA (Alateen and 12 step recovery) because of its Sunday school vibes and will sometimes reject sound advice because of the source, and so on.

During the early 1990s, I will be traveling widely, and with sufficient notice I may be able to schedule an appearance in your community. To make the best use of my time, you will want to make arrangements with the media (talk radio, TV interview programs, and newspaper reporters) ahead of time. Media representatives may call me at RRS headquarters in Lotus, California, for telephone interviews and program information. A typical community appearance will include at least one meeting for professionals and health care administrators, and one well-advertised meeting, a lecture with questions and answers, open to the general public. If the RR project is already up and running I can sit in on a meeting and contribute some ideas I've picked up from other RR groups, and if there isn't yet a meeting going I can announce the first meeting during the public presentation.

Recovery politics

In offering a rational alternative to AA, you may get resistance and criticism from established recovery programs. Keep in mind that AA is a private organization that advocates a philosophical viewpoint from the base of clinics, agencies, and hospitals that are funded by federal, state and local tax dollars and by insurance premiums paid without regard to one's religious or philosophical preference. RRS, a private organization representing scientific rather than religious values, has as much if not more of a "right" to a full presence in publicly supported organizations as AA has.

You may hear challenges like, "AA is a proven method for recovery and that's why it is so widespread. What's the track record of RR?" You may respond with the information that AA is proven, all right, but only to be as successful as no treatment at all, and that only about 15% of those who attempt AA are sober after four years. Worse is the fact that 50% percent of newcomers drop out within 30 days, and 75% are gone and presumably still addicted within one year. The point here is not that AA is a poor program, but that there is a need for alternatives for the majority who cannot be helped in a 12 step program. What is the RR track record? As mentioned earlier, fifty percent of those discharged from a residential treatment center in Long Island (APPLE) are abstinent after 2 years, using RET as the sole base of that program. That's better than many programs, but says little about which program is better. The question is, "Better for whom?" For those who cannot believe the 12 steps, RR is *infinitely* better, and for those who insist on depending on a higher power, AA is far better than down-to-earth RR.

Still others may say, "I've read *The Small Book*, and it's critical of AA. Why can't you just go about your own business without all the AA-bashing?" Here, you may simply acknowledge that TSB does contain an aggressive critique of the 12 steps, because — and only because — they are irrational as can be. RET is an irrationality-bashing approach to mental health, and criticizing the 12 steps is a matter of life and death for many chemically dependent people. Most newcomers to RR will want to ventilate their own personal frustration with the

226

strange and sometimes offensive ways of 12 step programs, so a certain amount of AA bashing is a legitimate function of the RR program. Remember that we are vindicating those who have been subjected to a powerful, forceful ideology that demands submissiveness and confessions of sin and personal impotence. Furthermore, neither RR nor AA are polite toward the other, as reading "The Big Book" will show; there is an ideological chasm between the two programs that is best not bridged. Since its inception in 1936, AA has been relentless and merciless in its attacks on humanistic values. Recovery in AA is largely a conversion to the spiritual values of surrender and faith, while in RR, recovery is an assertion of independence and a matter of learning to apply reason — to think rationally about oneself and the use of intoxicants. With RR now available in your community, the wages of "sin" (disbelief) need no longer be death.

The good news for Coordinators and Advisors is that most of the feedback you get will be positive and enthusiastic. What you have to say will immediately be recognized as sensible and important, as rational ideas usually are. But watch out for those who seem to embrace your proposals but then, when push comes to shove, change their minds because of political pressure. Agency directors are particularly vulnerable to this, as I have learned over and over. One said, behind closed doors, "You are exactly right. AA isn't for everybody, and AA is all we provide to the community. Frankly, I'm glad I don't have an addiction problem myself because I couldn't make use of the program I direct. I'm glad RRS is in town, and I'll help any way I can." This director later found it impossible to aid organizing efforts by encouraging referrals by his clinical staff, by encouraging the distribution of RR literature in his clinics, or by identifying and assigning personnel to the task of offering informed consent.

If you have a personal history of addiction and have been in a 12 step program yourself, you will probably have a good intuition about developing a local RR project. You understand the difficulties of poor meeting attendance, of overflow attendance, of getting the word out in the media, of maintaining a good relationship with the owner of your meeting place, of handling petty cash accounts, of publishing meeting schedules, of managing an answering service or machine and returning calls, and just "being there." You may also be able to provide a valuable service to the local AA establishment by removing their burden of having to be all things to all people. They won't appreciate it when you do, but everyone in AA, even the loyal old-timers, will know down inside that going to RR is far better than going to the liquor store.

Is it "fair" to recruit members from those active in AA? You bet it is! Again, they (AA'ers) won't like it, but we aren't in need of the approval of other organizations. In fact, the only way we are likely to get the approval of AA is to cease to exist. So let's be rational, and recognize that practically all of our members for a few years will come over from AA, and it doesn't make sense to wait until someone is "entirely ready" to go off the deep end to let him or her know about the rational alternative. Go ahead and contact your old AA cronies and tell them about RR. If you're still active in AA, you can talk about RR during meetings or afterwards. Of course, you won't try to launch a rational debate during a meeting, but to give someone who is obviously HP-resistant an RR flyer is an act of compassion as well as a program-builder. Just remember that our purpose is not to convert people from AA to RR, but to find those who simply aren't receptive to the spiritual teachings of that program.

Bottles and needles

What about alcohol vs. hard drugs? Shall we mix? For now, and perhaps for the long run, yes. Some believe it would probably be better to segregate alcohol and street drug abusers into separate groups for the following reasons:

(1) Drunks and junkies don't always get along with each other. Alcoholism is a "legal disease," while drug addictions, especially narcotics like heroin, crack and coke, are "illicit diseases." Drug addicts often look down on alcoholics as ones with "easier problems," while alcoholics sometimes view junkies as "crooks."

(2) Alcoholics commit their antisocial acts while under the direct influence of their intoxicant, while junkies commit their antisocial acts between their periods of intoxication. Junkies quite often commit antisocial acts in order to financially support their habits, while alcoholics are less likely to steal or commit violence in order to obtain their intoxicants. These differences may translate into prejudices and classism based on one's drug-of-choice. When alcoholics and other substance abusers are mixed in the same RR group, there will be some attention given to the above attitudes. With proper use of the ABC's of RET and frank discussion of the underlying issues of blame and guilt, these problems may be resolved. The project Advisor may be able to help with this problem by sitting in for a session or two and becoming actively involved.

"Running" the meeting:

As described in some editions of JRR, RR meetings are unstructured discussions of chemical dependency and living life. Each meeting can open with the overhead question, "Who's been thinking about drinking?" If that produces no input, then the second question, "Then who has a trouble to talk about?" may be asked. Here, a spectrum of issues may come out, and whatever problem is identified can very likely be traced to one of the common irrational ideas that cause the alcoholic drinking and relapse cycle, or as cited in TSB, "The Central Ideas of Alcoholism." The purpose of the discussion that will follow is to show to the speaker which of the irrational ideas he or she is presently believing and allow for a thorough disputing of that idea. The effect, when done clearly, will be (1) a change of feeling and a solution to the practical problem originally described, and (2) less chance of drinking/using or relapse. Whenever possible, use the ABC format, as on the Sobriety Spreadsheets. A few may get the big picture immediately and demonstrate substantial change, but usually it will be necessary to repeat the rational ideas over and over, week after week.

Coordinators should be careful not to get into the "therapist" role, where most discussion revolves around his or her remarks. Instead, it is better to develop the abilities of others in the group to make rational interventions. Some Coordinator input is good but too much is too much and will result in group dependency on you. While that may be flattering to some in the short run, interpersonal dependency will usually have undesirable consequences. This is where being an effective Coordinator becomes an art.

One way to get the feel for RR group process is by listening to RRS audiocassettes such as "Take it From Here," a series of short statements about 10 to 15 minutes in length, that can be played at the beginning of a meeting. The statements are brief, sometimes informative, and always provocative for the purpose of stimulating group discussion. They contain rational ideas that can help with integrating one's philosophy along rational lines.

The Coordinator role is complex, and can be challenging, stimulating, and fun. You will have a full-time administrator (me) to back you up with consultation and follow-up on your contacts as needed. You have a unique role in your community, and RRS wishes you well in your important work.

Disciplinarians vs. Anarchists
There are two schools of thought about how RR groups "should" be. One point of view is that because the meetings are intended to be therapeutic, they therefore should have someone who is well-versed in RET to more or less lead the group. The other point of view is that RR is a self-help experience based on "bibliotherapy" (self-help through reading) and spontaneous discussions of what has been read. This divergence of opinion could be called "The Disciplinarians vs. the Anarchists," provided that we keep our senses of humor. The disciplinarian viewpoint recognizes that RET is "uncommon sense," not easily understood at first, and therefore someone with expertise is needed to identify what's rational vs. irrational. The Anarchist

229

viewpoint recognizes that human beings do have the capacity to meet with others who share the same problem, creatively delve into their own personal problems, and work together toward a solution.

As with most dichotomies, both viewpoints have their merits, and RRS expects that each project will evolve according to the way that local leaders believe is best. So far, we have learned of a few groups that feel uncomfortable with potent leadership, and also of some groups that are uncomfortable with "no structure". RRS has these recommendations for both difficulties.

(1) If your group has trouble focusing on constructive discussion, urge the members present, if they have not already done so, to re-read *The Small Book* or other RET literature available through IRET, 45 E. 65th St., New York NY 10021. Although RR meetings may be light on structure, we are heavy on agenda, and the agenda is RET, especially as contained in TSB. There is much research showing that bibliotherapy is highly correlated with therapeutic change. People who don't know what to do at meetings often don't understand the agenda. Some groups have found the "Take it From Here" tapes helpful in stimulating discussion, and there is a growing body of self-help literature for RR groups in JRR.

(2) If your group is having trouble with too much structure, or members don't feel comfortable and spontaneous, rotate the facilitator role. This may dilute a group's resistance to facilitators who are perceived as "higher powers". Your RRS Advisor may be helpful in resolving problems. Remember that in RR, everyone is expected to be an expert, and all are expected to become rational therapists — first for themselves and then for others.

(3) Always feel free to contact RRS directly, and by all means read JRR for guidance. The following article by a veteran RRS Coordinator gives one good version of how the Coordinator functions within the group. *(JRR,* July - Aug., 1990)

The Coordinator's role in Rational Recovery

RR meetings are discussions that focus on the problems of chemical dependence and staying sober. We refer to *The Small Book* as a guide to no-higher-power sobriety. Everyone in the group, and especially the Coordinator, is supposed to know the contents of TSB well enough to mention specific sections that deal with certain problems. Other excellent material is available from the Institute for RET, 435 E. 65th St., New York NY 10021, and we often hear comments about books from their catalog. Unless people have a basic understanding of RET as described in *The Small Book,* they are unlikely to make the best of meetings. Even so, newcomers are often able to get involved in the discussion right away, because rational ideas make such good sense from the start. Rational Recovery is based on the assumption that human beings, motivated out of self-interest, are quite capable of gathering together around a common problem and working on it in a constructive way. RRS provides the conditions and materials that allow that to happen. While others may choose a course of endless recovery and dependence on higher powers, we are being empowered by RRS to break the chains of addiction on our own. We ask of new members that they come with a critical attitude but be willing to use their intelligence to find faults in their own thinking. We also ask of new members that they inform the group ahead of time when they intend to leave the group. It does take intelligence to participate in RR, but whatever amount of intelligence one has is always enough, as long as the individual uses it.

RET is a type of psychotherapy that is taught in most universities, but there is also a self-help version of RET that can be understood and used by anyone. RET self-help is so simple and so effective in solving personal problems that it has often been called "uncommon sense." One example of RET self-help is, "Sticks and stones may break my bones, but names will never hurt me." Another example is, "No use crying over spilt milk." These are rational sayings. In Rational Recovery, we learn the "ABC's," which is the method of analyzing and evaluating our own thinking, especially our ideas about drinking alcohol or using drugs. The Sobriety Spreadsheet is a worksheet that helps get our thinking down in black-and-white so we may dispute our own irrational ideas. Although doing ABC's is an important part of learning the RR program, it is important that the meetings be flexible and that we not get hung up on trying to stick to some format all the time. RET self-help is an attitude that is picked up through discussions and readings, and it is unnecessary to talk about ABC's in order to get to the point of what's rational or irrational.

One of the Coordinator's roles during meetings is simply to point out that certain ideas that are being expressed in the discussion are irrational, to explain why, and then to offer a rational concept as a better alternative. The best way to do this is by asking questions of a person who holds an irrational idea. For example, if I hear someone saying that it is hard to say "no" when offered a drink at a party, I assume that he or she irrationally believes that other people's opinions are extremely important, and that he or she needs the acceptance or approval of others in order to feel well. I wouldn't get very far by saying, "You think that you need everyone's approval and you have got to get rid of that false idea." But I would probably do better by asking, "What would happen if you refused to drink at the party?" Then, the member might level and say, "Everyone would think I'm weird and wonder what's wrong with me." Then I can ask another good question, "Why is it so important what those people think of you?" Now we are closer to finding this person's negative self-concept (shithood) that leads one to depend on the opinions of others to define one's worth as a human being. With further discussion, the coordinator or someone else may offer the idea that it doesn't really matter if other people like you, as long as you like yourself, and that can help the group focus on the rational idea of unconditional self-acceptance. This can be done without any discussion of ABC's and no one has to have a Ph.D. or an MSW to help out. This is really simple stuff and, as Albert Ellis has said many times, "Anyone can do it."

Consider my own case; I am a janitor by trade, without a high school diploma, although I did get my GED a few years back. Although I have a "rap sheet" of alcohol dependence the length of the entire nation, it is unnecessary for Coordinators to have a histories of chemical dependence in order to be helpful to the group. I understand that there are many RR groups where those coordinators were never addicted to anything, yet are doing well in helping their groups along. I personally like the idea that in RR we do not regard ourselves as a special breed of human being that can only be helped by another former drunk. The real problem in recovery from alcohol dependence is learning to trust others and accept and understand ourselves rather than demanding those things of others.

The job of the Coordinator is to set the stage for open and honest discussion, so that rational insights can be learned. If the Coordinator knows the contents of *The Small Book* reasonably well, he or she will have enough knowledge of RET to give the group discussion meaning and direction. The Coordinator needs to be kind, considerate and calm when working with others, but at the same time firm and assertive in pointing out the errors in others' thinking. We do not extol the crude expressions often heard in traditional meetings like, "Take the cotton out of your ears and stick it in your mouth."

We Coordinators should be careful not to take on the role of the all-wise counselor or therapist, not only because that would be dishonest, but also because that kind of role-playing feeds right into the dependency problems that most newcomers will have. A common viewpoint of newcomers is that they can't stand anything that is out of order or that seems to have no order. They expect perfect performance of themselves and others now, and then angrily condemn those who fall short of those arbitrary standards. Part of their drinking and relapse cycles come from their insistence that things should absolutely be a certain way for them and it's intolerable or unacceptable when they aren't. Therefore, new members of RR sometimes complain, "Hey, what's going on here? What's this supposed to be? What are we supposed to be doing here?" They are saying, in effect, "OK, here I am. Now, make me better." Meetings, many newcomers believe, should run like a precision machine, with an opening ritual, an "order of worship," spoonfed information, and no one interrupting or reacting to others.

When we hear these complaints, it is usually a good time to point out that two of the most important ingredients of Rational Recovery are that (1) we have no dogma, creed, or articles of faith to follow and (2) the meetings are unstructured. In these ways, RR meetings reflect real life, because there seem to be no absolute or perfect truths, and because life seldom provides us structure to keep us out of trouble or on the best course. In RR, we learn to give structure to our thinking, and then live an unpredictable, chancy life without resorting to drugs or alcohol. Houses may burn, relationships may fall apart, jobs may be lost, and other serious misfortune may occur, but we remain calmly in control of ourselves through rational insights learned from readings and in group discussions. Instead of predictable ritual and dogma, our meetings help members form an intellectual strategy for getting the most out of life, focusing on the realities of day-to-day living. This strategy for rational sobriety is based on objective information that can be read, told to others, discussed, argued about, and understood.

Most Coordinators welcome this chance to be a leader in a revolutionary self-help movement, and we know that we have a lot to learn about self-help, about alcohol dependence, and about the complex problems that human beings can have. Some of our best resources are the RRS Advisors, qualified professionals in our communities who are committed to seeing change in the addiction care scene. They can teach us more than we already know about the helping process because they have spent years studying about it and their entire careers practicing their skills. They are also able to help out when special problems crop up during the group meetings or when things seem to get out of hand. I am impressed that they do not charge a fee for helping the local RR projects, and that we Coordinators can have a real learning experience without investing money.

The Coordinator should be keenly aware of how very easy it is for an alcohol dependent person to become dependent on others, especially you. Dependency seems to be common to all groups, not just alcohol dependent people, and it is because of this that RRS Advisors usually keep a cordial distance from the groups they advise. While dependence is encouraged, even taught and required, in traditional programs, RR actively discourages dependency whenever possible. An RRS Coordinator is not a sponsor, a therapist, a leaning post, or a spiritual, financial, marriage, or sex counselor. We do not make decisions for others, and we are not responsible for how others live or die. What others do with their lives is their own choice; none of us in RR is the other's keeper.

To sum it up, the only qualifications to be an RRS Coordinator are an understanding of how to help others become more rational, an understanding of the limitations of self-help, and the desire to be an RRS Coordinator.

Summary:

Rational Recovery Systems (RRS) is a comprehensive national program providing self-help care for alcoholism free of charge. To achieve necessary social change for a widespread rational alternative, RRS coordinates the efforts of RRS Coordinators and Advisors in the community, social service, and health care systems. Subscribers to JRR may become Advisors by expressing intent to aid in RRS development. Patrons may disseminate RRS literature or, if qualified, become Advisors who supervise local RR groups. Professional presence in RRS is in recognition of the seriousness and complexity of alcoholic disorders and the requisites for recovery. Social change is a long-term project and RR patrons are highly committed and prepared for persistent effort, using the consultative and supportive services of RRS.

Bibliography

Alcoholics Anonymous, ("The Big Book") (1939) New York City; Alcoholics Anonymous World Services, Inc.

Beattie, Melody (1987) *Codependent No More*, New York, Harper and Hazelden

Bufe, Charles 1987) "AA: Guilt and god for the gullible," *The Match! an Anarchist's Journal*, Tucson AZ

Christopher, James (1988) *How to Stay Sober: Recovery Without Religion;* New York, Prometheus Books.

Gralnick, Alexander, "The Future of the Chronic Schizophrenic Patient," *American Journal of Psychotherapy*, Vol. XL, No. 3, July, 1986.

Ellis, Albert (1962) *Reason and Emotion in Psychotherapy*, Secaucus NJ, Citadel.

Ellis, Albert, et. al., (1988) *Rational-Emotive Therapy with Alcoholics and Substance Abusers*, Oxford, Pergamon Press.

Ellis, A. & Harper, R. A. (1975) *A New Guide to Rational Living*, N. Hollywood CA, Wilshire.

Ellis, A. (1978) *I'd like to stop, but.... Dealing with Addictions* (casette recording), New York, Institute for Rational Emotive Therapy.

Fox, Vincent (1990) *Mensa Bulletin*, May, 1990

Herman, Helen (Summer 1988) "The 12-step Program: Cure or cover?", *Out/Look: National Lesbian and Gay Quarterly*, San Francisco (reprinted in Utne Reader, Nov/Dec 1988)

Koenig, et.al. (Feb. 1988) "Religion and Well-Being in Later Life", *The Gerontologist*, Vol. 28 No. 1, Washington, The Gerontological Society of America

Peele, Stanton (1989) *The Diseasing of America: Addiction Care Out of Control*, Lexington Books

Schaef, Ann Wilson (1988) *When Society Becomes an Addict;* San Francisco, Harper and Row.

Stein, Benjamin (1988) "Hollywood: God is Nigh," My Turn, *Newsweek*, Dec. 12

Harvard Guide to Modern Psychiatry, Nicholi, 1978

Diagnostic and Statistical Manual, Third Edition, American Psychiatric Association, 1980

"Differences in Platelet Enzyme Activity Between Alcoholics and Non-Alcoholics," *New England Journal of Medicine*, 1988; 318:132-9

Heavy Drinking: the Myth of Alcoholism as a Disease, Herbert Fingarette, 1988

"On Professional Therapists and Alcoholics Anonymous," Westly Clark, M.D., *The Journal of Rational Recovery;* Lotus Press

Journal of Psychoactive Drugs, 19(3) July-Sept. 1987

Trimpey, Lois and Jack, *Fatness: The Small Book;* Lotus Press; 1990

"Beyond the Supreme Court Ruling on Alcoholism as Willful Misconduct: It is Up to Congress to Act," *JAMA*, July 8, 1988, Vol. 259, no. 2

Appendix A

CONFIDENTIAL RESEARCH QUESTIONNAIRE

Readers of *The Small Book* are requested to participate in a study being conducted by Harvard University Medical School. Little is known scientifically about the individuals who achieve sobriety outside of the traditional recovery programs based on the 12-step program. Even less is known about the reasons people drop out of AA, and about what becomes of them. If you have or have had a problem with alcohol or drug dependency, please assist in this *very important* piece of research.

Our study will be longitudinal over the next several years, with results published in scientific journals and *The Journal of Rational Recovery*. Participants are requested to keep Rational Recovery Systems notified of address changes.

The study will request data on your personal philosophy, your experiences with alcohol, your health history, your means for remaining sober. Length of sobriety does not matter to participate. Your information is needed even if you are still struggling to get sober.

Although you will not be anonymous to Rational Recovery Systems, your records will be given the highest degree of confidentiality, just as you would expect from any professional health service organization. If you are willing to participate in this extremely important study, please send a short note containing the following initial information to Rational Recovery Systems, Confidential Research Questionnaire, Box 800, Lotus CA 95651.

(Your name will be deleted from information submitted for scientific study.)

Name: Age: Sex:
Address:

Education:
Occupation:
Which term best describes your personal philosophy?
Agnostic, Atheist, Christian, Humanist, Jew, etc.
(be specific)

Type(s) of chemical dependency:

Age at onset of chemical dependency:
Presently using or sober?   If sober, how long?

Previous periods of sobriety? (dates)

Did or do you attend AA meetings?
How many/How long?
If you discontinued AA, why?

Summarize your means for becoming sober. (You may use separate paper for any of these items.)

This research is being conducted by Harvard University Medical School to describe the population of people who recover through means of self-reliance and personal responsibility. Please fill this out promptly, as this is one way you can help others to gain access to the rational mode of recovery.

Appendix B

MORE RATIONAL IDEAS FOR RECOVERY

1. I am aware that I have become chemically dependent, and the consequences of that dependency are unacceptable.

2. I accept that, in order to get better, I will have to refrain from any use of alcohol, because any use will very likely lead to more, and then a return to my previous addiction.

3. I accept that I will likely benefit from some outside help in accomplishing this, because I have been unsuccessful in previous attempts to resist my desire to drink.

4. Although I may have serious personal problems, I still have the capacity to learn about myself, new ideas, and how to achieve a durable and meaningful sobriety.

5. The idea that I need something greater than myself upon which to rely is only another dependency idea, and dependency is my original problem.

6. I surrender all ideas of perfection, for myself and others, and my first goal is to learn to accept myself as I am, a fallible, yet very worthwhile, human being.

7. I place a high value on the principles of rationality, learning, objectivity, self-forgiveness, and on my own self-interest.

8. Recognizing that others will benefit from a Rational Recovery plan, I may take these ideas to them, as a way of creating a larger society of sober, rational people.

9. Recognizing that there is much more to life than a constant struggle to remain sober, and having gained a reasonable expectation that I can live a meaningful life without alcohol or drugs, I will gradually separate myself from my RR group or therapist, with the understanding that I may return at any time that I wish.

10. I accept that there are no perfect solutions to life's problems, and that life is in part a matter of probability and chance, so therefore I am willing to take risks to achieve my own self-defined goals.

11. Now certain of my inherent worth, I can take the risks of loving, for loving is far better than being loved.

12. With the passage of time, I will find that refraining from mind-altering drugs is no big thing because they have little intrinsic appeal to a physically and mentally healthy person.

13. In addition to addictive substances, I also choose to give up ideas of guilt, blame, and worthlessness as a matter of principle and because they are inappropriate emotions for adults.

Anyone can make up ideas for rational recovery. Make up some yourself! Rational recovery isn't written in stone. It is a process of applying reason to human problems.

An update

Since the fourth printing of *TSB* in November, 1990, there has been explosive growth of RRS across America. Today there are over 150 cities that have RRS projects, and we sincerely hope that within a year or so every chemically dependent American will have access to our recovery groups. Professionals and others who want to bring this important program to their communities may call RRS at (916) 621-2667.

I can say without hesitation that readers of TSB are defining a level of care that is unrecognized in professional literature and that has been unseen in the American media — the *home* level of care. Many people have written or called to report that they are recovering in the privacy of their own homes, using the principles of RET described herein. I personally salute these individuals who are affirming the human capacity for self-correction. Others will find the groups and residential programs an excellent way to streamline the recovery process.

As of January, 1991, RR-Residential has been helping substance abusers to learn to abstain and avoid the emotional pitfalls of relapse in a 28-day, residential setting in rural California. Also, RRS is implementing inpatient treatment programs at various hospitals in Southern California and New England. Now RRS offers all levels of care, including one available nowhere else — home care.

This will be one of the last printings of *TSB* by Lotus Press, the self-publishing adjunct of RRS. In the future, *TSB* will be published by Delacorte, thus freeing us at RRS to devote more of our time to planned social change. Many happy changes to you.

Warm regards,

Jack Trimpey

Jack Trimpey, LCSW
Director, RRS
Editor, *The Journal of Rational Recovery*   June, 1991